The Squaring
of the
Triangle

Arthur Sweet

THE SQUARING OF THE TRIANGLE by Arthur Sweet

Copyright©2015 by Arthur Sweet

Designed by Ellie Searl, Publishista®

ISBN-13: 978-0615936178
ISBN-10: 0615936172
LCCN: 2013957178

Diamond of Life Publishing
Encino, CA

PROLOGUE

P RESIDENT THOMAS JEFFERSON LOOKED OUT of his window at the White House. He was the third president of the infant nation. He saw the American flag fluttering in the July breeze. This flag celebrated the birth of a new nation with but a quarter of a century's existence.

As the third president of the United States of America, he suddenly realized that he was in for the fight of his political life as well as that of this tiny nation. It seems that the former president, John Adams had had a personal vendetta against his Vice President Jefferson. The reason for this feud was simple. President Adams ran for re-election. His opponent was the sitting Vice President Jefferson. The man who won the presidency would determine policy for this young nation. It was expected to be a close race.

When the votes were counted and totaled, Adams was no longer the president of his country. This upset affected how the thirteen states of the nation would be governed.

Ex-president Adams was defying a basic element of the U.S. Constitution, namely that there were three co-equal branches of government. These laws provided that the legislative branch would enact the rules of government, the executive branch headed by a president would run the country according to these laws, and a judicial branch would adjudicate the laws.

President Thomas Jefferson was being inaugurated in 1801. The country's frontier forces were fighting the various Indian tribes that were being pushed west by the American frontier forces. The soon-to-be-installed president was none other than the existing Vice President, Jefferson.

Briefly, this American expansion process was happening west of the Appalachian Mountains. Settlers were moving into Indian tribal lands. The raids by the Sioux Indians and the Shoshone tribe were being fought effectively by the frontier forces. The infant American government and its army had been attempting to control Indian attacks on the settlers.

Historically, the Declaration of Independence had been issued on July 4, 1776. In the years that followed, Thomas Jefferson was involved in writing the U.S. Constitution. Also, he was becoming politically active by serving as the Vice president of the United States of America during the John Adams Presidency.

During the election of 1800, the then Vice President Thomas Jefferson received more votes to become the third president than did "the sitting president" John Adams. Thus, in the 1800 national election Adams lost his bid a second four years. In a word, President John Adams became an ex-president with personal influence but no authority to run the government.

After this defeat there was "hell to pay" because Adams was a sore loser. The defeated John Adams swore, "I won't get mad, but I will get even!"

Two weeks before Thomas Jefferson was to be sworn in as president "lightning struck." It was a message from Secretary of State, James Madison. It read as follows:

February 14ᵗʰ 1801
Urgent
My Illustrious Friend Thomas Jefferson, President Elect,
Dear Thomas,

There are 218 federal judges needing to be sworn in as Federal Judges immediately upon your "being sworn in" as the new president of the United States of America. Today you are the sitting Vice president of your country and you will continue to be so until March 4, 1801.

You must know and I just learned that your Predecessor the Honorable President John Adams appointed his friends and cohorts to serve as these judges in the federal courts of our nation

Mr. President Elect on the above date March 4th 1801, President John Adams will retain no power to appoint a garbage collector let alone a federal judge. You, Mr. President, will be hamstrung by these 'midnight appointments.'

This letter will serve as notice that I intend to review this matter legally and personally sue Adams's first judicial selection, Judge John Marbury, as being a fake, a charlatan, and an imposter in all of the United States or its possessions.

I am sure that any decisions rendered by such misguided and unlicensed imposters will be ruled null and void. These so-called judges will be not be allowed to practice law in any federal court throughout the 13 states, and he will be enjoined from doing so.

Our country's jurisprudence will not be "bastardized" in this high-handed manner. No lawyer I have consulted thinks his appointment by Adams will stand a test in court. Both parties to these appointments will be sued and punished to the fullest extent of the law.

John Adams hopes to become the Chief Justice of the United States Supreme Court.

The appointment of even one judge would violate the constitution basis of Separate and Equal clauses and any such actions and opinions would be unconstitutional. Such improprieties should and will be stopped before they start and I intend to do so.

I offer my country my services to stop this affront to our constitution. I am filing a case against Judge Marbury's appointment before the sitting U.S. Supreme Court today.

This "act of skull-duggery" involving you as the newly elected president of the United States of America, will damage your power to govern. In my humble opinion you would be unable to make your own Presidency's appointments during your first term.

Please take immediate action to prevent this from happening.

Your Obedient Servant,

James Madison,

Private Citizen

This was the spirit of the founders of the United States of America and the colonists who fought and died in the Revolutionary War. It was felt by all of the signers of the U. S. Declaration of Independence. Similar bravery was displayed when Washington crossed the Delaware River during the Revolutionary War and had the red, white, and blue flying as General Cornwallis surrendered.

The flag became a symbol of our new country soon after it was formed. The adoption of a flag was a rallying point for the country and made Betsy Ross a heroine. She was commended, paid for her work, and the flag was flown daily—dawn until dusk. The flag was a symbol of the right for the states to band together for a common cause under the rule of law.

As a result, the Congress of the United States adopted the flag and the infant country had a symbol to show to the world that a new country had been created and was under the rule of law and governed by a court, which would decide whether the operations and activities followed the road map set up under the Constitution.

Since then the American flag has reigned supreme and flutters in the breeze. The United States of America continued to flourish. The population was growing as was the land area, which had almost tripled, indicating that the new country formed had the Federal Army backing it up.

During the first decade of the 19th Century, when Jefferson took office, a decision had to be made. Was the government of the United States capable of doubling its size with the "Louisiana Purchase"?

President Jefferson thought so, and he got Congress to fund an expedition to find "The Northwest Passage." It took nearly three years and the efforts of over thirty people, including two Army Captains, to demonstrate that there was no such route.

The two Captains Meriwether Lewis and William Clark made the perilous journey and braved unheard of dangers to prove that there was no water route from the Atlantic Coast to the Pacific Coast. The story starts in the office of President Thomas Jefferson and ends in the Grinders Travelers Inn with Captain Lewis face down on the floor and the door locked.

FOREWORD

PRESIDENT-ELECT THOMAS JEFFERSON RECALLED his father telling him how tough living in the British Isles was in the early 1700s. To escape the poverty that prevailed in Britain, the Jefferson *pater familias* emigrated and settled in the state of Virginia. It was a wonderful move.

The Jeffersons became tobacco farmers. They grew the crop most prized by those British citizens who came over to North America. Jefferson senior met a political savant, William Randolph who said to him, "I love to live here and will stay here till the day I die!"

Randolph had a daughter who caught Jefferson Junior's eye. A marriage followed and Jefferson's mother, being a Randolph, had raised her children as if they were of the manor born.

Accordingly, Thomas Jefferson was born in 1743, forty years before the United States won its independence. He grew up as the son of a rich plantation owner in the Monticello area of Virginia.

Thomas Jefferson was educated by a tutor. After studying law, he became an attorney, a circuit judge, and managed the Randolph land, which improved both Jefferson's reputation and his bank account.

This tobacco plantation had become a family business, which used a great deal of slave labor. It employed a work force of a hundred slaves that made his growing tobacco "a cash cow" for his political ventures.

This Randolph-Jefferson estate became substantial. However, the estate was heavily in debt and Jefferson was obligated to operate it for the

Randolph's as well as for the Jefferson's. Unfortunately, Thomas Jefferson did not realize how much debt there was or he wouldn't have become its manager. It took him and his cousins many years to overcome the heavy obligations.

Thomas Jefferson was well-schooled in church schools as well as having a private tutor during high school. He went to William and Mary College, and upon graduation, ran the family tobacco business.

Thomas Jefferson was in favor of the movement to break away from Great Britain because of the British Government's Stamp Act. While not in the continental forces, Jefferson publicly denounced Great Britain for taxing the settlers on the tobacco that was grown in America.

The Revolutionary War started in 1776 and ended in 1783. After a peace treaty was signed, the colonies became the United States of America. A Continental Congress was formed to create the U.S. Constitution. This body politic provided a written document by which the new nation would be governed. Thomas Jefferson was one of the three principals who wrote the document.

The U.S. Constitution was adopted, ratified and an election was held. General George Washington became the first president of the United States of American in 1788.

One of President Washington's acts was to appoint Thomas Jefferson to be the new nation's first Minister to France. As such, his Excellency, Minister Thomas Jefferson was in a very precarious position because of the French Revolution. Napoleon Bonaparte had become an Emperor surviving the riots in Paris during which the French monarchy was overthrown.

At this juncture, Thomas Jefferson returned to the United States and joined a political party called the Democrat/Republican Party. This action resulted in his deciding to be a candidate for the US presidency.

However, Massachusetts Senator, John Adams, ran for the presidency against Thomas Jefferson and won. Thomas Jefferson came in second and thus became Vice president to John Adams. This "pecking order" election position lasted until the election of 1800.

The presidential election of 1800 turned out to be a dog fight between Jefferson and Adams. It was almost a tie until the last vote was counted.

Thomas Jefferson defeated John Adams and became President Jefferson, the nation's new leader.

There was hell to pay. A weak President Jefferson faced a hostile bureaucracy. It became an exciting time in Washington, D.C. The White House had been finished and opened up for President John Adams and his wife Abigail Adams to occupy. However, the results of the 1800 presidential election changed Adams's plans

President John Adams was a disappointed runner-up and proved to be a poor loser. During his last month in office, he appointed as many federal judges and other office holders as he could before March 4th, 1801, the day president-elect Jefferson would be sworn in and John Adams was to move out of the White House.

During the election campaign in 1800, widower Thomas Jefferson was hounded by the talk around D.C. It was that *Jeffy* was *a nigger lover*. It was based on his having a housekeeper Miss Sally Hemings, one of the 100 slaves he owned. She lived in Monticello and was its manager.

Thomas Jefferson had led a solitary existence from 1782 the day his wife died. Although the rumor in the District Columbia was that Sally Hemings was President Jefferson's plaything, his mistress by night, facts show that Sally Hemings was a competent employee, ran his home despite being his toy, his mistress.

It was a dirty campaign. Tales about Jefferson's personal love life were highlighted as the battle to become president was fought in the press, with scandalous leaflets, and with whispered half-truths. Even poetry sullying the reputation of then Vice President Jefferson were bandied about the sacred hall of the U.S. Congress. One such ditty was:

"Little Miss Sally causes the Veep to dally
On his way to her White House soft bed,
A fly on the wall could really tell all,
But what happened is better not said!"

Once Jefferson was elected, he became the sponsor of the Louisiana Purchase. This deal was one of his first efforts as president. He was instrumental in getting congressional funding and closing the deal.

The countries of France, Spain, and America had to approve the treaty to acquire this territory. A vast amount of land owned by the French, it included 800,000 square miles of territory. The price was steep— $15,000,000. Jefferson was criticized by the press, the politicians, and the public for buying *a pig in a poke.* Every Washingtonian had known there had been many previous explorations looking for the Northwest Passage.

Mammoth land acquisitions had been proposed, but nothing of this size had been successfully completed. President Jefferson knew this. He also knew that this unexplored territory could belong to the USA if the new nation acted promptly. The deal was completed during the year 1803.

One of Jefferson's first actions as president was his appointing a private secretary, Meriwether Lewis, to serve him in the White House.

Much of this story takes place 3000 miles away from Washington, D.C. It involves Thomas Jefferson's dream, in which he, as the newly elected president, could be remembered as the man who doubled the size of his infant nation and made it stretch from sea to shining sea.

It was a politician's dream—add new territory to the country and people it with settlers and immigrants. The president's main task was to explore, explain, and excite the world about the new nation's effort to double its land mass and population for just fifteen million dollars. AND against all odds, he did it by the time he was sixty years old.

CHAPTER 1

The Dream

A CANDLE WAS BURNING ON President Thomas Jefferson's desk. The president's eyes were misty as he recalled the fervor with which he had served his country as the United States Minister to France. During his five years in Paris, he had been kept abreast of the French Revolution, its news, and how it affected the politics of both nations. He noted that in the future, the two countries were intertwined.

However, both he and his two daughters were glad to have returned to his vast tobacco plantation called Monticello. President George Washington, the father of his country, had offered Jefferson the cabinet post of Secretary of State with these words, "I need you to help me organize the executive branch of our government, Thomas. You are well versed in the U.S. Constitution. You will be one of five members of my new cabinet. You know our government like the back of your hand. You are just what the United States needs."

It was late in the day and Thomas Jefferson said to himself, "That was ten years ago. I'm president now. The Louisiana Purchase is a done deal. The Triangle is complete. I must square it with all parties involved. I will give this plan the code name "The Squaring of the Triangle."

As he paused to leave the president's office and go to the living quarters in the White House, he said good night to his private secretary, Captain Meriwether Lewis and went upstairs to rest.

The next morning the president arose and returned to his office. He looked out the window behind his desk, glanced at the early morning sky, and saw the green velvet lawn sparkling with drops of dew. He remembered that the French Ambassador had told him that the Louisiana Purchase would have to be completed immediately and according to international law.

To do this, the United States must form a party of American explorers to traverse the new territory, crossing it from east to west, and make its claim to the new territory. This could be accomplished by raising the American flag and notifying the Indians and fur traders who lived there that they were now American citizens. As such, they owed allegiance to the *Great White Father in Washington, D.C.*

President Thomas Jefferson pulled a sheet of white paper and started to draw up his plan for the Louisiana Purchase. He wrote across the top of the page "The Squaring of the Triangle." He added a second line in brackets (The Voyage of Discovery). Just seeing the words gave him a thrill.

He thought for a minute and started sketching an outline of a plan. It showed the Capitol with the words Congress underneath it. An arrow led down to a triangle with the words Leader, Co-leader, and Explorers written in it. Another arrow led down to a square with the words Fort Clatsop and in brackets underneath were "The North West Passage Up the Missouri River" and an arrow pointing down to The Pacific Ocean.

The sketch was completed. The president signed it with a flourish— Thomas Jefferson, 3rd president of the United States of America, and dated it July 4, 1802. He got up, walked over to the shiny potbelly stove at the back of the room, and poured his morning cup of tea. He walked back to his desk and sipped the tea.

As he was enjoying his morning break, he picked up the sketch he had just made and said to himself, "Not bad for an amateur. I'll have the Congressional Cartographer make it official on parchment."

He rang for his private secretary, and a slender young man with curly black hair entered the room. He walked to the front of the desk, clicked the heels of his army riding boots, and said, "Good Morning Mr. President. You rang sir?"

The president replied, "Yes, Captain Lewis, I need you to take this sketch over to the National Cartographer. He's done some work for me. After showing it to me for my approval, tell him to make a half a dozen copies.

You can send a copy to the president of the Senate, the Speaker of the House of Representatives, the Washington Post, The New York Times, and The Philadelphia Inquirer. Then frame ours and I'll hang it on the wall in the president's office."

The president's sketch, entitled "The Squaring of the Triangle," showed the Capitol Building at the top of the page labeled Senate and House of Representatives Approval. Immediately below that was a moneybag with a dollar sign and 15 Million on it. Below was the Corps of Discovery, two Captains, four Sergeants, twenty-six Privates, two Guides, one French Canadian guide, one Indian Woman, and one Black Slave.

History shows us that after 1492, the year that Columbus reached North America, explorers wanted to find a shorter route to the west coast of North America. It took much longer and was more hazardous to travel around Cape Horn. The seas were rough. Towering icebergs were floating by the sailing ships. There were no medications for seasickness, and those passengers who hadn't died during the trip wished that they had. Despite all the danger and discomfort, the sailing ships kept making the ocean passage.

The cry from European countries was *go west young man, go west!* It was heard around the world, and especially in the eastern section of the United States of America. The population of the country was on the move. Even Thomas Jefferson was bitten by West Coast fever. The Louisiana Purchase was just a symptom of the times.

If Americans wanted to travel to the Pacific coast from the Atlantic Coast, they had to travel by sailing ship.

President Jefferson believed that when the United States acquired the 800,000 square miles of territory from France that would be his moment of greatness. James Monroe, United States Minister, sent President Jefferson a dispatch saying, "Congratulations, Mr. President. The Louisiana Purchase will be your crowning glory. Your citizens and the whole world admire your vision."

Jefferson thought to himself, "How different was George Washington's way of governing our people. George had ideas that came from the governed, while Napoleon dictates to his countrymen from his perch as the Emperor of France. My country is the only one of its kind in the world today."

The dispatch from which Jefferson was reading had arrived from Paris. It was the president's special envoy, James Monroe. It encapsulated what the United States President Thomas Jefferson wanted to do to make the new country of thirteen states unite and show the rest of the world how to create and govern a country and its people. This was part of the constitutional duties assigned to him when he was inaugurated as the presiding officer of this infant nation. It was Jefferson's special goal, which he called "the dream."

When he was elected the third president of the country less than two years before, he had talked to John Adams, his predecessor. He had learned that France would sell its claim to 800,000 square miles of North America, all the land area that France had title to. This transaction called "the Louisiana Purchase" would end French interests on the North American continent.

The president had named it "My Louisiana Purchase Plan." He had kept this in mind during the two years since he had occupied the president's office in the White House. That morning he summoned his personal secretary, Captain Meriwether Lewis.

Meriwether Lewis was a young man of twenty-eight years of age. The president had known Lewis for a number of years as both grew tobacco on separate plantations in Virginia. Meriwether Lewis was a handsome man. He was less than six feet in height and slight in build but had curly black hair and a light complexion showing his English ancestry. He was popular and an average student. He was a great horseman, a good rifleman and would have gone to the University of William and Mary had his mother not been widowed when he was in his teens

The president's spread, Monticello, was much larger than the Lewis farm. The president was thirty years older than his fellow Virginian.

Standing in front of the president's desk after delivering the special dispatch from France, Lewis said, "Mr. President, this was sent by our diplomats who are in Paris. It must be the one you have been waiting for."

President Jefferson motioned for Lewis to sit down in a chair at side of his desk as he said, "Meriwether, I need to talk to someone who is familiar with the frontier country. I need to know about what you call the back country.

"You served there after receiving a promotion to the rank of Captain of the United States Army. You know about the Indian tribes and the fur trappers found there. I need to get information. Tell me what you can."

Jefferson went to the window and looked out upon Pennsylvania Avenue. He continued his ramblings. "This concerns a grandiose scheme I have had in mind. It occurred to me while I was vice president in the Adam's administration. If adopted and funded by Congress and approved by me, it will make the United States of America a major player in the world. While it involves some risk, I sense that it is my path to glory, and I must go ahead. I know it will succeed!"

Jefferson turned away from the window, walked back to his desk, and asked with a smile, "Meriwether, how long have you been with me?"

The secretary turned his head and told the president, "Mr. President, I have been with you as your private secretary for over two years."

Jefferson said, "It seems longer than that."

Then Captain Lewis added, "Maybe it is because your family lives close to mine. We have gone to the same tobacco auctions. I have only been here since 1801 serving as your private secretary."

The president said, "Yes, I do appreciate your taking care of my secretarial needs, but now I wish to tell you a plan that I've been going over in my mind since my inauguration. My idea will double the size of our country overnight. Yes I said over night!"

Looking Captain Lewis straight in the eye, Jefferson added, "Both your country and I need your services."

Clearing his throat, the president went on. "I want you to think about spending the next three years of your life working for our country. I won't tell you all about it until tomorrow, but be prepared to say 'yes' after thinking about the concept. That will be all, Captain Lewis."

The secretary arose, saluted, and left the president's office. He was dying to hear more. However, he realized that President Jefferson was trying to whet his curiosity. It was one of the oldest sale's gimmicks known to man and the Captain chuckled as he sat down at his own desk just outside the president's office.

Now it was Private Secretary Lewis' turn to dream. He rolled over his own thoughts about the president's secrets. *We have been undergoing great changes in our new country. We have become a fully operative nation*

springing from the thirteen colonies. We ended our conflict with the British.
Our country is just eighteen years old.

As a new country with a president, a congress, and a legal framework
pointing the way, we now have doubled the size of the land we control. Many
more states will add to our national stature. President Jefferson as a
Democrat-Republican will want to add states to the Union. They will be
formed from the territory now controlled by the United States. Our own
citizens will move west to be joined by immigrants from Europe.

Lewis could not remember the battles of the Revolutionary War
because he was too young, but his mother and brother could. His brother had
joined the colonials fighting for freedom and opposing taxation without
representation and its being forced on the American people.

At every Thanksgiving celebration, Meriwether heard stories of the
English Red Coats being beaten back by the *ragtag* revolutionary troops.
These bits of Americana were bandied about. The Lewis family members
told Meriwether about fighting the British and about the midnight ride of
Paul Revere as he announced far and wide, "The British are coming. The
British are coming." They told of how Washington crossed the Delaware
and how the war ended in 1783. This story was told during the Thanksgiving
holiday, the time the Lewis Clan got together and recalled the past and
feasted on roast turkey and pumpkin pie.

Tom Lewis, the oldest son, made a toast to the United States of
America, "Here's to our new nation—thirteen states with freedom of
religion, freedom from the crown, freedom to think and say what we want
to. We raise our glasses high."

This year, after the festivities were done, the election of Thomas
Jefferson was hailed by the Lewis family as a gift of God and how Jefferson
would lead the nation by reaching for the golden grail.

After the Revolutionary War had come to a victorious end, Jefferson
returned to his home in Virginia. As a practicing attorney rather than a
politician he spent much of his time in Philadelphia, then the capitol city of
the United States.

At the end of the 18th Century the French were up to their ears fighting in the Napoleonic War. Jefferson heard from aides that Napoleon was ready to make a deal. He wanted to sell the Louisiana Territory and all of the French land interests from the 54th Parallel to the Caribbean Sea. He was offering Louisiana and the area bounded on the east by the Appalachian Mountains and the West by the Rocky Mountains. This was 800,000 square miles of uninhabited country but for the American Indian tribes.

Jefferson was in France as the United States Ambassador and was approached with the idea of the Louisiana Purchase. Jefferson heard rumors that French territory was for sale, the price mentioned was two million dollars for Louisiana only. John Adams, the successor to George Washington, did not favor the deal, but its representatives and senators did and they won the day. The necessary legislation was approved by Congress.

This Missouri Mississippi watershed would be sold for fifteen million Yankee dollars. It must be cash on the barrelhead and right now. No ifs, ands, or buts. The offer, once accepted by the United States, was final.

Jefferson's dream for his country's future was happening right before his eyes. The path to capitalize on France's offer was uncertain. But President Jefferson knew that it would require strong leadership. The leader he chose must have a firm hand on the reins. It was his choice to make, but who should it be?

The next morning Captain Meriwether Lewis was prepared to make the decision of his life. He knocked on the door of the president's office. He heard the president say, "Come in Captain Lewis. Come in."

Lewis entered, stood at attention, and saluted.

Jefferson said, "I hope you slept well."

Captain Lewis answered hesitantly, "I did. I did, Mr. President."

Jefferson said, as if he knew what the answer would be, "Well, can I count on you for the next three years? The country needs you. We have made the Louisiana Purchase. Now, the people of our country must see what we have bought. You are the man to do it. You have to stake our claim. Will you?"

Stunned, Captain Meriwether Lewis said, "My answer is yes."

The president rose and silently walked to door of his office, closed it and returned to his desk. As if Lewis wasn't there, the president said, "My fondest hope has happened. While I was Ambassador to France, I heard a rumor that Napoleon Bonaparte needed funds. He was preparing for a battle at Waterloo. Fighting wars is not cheap. He wanted to get on with it. 800,000 square miles for fifteen million. That's a bargain for sure."

The president talked as if he was thinking aloud. "You know, Lewis, you have been my sounding board where my ideas are bounced off of. I want to be sure I am on the right track.

"Sometimes while I am ruminating, I look out the window and try and conceive what our life would be like in a large country. With only the thirteen states, we are so limited in what I can accomplish."

"Last year's memories are perfection. Next year's guesses are just that, guesses. The only thing you can change is what I call *the now*. Yes, you can change *the now*.

"The entire continent of Europe has seen people fleeing their countries because of war, rebellion, conflict, and poverty. These immigrants are coming to a free world."

Jefferson cleared his throat and said, "Lewis, you've been with me for over a year now and are a native Virginian. Your family has farmed and raised you. You are young and single."

Picking up his pipe from the top of his desk and stuffing it full of leaf tobacco, the president started to puff on it, smoke curling up overhead. It was Virginian tobacco at its finest. While Lewis had not yet picked up the habit, he was used to it. The president's smoking was not a problem.

The president said, "Lewis you have the native-born instincts of being a tobacco farmer, a soldier, and now my private secretary. While you are not yet thirty, you have talents that I do not possess. You are a good listener and keep excellent notes on our conversations. See you tomorrow at nine. That will be all, Captain Lewis."

As his private secretary left the office, President Jefferson thought "*He will do nicely as overseer for my dream. Tomorrow I will outline the plan I have for him. Hopefully dreams sometimes come true!*"

CHAPTER 2

Squaring the Secret Triangle

THE PRESIDENT SUMMONED HIS PRIVATE Secretary Lewis into his office and said, "Sit down Captain Lewis. You've been with me since I have been president?"

Lewis answered the rhetorical question, "Yes, Mr. President, it has been almost two years."

It was unusual for President Jefferson to be so informal. This caused Captain Lewis to be excited. His two-year career as the private secretary to President Jefferson had altered Lewis' future. He had been a tobacco plantation owner and farmed 1,000 acres for several years. Lewis could not picture himself as such and volunteered to enter the U.S. Army as a Captain. He was enlisted in the frontier forces keeping the Indian tribes at bay in the territory of Ohio, west of the Cumberland Gap.

At the start of his first term, President Jefferson wanted Captain Lewis to function in the White House as his right arm rather than fend off the American Indians in the Ohio territory. Captain Lewis became the gatekeeper of the president's office, keeping people from bothering the president.

It was not a pleasant task but an interesting one. He was privy not only to the president's mail but also to his secrets. The most important of these events happened in 1801 when President Thomas Jefferson became the successor to John Adams.

As president, John Adams had abhorred centralized government. On the other hand, his successor, Jefferson, was a Federalist. Just before President Jefferson was to be sworn in, the then president Adams showed his displeasure. Before a joint meeting of the Congress, President Adams had said, "I will teach that SOB Thomas Jefferson who's boss. Wait till his inauguration in March 1801."

Two weeks before the March Inauguration, John Adams did the following. He appointed over two hundred federal employees, knowing such midnight appointments would hamstring his successor for many months. And he appointed federal judges, among whom was Judge Marbury, an unknown. In the opinion of James Madison, the U.S. Attorney General, this appointment violated the U.S. Constitution. Madison filed a lawsuit, attesting that such an appointment by the executive branch violated the right of the judicial branch to be involved in the selection process of judges.

It turned out that the appointment of Judge Marbury by President John Adams did violate the U.S. Constitution. The ruling of the Supreme Court declared all such John Adams' appointments unconstitutional.

Finally, after his March inauguration, President Jefferson moved into the White House only to find John Adams had added insult to injury. As the Washington newspapers put it, "Adams Loots White House." Adams apparently had scurrilously removed from the White House everything he could carry.

President Jefferson's stature as seen by the American public was horribly low, He said to Lewis, "Never fear, we will overcome Adams and his chicanery. You will help me by making the Louisiana Purchase my crowning glory!"

In his own mind. Jefferson had dubbed the Louisiana Purchase a triangle because there were three countries involved, and each was an integral part of the transfer of territory owned by France and Spain.

President Jefferson had drawn a sketch showing the details of the exploration searching for a Northwest Passage to the Pacific Ocean. The previous attempts by Spain and France to do so had discovered nothing. Many other explorers had tried but all had failed!

The land area was unexplored and unoccupied except by Native Americans, hunters, fur traders, and some farmers.

The words that Captain Lewis heard from the president's mouth were "The Louisiana Purchase is now signed, sealed, and delivered. The future growth of our country is in your hands Captain Lewis! You have a week to decide to head this exploration or reject my offer to lead it."

Captain Lewis left the president, entered his own office, and packed a saddlebag with unfinished work. He wanted to spend the next week deciding if he could do as the president had asked.

The twenty-four-year-old former tobacco plantation owner remembered President Jefferson saying, "If you are the man I think you are, you will say 'yes' and astound the world."

This statement had so amazed the young man that he gasped and said "Thank you Mr. President."

Meriwether Lewis wanted to go to his home in Monticello and come up with a plan. He left his office hurrying down the winding staircase and went to the stables behind the White House. He saddled up, mounted his horse, waved goodbye to the White House groom, and headed across the Potomac River toward his Virginia home—some 130 miles away

It was a beautiful summer day, not yet hot and humid as is often the case in Washington, D.C. Jefferson traveled at a leisurely pace. It provided a restful interlude for Lewis to think about President Jefferson's offer.

Lewis reasoned why Jefferson had selected him. He could come up with several reasons. He was a good leader and a dependable group member with army experience. He had led a U.S. Army company of soldiers in the frontier country in the Ohio Territory. He was used to taking orders from a superior and most of all to carry them out to the letter! He was a good tobacco farmer. His family lived just ten miles from President Jefferson's home. President Jefferson had recognized Lewis's abilities as a plantation manager. He was single and had no immediate family commitments. He was moral, not profligate. And he was compassionate, helping his mother survive his father's death from small pox.

On the negative side were his bouts of depression due to unpleasant or difficult events. His education was minimal, he had never finished his schooling. He realized that he often made decisions quickly because of insecurity.

In Washington, D.C., he was known as a *short timer* because of his inexperience in the political community. Also, he still felt guilty for running away from the tobacco plantation to go fishing when he was eleven years old. His father had found him at the river. His dad viewed this event as an act of insolence because he did it even though he knew it was against the rules. When caught, Meriwether was locked in his room for a week except for meals and going to the outhouse.

Such thoughts occupied Lewis's mind during most of his first day's ride home.

In late afternoon, Meriwether watered his mount. The sun cast long shadows on the dusty path. The captain found a tavern where overnight visitors could rest before continuing their journey. It had been a tiring day but so inspiring. Meriwether thanked the lord for his wisdom and help in this possible adventure.

Rising at sunup, feeling much refreshed, and wanting to get back on the road, Captain Lewis ate a quick breakfast, saddled up, and headed out. His favorite horse could sense that he was nearing home and tugged at the bridle trying to get his rider to increase the pace.

Lewis finally saw his home in the distance. It was painted stark white. It had a weather vane on the roof, the metal bird pointing upwind. As his horse turned into the gravel private drive, the captain was greeted by the barking family English bulldog, Britt.

After he dismounted, his older brother Tom gave him a hearty handshake and a wide smile. Tom said, "I thought you would be running the country by now, Meriwether. What has brought you back to Virginia?"

Meriwether answered, "I came down for a week to see how things were going here at the plantation. I have an important decision to make, but I am dead tired. I will tell you and Mom all about it in the morning. I've got to hit the hay."

With this brief greeting Tom said, "Good night and God be with you."

Meriwether Lewis had a fitful night. As he dozed off to sleep, he had a horrible thought. *What if I fail to measure up to my parents' expectations?* He dreamed about his past, having visions of growing up in this verdant farming area. He dreamed about his parents wanting him to work in the fields after school and all day Saturday. He had worked the farm with Tom. On Sundays, the two boys would go to church, sit in the family pew, and listen to the pastor preach about the good Lord, going to Hell, and experiencing

Damnation. He awoke in a cold sweat as the thought of failure consumed him.

However, waking up to reality, Meriwether started to plan his future. This week spent at home would allow the captain to decide what action to take to meet the president's wishes. His head swirled with ideas of his new project. The fact that the president of the United States had offered him this unbelievable opportunity was mind-boggling and gave him pause.

Meriwether Lewis was unsure of himself. He wondered *would I, at only twenty-nine, be able to head such an exploration?* He thought that such an endeavor needed an older man who had knowledge of astronomy, meteorology, medicine, Indian lore, and sign language. Then Meriwether immediately dismissed this thought. He could prepare himself in these skill areas with intensive instruction. He recalled his dad telling him, "practice makes perfect, Meriwether. You'll learn as you go along."

The intangibles bothered him. *How do I overcome insecurity? How do I combat lack of drive? How do I overcome the lows of dejection?*

He had always felt inferior in the area of leadership. When a decision faced him, he usually delayed making it because of his uncertainty. This made his parents look to his older brother Tom for leadership. Most of the time Meriwether was willing to be a capable second in command.

He had done well and had become a captain in the armed forces protecting the settlers and maintaining the peace. He liked his great opportunity of being Jefferson's private secretary. *Do I need any more than that?*

If I fail in what I am being asked to do—lead the Corps of Discovery-- I have much to fall back on. I have a good track record as private secretary to President Jefferson. And a career in the army would be mine again. Insecurity does not matter in an army career if I follow regulations and keep my nose clean. Lewis tried to keep these thoughts in the back of his mind.

His final gut feeling was his two years of service in the White House had been beyond reproach. He had served the president well. He knew his military record had been spotless. But the extent of his experience was limited. His major benefit was that he came from the Monticello area in Virginia and had managed the tobacco business. With that thought, he closed his eyes and fell asleep.

The week that the president had given him to decide sped by. He kept having random thoughts. *Would I ever meet the Emperor of France, Napoleon Bonaparte? Would exploration be my career? Who else but President Jefferson could have visualized the Louisiana Purchase? Would my leading the Corps of Discovery be great for my future? How would I have negotiated the Louisiana Purchase? How did the U.S. Treasury find the gold bullion to complete the purchase?*

His assignment to find the Northwest Passage to the sea would be a first. Many had tried to do so and none had succeeded. The odds were he, Captain Lewis, would fail, too.

By the time a week had passed the Captain mustered all his courage. He had debated the pros and the cons with himself. He could not see himself a private secretary all his life. It meant being a *toady* to the rich and famous. Having reviewed his options, he decided that he was enough of a daredevil to give it a go!

Yes, Captain Meriwether Lewis would accept the leadership role, but he had two conditions that must be met. The first was that a co-captain be appointed by the president, and that it be the man that Meriwether wanted.

The choice of his co-captain would be so vital that Lewis must pick his own man. President Jefferson must be told that he, Meriwether Lewis wanted to contact a United States Army Lieutenant he had served with while in the frontier forces in the Ohio Territory.

The choice must be immediate and Lewis had already corresponded with this man. Even though he was of junior rank, Captain Lewis knew that Captain Clark would be up to the task.

He sent Captain Clark a dispatch:

New development will delay my making an offer to you. Please keep me posted when you move your command. I will tell you more within the year.

Your Obedient Servant,
Captain Meriwether Lewis Corps of Discovery.

The second requirement was that there would be no recrimination if the co-captains failed. This venture was to be a best-efforts endeavor. If it was unsuccessful, so be it!

Having decided these factors in his own mind and having no wife to talk it over with, he spent Sunday with his family and neighbors and saying goodbye. Captain Meriwether Lewis returned to Washington, D.C. in high spirits. He was anxious to be prepared for the leadership role in the Corps of Discovery.

The responsibility of this epic adventure was to be split between two co-captains. One would be responsible for collecting and recording all the scientific data and natural specimens of the new territory. This was to be Captain Lewis's function.

The other leader was to be elevated to captain in the U.S. Army. His responsibilities were to handle all the operational functions. These would include organizing the work crews, assigning duties, setting up camp, and travel details, including running the organizational features such as assigning functions of day-to-day duties, preparing daily schedules, mapping the route in detail and keeping a log of the trip.

It was to be organized as it was an army command. Each half of the expedition would have a sergeant and fourteen privates under a Captain's command. All major decisions that affected the entire Corps of Discovery would be decided jointly by the captains. If they disagreed, the sergeants would vote to break the tie.

The time line set up by the president with the approval of the United States Congress involved Captain Lewis planning all preliminary functions. He was to bring back his thoughts of what skills he needed to learn in order to get the expedition started by spring of 1804. The exploration was to depart from St. Louis in the Missouri Territory and proceed up the Missouri River by boat.

An immediate start was vital to prevent Great Britain from sending its explorers south from Fort Vancouver where they would file claim on the same territory. This involved the 54th parallel and it being mentioned in the Louisiana Purchase. The 54th parallel was to be the northern boundary of the search area for the Northwest Passage. All the details seemed overwhelming to Captain Lewis.

The week at his home allowed Lewis to think as to how to conduct the Voyage of Discovery. The horseback trip from D.C. to the Monticello area of Virginia had refreshed his mind. Marveling at the beauty of the Virginia countryside, the warmth of the summer heat, the vibrant green of the tobacco fields, and the natural beauty provided a pleasant backdrop for the thoughtful Meriwether Lewis.

The following day, Captain Lewis traveled by horseback to Washington, D.C. He was to tell President Jefferson that his decision was, *Yes, but first the president must accept two changes in his plans.* The Virginia splendor of the clover green tobacco fields looked as if some super-being had pasted them to the blue sky above. It was a scene he had seen many times in his life, and it always gave him a sense of peace and tranquility.

Captain Lewis entered the White House and climbed up the stairs to give the president his answer face to face.

He said, "President Jefferson I have enjoyed being, and would be greatly honored to remain, Private Secretary Lewis. But I am doubly honored to serve you as a leader of the Corps of Discovery. I do think it is a tremendous task and too big for one man, no matter how talented he is. If I can pick my own man to share the burden and co-lead the Corps of Discovery, I accept with pleasure."

The president said, "So be it. You, Captain Lewis, will command. The men involved with data collection and your co-captain will be in charge of other activities in operating the expedition guard duty, cooking, store keeping, discipline, and mapping. Meeting with the Indian tribes, showing off our weapons, holding celebrations and awarding medals will be done by the entire Corps of Discovery. This will be the best method of Operation Discovery."

Without further elaboration, the president added, "Losing a personal secretary but gaining a co-commander of the corps, I bid you farewell, good luck, and Godspeed. Please let me know whom you choose to be your partner, Captain Lewis. I will be gaining two leaders of a mission into the unknown future. I am a lucky president."

The president watched Captain Meriwether Lewis leave the office with a salute and a smile. Jefferson rubbed his hands together in anticipation. "The Corps of Discovery is about to become a reality and I, President Thomas Jefferson, can't wait for the nebulous search for the Northwest Passage to begin!"

CHAPTER 3

The Preparation

*W*OULD MY FATHER HAVE LIVED was in Captain Meriwether Lewis' mind as he approached Williams and Mary College. Much of the past two days had been spent on horseback. It was late in the afternoon when he arrived at this small college. It had a great reputation. Captain Lewis would prepare here for the next six months.

The school seemed old. Its setting was almost the same as in 1632, the year the college was founded. It was located between the James and York Rivers, 152 miles from Washington, D.C. Many senators and congressmen had been educated there. President Jefferson had selected this university to be the captain's seat of learning. "Prepare yourself for the Voyage of Discovery." President Jefferson had said to Lewis. "Intensive study is essential, Meriwether. I am sending you to the best school in our nation."

Lewis answered, "I am sure it must be or I would not be going there."

Captain Lewis had accepted the leadership of the Corps of Discovery. It was a completed deal. Captain Lewis was aware that it would be a difficult task. He did not look forward to some of the problems he would face, but he was thrilled nonetheless. In fact, he relished the idea!

The president had handed a letter to Lewis. "Take this letter to George Strong, the president of William and Mary. He will be your mentor while you study for the expedition. The education you seek will serve to prepare you mightily."

Captain Lewis replied, "You honor me Mr. President. As you know, I am only twenty-nine years old and to be put in charge of a multi-year expedition, costing our nation five hundred thousand dollars seems preposterous."

Jefferson answered, "Who is president, you or me? You'd better be on your way, Captain Lewis. It is a two-day journey, and it may take you more time if it rains. If it does, I pray the creeks don't rise." The president added, "Send me a message that you have arrived and have met Doctor Strong. God Bless"

Meriwether Lewis stood up, saluted, and left the president's office. He went to the stable and told the groom to saddle up his horse.

It was to be nice a summer day in Washington, D.C. The sun shone brightly overhead; Captain Meriwether Lewis left Washington early because it was a good two-day ride.

He was about to receive special training for his search for the passage to the north, and it rattled his mind. He was to lay claim on the new territory for his country. He was both excited and concerned. One of the thoughts that Captain Lewis had mulled over while traveling along the dusty path was the fact that congress had committed a budget of one-half a million dollars to this exploration.

His mission was to survey and report back to the president and congress the findings as to the environment and residents of the area. Furthermore, he was to send specimens reflecting physical conditions of the territory and its resources. It would be a fact-finding mission—one that had never been done before.

The letter Captain Lewis carried from President Jefferson to Doctor Strong asked the good doctor to:

Please give Captain Meriwether Lewis your best professors in order to prepare him for his exciting visit. I need him to spread the news, far and wide, that the United States has become a major player on the world's stage. Please report his progress directly to me. Your country and I, as its president, thank you in advance for your courtesy.

Little wonder Captain Lewis would be given special treatment.

Lewis reflected how this Corps of Discovery effort was similar to Christopher Columbus fulfilling Queen Isabella of Spain's command voyage in 1492. Columbus had been commissioned by the queen to sail west until he found the new world. His voyage more than doubled the size and importance of Spain on the world's stage. But Captain Lewis knew that his Voyage of Discovery commissioned by the president could overshadow the voyage of Columbus. It made Lewis shiver with delight thinking what his future might hold.

Meriwether Lewis donned his captain's uniform and took time to look around the campus. The school was well known. It was small and stately.

His first order of business was to call on the president of the university who greeted Captain Lewis warmly.

Captain Lewis said, "I have a letter from the president of the United States for you President Strong."

The university president said, "Captain, let me read the letter, and then we can discuss what it contains and what information I need to get you ready for this trip."

Captain Lewis looked around and asked, "May I sit, your Excellency?"

The president laughed and said, "Forget about this *Excellency* bit . . . just call me Doctor Strong. Excuse me for several minutes, as I want to read the president's request. I'll return from my private office as soon as I've finished reading it."

Five minutes later, the president came out and said, "Come in, come in, Lewis. President Jefferson has given you high marks as his private secretary and asked me to give you all the information possible to prepare for your trip to find the Northwest Passage."

"You are to find the shortest route to the Pacific Coast from St. Louis, Missouri. He said that you should be able to lead this mission, and I eagerly want to start your training from my own private office. Come with me."

The two walked into a barn-like office that doubled as a conference room. It was on the second floor in the administration building. The building appeared to Lewis to be fifty years old—built before the French and Indian War.

"Sit down Mr. Lewis," was the president's next statement. "Would you like coffee or tea? You may smoke if you like."

The president sat at his desk, picked up the letter, and started to re-read it. Lewis looked around the room as he waited for the president to finish reading.

The room was sparsely furnished with a large desk and a bookcase behind it filled with the latest books. A large globe sat on a pedestal to the right of the desk. Two chairs faced the desk. Captain Lewis sat in one of the chairs.

The president moved to his globe and said, "So you are going to form a Corps of Discovery to explore the Northwestern Territory. I know that we have recently purchased it from France. President Jefferson has indicated your exploration will be to find the shortest way to the Pacific. As you explore, you will collect specimens of the flora and the fauna of the territory. You will attempt to find what many have tried and all have failed . . ." Doctor Strong paused for a few seconds, ". . . to find the Northwest Passage . . . the magic way through the Rocky Mountains."

Dr. Strong took Captain Lewis by the arm and said, "It's this way to my carriage."

The two men left the office. Dr. Strong told his secretary that he was through for the day and if she needed him, he would be at home.

As they drove to the president's house, he pointed out certain locations such as the Williamsburg library, the grade school, the junior high school, and the college buildings. They arrived at a modest two-story home as the sun was sinking below rolling hills. The two men walked down a gravel path to the front of the president's home where his wife was waiting.

After introductions, Dr. Strong said, "Let me show you your quarters Captain Lewis. I hope you find them comfortable. The toilet is behind the kitchen with the usual facilities attached. Dinner will be served at seven."

With that he left Captain Lewis to freshen up and wait for dinner. Lewis thought to himself, *what a wonderful education I should get. I will be under this man's guidance as he provides teachers to prepare me for this once in a lifetime chance to explore and look for a shortcut to the Pacific.*

The next morning Captain Lewis arose, and after eating breakfast, walked into town. He wanted to go to the library to find out what he could on his own about his great opportunity.

By the time he reached the front door of the library he had mapped out his next six months. He would study with the professors at the university.

He would collect information about the Northwest Territory. He would study astronomy, medicine, mineralogy, botany, and woodcraft.

It was in Dr. Strong's office that Captain Lewis met his astronomy professor, who told Lewis that that they would start by viewing the evening skies intensely for the next week or so.

Captain Lewis said, "Thank you sir, I will meet you this evening on the parkway at ten o'clock, and you can start educating me in astronomy."

At the appointed hour Captain Lewis met the astronomy professor and they went outside to see a beautiful night with the crickets chirping and the new moon looking like a silver slipper—a crescent in the sky.

The professor went to the rear of the school, set up his telescope, and adjusted the height so Lewis could look through the eyepiece.

The professor turned to Captain Lewis and asked him bluntly, "What do you know about the stars?"

Captain Lewis said, "Professor, honestly nothing. I am a farm boy. While I was in the U.S. Army in the frontier forces, we normally did all our work during the daytime. What we did was to get ready for the next day."

The professor said, "I'll start with basics and by the time we're finished, you will know where the North Star is and whether an individual star is part of a constellation or not." He continued, "The North Star is part of Ursa Minor, or the little dipper, a group of stars. See there it is."

After two weeks Captain Lewis was able to function at night and knew how to locate not only the stars, but also the planets, of the solar system.

The next month was spent in geography. Lewis would need to learn about the principal geographic features and their relationships to local flora and fauna.

Lewis knew that accurate mapping was necessary. Dr. Strong told Lewis that most of his other subjects could be learned in six months, but not mapping the trail that the corps would explore. That would be completed on the journey itself—mapping geographical features so that future visitors would be able to find their way into and around the territory.

One of the objectives of the Voyage of Discovery was collecting information from the indigenous people. Those who knew about the far-reaching land were local Indian tribes, fur trappers, hunters, and farmers.

Captain Lewis realized he would need to learn basic medicine because he would be the one to handle medical emergencies. He was no doctor nor could he hope to become one, but he did confer with doctors discussing medicines that could be delivered by a member of the corps.

Another problem to overcome during the voyage was communicating with the Indians and French residents of the territory. He knew that part of his mission was to inform the Indian tribes and other inhabitants of the territory that they now owed their allegiance to the United States. Captain Lewis only spoke English. It was essential to the mission to hire guides and crewmembers who could translate the local languages.

He knew that he and members of the corps needed to know how to sew their own clothes, make shoes, and cook foods that they could carry with them or find along the way.

And at the end of the training, he reported to President Jefferson that the six months he had spent in Williams and Mary had been fruitful. He had been able to secure the necessary skills to lead the Corps of Discovery into the wilderness to find the Northwest Passage and secure the Louisiana Purchase Territory--just as the president desired.

Lewis traveled back to Washington, D.C. by stagecoach because it was faster than on horseback. By the end of the first day Captain Meriwether Lewis had his report for the president.

Lewis had written: *Mr. President, I am ready. My education has been accomplished. I am ready to acquire supplies and assemble a group of men to become the Corps of Discovery. I have someone to help the cause. I would like to meet as soon as your schedule permits. Signed Respectfully, Your Obedient Servant, Captain Meriwether Lewis Corps of Discovery.*

President Jefferson had replied: *Captain Lewis, Congress is meeting now. Bring the papers you showed me. We will visit Congress tomorrow and report that you and the Corps of Discovery are ready to find the Northwest Passage and the shortest land route to the Pacific Coast. What a feat that will be!*

CHAPTER 4

Stocking Up

"IT'S AS COLD AS A witches tit," a shivering Captain Meriwether Lewis mumbled to himself as he took a deep breath. The ice cold air made his lungs burn as if he had inhaled a blast of hot air from his fireplace. The wind came from the north and was gale force. The captain suddenly realized that his duty in the Fort Pitt area of Pennsylvania could be troublesome and difficult.

Be that as it may, with the needs of the Corps of Discovery foremost in his mind, the trip to Fort Pitt in mid-winter was the assignment straight from the president himself. It was tough duty as he knew it would be.

Captain Lewis waited for the guard at the gate of the Fort Pitt stockade. The guard saluted and escorted the captain to headquarters where the executive officer on duty said, "I will tell General Peters you are here, sir." He saluted and left.

Captain Lewis looked around the small outer office. It had a stuffed American eagle hanging in the corner with a flintlock rifle leaning against the wall.

The inner office door opened and Captain Lewis was greeted by Brigadier General Peters of the U.S. Army Frontier Forces.

The two officers shook hands and walked inside. General Peters said, "The President's letter accompanying your orders says that he would appreciate any service Fort Pitt could offer you and the Corps of Discovery. Please sit down tell me all about it."

Captain Lewis started by saying, "General Peters, sir, I want to thank you in advance for your offer. I realize how overloaded you are with military functions. You maintain the peace in our frontier country. However, I have been ordered to make all the preparations for making the Louisiana Purchase a great deal for the country. I must see to it that the settlers, Indian tribes, and others living in the territory become part of the United States of America. I've got four months of tough duty facing me. I will need your help in provisioning our corps."

"I have been ordered to prepare for an expedition to explore and survey the Louisiana Purchase territory. Congress budgeted enough money to carry the corps for several years."

"In a nutshell, I need frontiersmen and any knowledge you have that will enable the Corps of Discovery to make this a reality."

General Peters said, "I will do what I can."

Captain Lewis said, "In addition, buying everything we might need for a lengthy exploration will try my talents. Organizing, training, and providing leadership for this plan made me think twice before I took on the job!"

After hearing Captain Lewis expound his story, General Peters said, "No sooner said than done."

He called an orderly and said, "Take care of Captain Lewis' needs while he is here at the fort."

The orderly snapped, "Yes, sir"

Rising from his chair, the general added, "Captain Lewis, let me know if there's a problem."

After saluting, Captain Lewis walked down to the settlement below the stockade. There Captain Lewis said to the lieutenant, "Please stable my horse at the fort Lieutenant. Come get me at dawn. Have a good night."

Early the next morning the mountains of the Pennsylvania countryside sparkled in the winter sunshine. Captain Lewis ate breakfast and left the inn with the lieutenant showing him around the village. He saw that the hills leading to the two rivers were covered with snow—pristine white and sparkling in the early morning sun, The Monongahela and Alleghany Rivers met to form the Ohio River. These rivers provided a natural barrier surrounding Fort Pitt.

It was wintertime and the rivers were frozen over. It covered the emerald green water protecting Fort Pitt from being attacked. Captain Lewis saw that the fort was on a bluff nearly one hundred feet high. It provided protection to the settlers, small manufacturing shops, fur traders, and merchants from the Indian tribes. The Huron and the Erie Indian braves raided the settlements of Pennsylvania. The sparse population and shops were the businesses selling to Fort Pitt and its complement of frontier soldiers of the United States Army.

The Lieutenant assigned to Captain Lewis, greeted him saying, "I have been assigned to help you, sir. My name is Carter, 1st Lieutenant Carter, sir." He continued, "It is late in the day. Could we start tomorrow morning after chow?"

Captain Lewis answered "Yes" as the two officers saluted each other.

Awakening early, Captain Lewis turned over in his bed and smiled as he thought what this new day would be like. *First off, I will need to ask Carter where I can get extra uniforms and other personal necessities that I can buy while I am in Pittsburgh. Secondly, the treasury gave me enough cash to pay for what I need to order and have delivered to St. Charles near the mouth of the Missouri. Lastly, what is the best way to get to the Ohio River so I can travel back and forth to the starting point of this adventure?*

Captain Lewis got up and met Lt. Carter after breakfast. The two officers went into the captain's quarters and sat side by side. The captain pulled out a long list and started by saying, "I need boats, men, and a source of information to help me realize the presidential dream. I think Fort Pitt might have such a man to *Square The Triangle* leading to success. Do you have a source of men to help me?"

The Lieutenant said, "I am ready to help. You can find men along the Ohio River. Do you have any limit as to age, race, skills, and so forth?"

Lewis replied, "Let me get my thoughts together. Five days on a horse has burned my candle down. Tomorrow at sun up."

A salute by both men and Lt. Carter walked out of the officer's quarters.

The list of the needs of the corps was long and in great detail. Being away from civilization and living off the land tested Meriwether Lewis' ingenuity. The end of the trail being far distant and undefined made this task much more difficult. Captain Lewis began to wonder *will I be able to handle this assignment for the United States of America?*

Ignoring this feeling, Captain Lewis began to look at the timing and decided that the boats to go up the river was his main concern. The survey of the Fort Pitt settlement he had made troubled him. Having very few places to buy the boats caused both the quality of what Captain Lewis bought and its need for prompt delivery to be very important. Failure on either score would be a major problem.

Lewis decided to start at the top of his list: buying boats to go up the river. He laughed aloud when he remembered the saying: *up the creek without a paddle*. He looked around Fort Pitts and found one place that made birch bark canoes.

Entering a compound he saw a half-built forty-foot boat called a keelboat. Being a *landlubber*, Captain Lewis asked the owner if he had experience in making larger boats. The owner pulled out a sketch and showed it to Captain Lewis.

The builder said, "See this here board running lengthwise down the bottom, this is called the keel. Well, if the wind blows the wrong direction, this keel keeps the boat from tipping over in the water. You'll need this kind of boat, Captain."

"The mast and sail will help you go up river when the wind blows. It's mighty hard poling the boat up river against the current anyway. We'll put a twelve-foot sail on it to save your crew effort. OK?"

Nodding in the affirmative Captain Lewis proceeded to order two canoes called pirogues, and finally, a barge which would carry all the items being bought by Lewis.

Having ordered the boats, Captain Lewis turned his attention to protecting the Corps of Discovery itself. He estimated he would have up to fifty men, twenty-five of whom would be permanent members of the total. The balance of the corps would return to St. Charles with the logs (journals) of the progress. This group of returnees would go back to St Louis after one year no matter where the expedition was located at the time.

Lewis wanted to purchase clothing for the twenty-five permanent members—from coonskin hats to moccasins. He bought two sets of clothing for each permanent member of the corps, and one set for anyone else who was traveling with the corps, such as local settlers who signed on to pole the boat going upstream.

He purchased several barrels of gunpowder, flint, and steel for firing the muskets, bayonets for the muskets, first aid supplies, extra cloth sails for the keelboat, twenty-foot poles for going up river, two box compasses, two telescopes, and food that could be stored.

He also bought the latest map of the western part of the United States, assorted trinkets to trade with the Indians, eighty gold peace medals minted by the order of President Thomas Jefferson, and citizenship certificates hand written on parchment and signed personally by the president. The task for Captain Meriwether Lewis was mammoth and the trouble he had was getting the keelboat and barge delivered in St Charles by the April 30, 1804. Captain Meriwether Lewis likened it to a mystery thriller where the hero is about to get trampled by a herd of buffalo but it gets scared off by his friend. Thus the hero is saved for the next chapter of the story

CHAPTER 5

The Deal

CAPTAIN LEWIS STOOD STRAIGHT AND tall. He had booked a trip down the Ohio River. He felt very prosperous. He had ordered his keelboat and barge from the Pittsburgh Custom River Boat Company. It was to be thirty-five feet long and had to be ready by March 1804. He picked out a design copying a smaller riverboat he saw at the boatyard.

He placed the order with a master carpenter who owned the yard. The line of credit was based on the U.S. Treasury Certificate of Deposit that President Jefferson had secured from the Federal Budget of 1803. The deposit was paid in $20 gold coins from the National Treasury.

The carpenter asked Lewis, "That thar is river craft and ye' must be takin' a long trip up an' down the Mississippi river. It'll take ten in crew at least, an' be a vessel with a sail to match to help 'em go up river. I'll need the balance of the money before I'll let go of tha boat. Understan'?"

Captain Lewis answered, "There is much more where this came from," and he patted his coat pocket.

Lewis turned to leave the yard as he noticed a red Spaniel tied up. He reached down to pat the pooch. The dog growled and whined as Lewis said, "How much for him? I need a dog liked that."

Carpenter said, "Ya gave me a beeg order. When ya pick up yor keelboat and barge, I'll give him to ya. His name is Seaman. If ya need another, I have a new litter, and ya can buy one 'o them, too. See ya in March, but make it end of the month."

Captain Lewis left the boatyard and returned to the Traveler's Inn. He took the list of all the purchases he had made and crossed them off his list. When he had finished his booking on the ferryboat, he returned to his lodging and started a list of his efforts in the town below Fort Pitt.

Working at a table in the lobby area, Captain Lewis prepared his letter to the president—a summary of his stay at Pittsburgh.

It had been eight months since had left Washington, D.C., but he had not forgotten the administration's legalese. He had given the president preliminary reports of *The Voyage of Discovery*. The information included his stay at William and Mary. He listed what men, supplies, and equipment he needed.

Lewis would need between twenty to thirty frontiersmen to be trained after he had completed his enlisting trip. He wrote that he was starting now to get organized and would send a monthly report by messenger.

He added an outline of what he had to accomplish before he could start advancing Jefferson's dream. He ended with," I have not rested since I left D.C. I have had everything we needed for the departure sent to St. Louis. I am following your departure deadline exactly. I am treasuring each dollar I spend as if it were my own. I remember your difficulty in having half of a million dollars set aside by Congress. Whether this is enough is very chancy. My purchases must be boated to St. Louis. I remain your obedient understanding respectful servant, Captain Meriwether Lewis."

Traveling the road to the Ohio River, Captain Lewis wanted to get his platoons assembled. At the Travelers Rest, he had a hearty dinner and proceeded to transcribe this organization. He had made a chart that he had shown to no one. He had not flushed out his plans for the trip. This effort required several hours, after which he blew out the candles and went to sleep.

Day three and day four were the same, except in the evening when the entire inventory was put to bed. Some details were recorded as the ferryboat was traveling. On the fifth day of travel, it rained all day and Captain Lewis had a chance to read his paperwork listing what supplies would be needed for this trip. He had to project himself into the future—to consider the needs of the men going on the trip with him.

This mental process meant his facing the conflict of reality and desirability. This mental exercise was as intriguing as it was exhausting. His plans would be modified from time to time. Captain Lewis said to himself more than once, "I'm glad that I am twenty-eight, stand nearly six feet tall and have the ability to look into the future and plan."

It was noon on the sixth day of travel that Captain Lewis reached Fort Pitt.

The fort was at the junction of the Allegheny and Monongahela Rivers. It was a beautiful site for Lewis to observe. On the crest of a rugged mountain, the fort was an example of the pioneering spirit of the settlers.

The town of Pittsburg was being built with more and more businesses and population moving into the area. Captain Lewis surveyed those residences and businesses that made up the community. This was the beginning of the frontier.

The purpose of the visit by Meriwether Lewis had been spelled out during his discussion with President Jefferson. First and foremost was to order all the equipment, supplies, and river craft needed from the tradesmen that were in the Fort Pitt area, and second was to find an assistant to operate the Corps of Discovery.

That night Meriwether Lewis stayed in a travelers rest tavern in a newly inhabited area of the city surrounding Fort Pitt. He made a list of the items and supplies he would need. First and foremost, he would need a boat built to his specifications in order to carry the men of the Corps of Discovery and all the supplies.

The next day he searched for a boatyard where he could pick his boat. He found a boat builder and looked at his stock of pirogues and other types of canoes. He also wanted a larger boat to get across rivers that were too deep to wade and too wide to attempt by a horse and wagon.

One boat caught his eye. It was named a keelboat. It was approximately thirty feet long and nine feet wide. It was designed to go up and down rivers ten feet deep. It had a keel on the bottom to steady the boat and keep it buoyant. It came either with a mast and a sail or without. Looking at the craft, Captain Lewis ordered a forty-two-foot keelboat to be built. He bought a barge that was available and two pirogue that were on hand. The later would carry six people.

The keelboat former was to carry two cannons, a sail that was twelve feet high, and the supplies to be purchased from the merchants surrounding the fort.

Getting the boat builder to build the special boat required a deposit of five thousand dollars. He would build the vessel and have it ready within a four-month period. Meriwether Lewis wanted a pirogue and he had two immediately in stock. This buying spree took several days to accomplish. Every night he went up to the Travelers Rest Tavern and worked in his room and updated his list.

It was an expensive trip. He purchased gunpowder, a hundred cannon balls, one pound each in weight, and forty automatic rifles, which could shoot up to twenty rounds before reloading. One man with this rifle would be able to discharge twenty bullets before having to reload. The rifles would be flintlock whereby the powder would be ignited by flint hitting steel in the standard way. These were extremely accurate. The tradesman demonstrated the rifle showing how the powder would penetrate a one-inch wood plank at a hundred yards.

Then Captain Lewis went to a sail maker for custom-made canvas sails. The captain requested two sails each to be twelve feet wide by fourteen feet high. These could be raised or lowered on the mast of the keelboat. All the clothing for the expedition was purchased including moccasins, coonskin hats, and leather outer garments for the men to wear as they proceeded up the Missouri River.

All under garments were stock and extra buckskin was for outerwear. They needed stockings and raw materials to make garments to protect the men against snow and rain. As a means of identification, Captain Lewis ordered forty coonskin hats.

Various types of foodstuffs were ordered so as to be prepared for two weeks so that Captain Meriwether Lewis could go down the river toward the Mississippi-Missouri junction where the Voyage of Discovery would start. St. Charles and St. Louis settlements were on either side of the Mississippi-Missouri Junction. Captain Lewis' purchasing stay at Fort Pitt was accomplished within two weeks.

Leaving Fort Pitt and saying goodbye to the Lieutenant Colonel who was the commanding officer at Fort Pitt, Captain Lewis got in a canoe, picked up several boatmen, and hired them to take the five hundred mile trip down the river.

The purpose of this trip was to select men to man the voyage, man the boats, and be privates in the Corps of Discovery. Also two of the men would be selected as sergeants and two others would be corporals with the promise of becoming sergeants in the event anything happened to the sergeants.

Captain Lewis had completed the purchasing of his supplies and mode of transportation. He had bought other incidentals from the tradesmen from around the port such as compasses, two telescopes, a map of the area drawn by a cartographer, trinkets, and other gifts to give upon visits to various Indian tribes and their chiefs.

Perhaps the most important items were from Washington, D.C. One was the *Proclamation of The Louisiana Purchase* signed by President Thomas Jefferson. At each stop within the area being explored, the chief of the tribe would be sworn in as an America citizen and presented with an original copy of the proclamation and a gold Friendship Medal, designed by the president, showing the two races shaking hands.

These items were used to prove to tribal chiefs that they were new citizens and as such awarded these gifts from their president. These tokens from their *Great White Father* in Washington, D.C. were to be given to the new citizens and would be given to all such individuals who lived there.

President Jefferson had given specific instructions to both Captain Lewis and Clark to parlay with the Indian chiefs—to exchange gifts and celebrate the joining of the two societies.

President, Jefferson said to Captain Lewis "You are our ministers of goodwill. Do not take this duty lightly. The value of the Louisiana purchase is in your hands."

It was agreed that Captain Clark would pick up the keelboat and the other two pirogues that Captain Lewis had purchased. Captain Lewis paid half of the cost to the merchants at the time the order was placed and the other half would be paid at the time of delivery.

Meanwhile Captain Lewis decided to explore around Fort Pitt and traveled up to the border of West Virginia. He entered a town called Weston, which consisted of a glass making facility and fifteen families that worked there. It was created in a typical country village, which had pine trees, clear streams, and native animas such as deer, gophers in the foothills, and beavers damming up the streams flowing into the Monongahela River.

Captain Lewis visited the glass blowing area and was surprised to find that the sand available for glass making was available and that fuel used to heat the pots of glass was abundant.

The small community entrepreneurs would blow various objects like drinking glasses and tableware. Having gone some eighty miles away from Fort Pitt, Captain Lewis retraced his steps and visited the various merchants to see how the orders he had placed were progressing. He prepared to go down the Ohio and stop along the way filling the corps to the twenty-five privates required.

When he took delivery of the boat, he collected his new guard dog as a free bonus. Seaman became a major player in the drama. He wagged his tail in appreciation and licked the hand of his new master. It was down the river of opportunity and up the river of destiny. Was the search for the Northwest passage about to be found?

CHAPTER 6

Getting the Corps on the Road

AFTER HE SCRUTINIZED THE DOCUMENTS that had been signed by President Thomas Jefferson, Captain William Clark grabbed Sergeant Pryor by the arm and commanded, "Keep these here Indians from comin' aboard. They'll wreck the place. That's an order, Sergeant Pryor, and I mean look to it now!"

Sergeant Pryor snapped to attention, and said, "Aye, aye sir." Then he handed the papers to the French Canadian official, a Canuck who ruffled through the documents, and said, "Zees papers seem to be okay. You corps or whatya call ya self can be here in Missouree for a week. N'est pas?"

Having no objection, Captain Clark said, "Come aboard."

The small group of French officials came aboard and looked the keelboat over from stem to stern as Captain Clark said, "You are the first to greet us in St. Charles. My co-captain Lewis is in St. Louis presenting our official documents to your governor and staff. For starters, we will show you our latest cannon. You will note that it shoots a one-pound canon ball over a thousand feet. It is the greatest gun ever invented. It doesn't use gunpowder or shot. It reloads itself. Next week it will be ready to demonstrate. Do you want to see it work?"

Without waiting for an answer, Captain Clark continued. "When I get it mounted on the bow of our keelboat, I will show it in operation. Then, you can try it out if you want to. But now you, as the French official, must figure out how much you will charge me for tying up to your dock. Lieutenant Lewis is the one with the money, but he had to leave for government business this morning. Your paths must have crossed."

According to plan, Captain Lewis had gone to the Traveler's Roost on the Mississippi near St. Louis. This was the spot the captain had selected as his living quarters, the one Captain Lewis would use while in St. Louis honoring the wishes of President Jefferson.

In the meantime, they would look around the Missouri Indian Tribal territory east of the Mississippi River. While in the St. Louis settlement Captain Lewis would acquire the supplies he needed.

That morning Captain Lewis had received a dispatch from President Jefferson. It reported that the U.S. patent office had a patent filed a few weeks before. The patent modified the standard muskets used by the frontier armed forces. It converted muzzleloaders to breech loaders. They could fire up to twenty-eight rifle rounds before needing to be reloaded.

Captain Lewis knew this would make the army musket obsolete. Getting the new guns into the hands of the Corps of Discovery was the problem.

The kickoff date of this expedition had been set for May 14, 1804. However, Captain Lewis and Captain Clark had a decision to make. Should they start the Voyage of Discovery without the president's order? Or delay leaving until the diplomacy between France and Spain was completed with a signed treaty? It could mean the better part of a year.

A major purpose of the expedition was to inform the residents of the Northwestern lands that the territory was now owned by the United States of America. President Jefferson thought that any delay would allow British General Vancouver to head south and occupy the land south of the 54th parallel, which would cause the settlers and Indian tribes in the Louisiana Purchase territory to suffer.

President Jefferson had said to Captain Lewis, "You are our ministers of goodwill. Do not take this duty lightly. The Louisiana Purchase is in your hands. Keep me informed of your progress as you explore the Missouri River basin and find the Northwest Passage so that we can reach the Orient from the Pacific Coast now that we have the land of the Louisiana Purchase. It will make our fur trade much more valuable by using the Pacific Ocean. It will cut the distance to market in half."

Now everything was on hold waiting for the European countries to sign the treaty.

Captain Meriwether Lewis had prepared for the voyage at the University of Pennsylvania. While preparing he learned about unusual medicines, such as Dr. Rush's Elixir of Life, the standard type of medication for what might ail the members of the corps as they traveled toward the Northwest Territory.

However, this elixir failed as a nerve medicine. Captain Lewis had the jitters because of the delays. He blamed himself for failing to make an independent decision to proceed and act on his own rather than wait to hear from President Jefferson to move ahead.

It was an internal conflict involving assumption of authority by Lewis. Having been President Jefferson's private secretary, Meriwether Lewis had decided he'd rather be safe than sorry, so wouldn't act on his own.

Captain Clark was so new to command that he told Captain Lewis, "It's your neck Meriwether."

Captain Lewis said to himself. *My butt is on the block. If we don't keep on the president's schedule, and his corps does not make up for lost time, will it be my fault? Or will President Jefferson subscribe to, and support, whatever action I take?*

While working to assemble men and material for the Voyage of Discovery, Lewis's decisions were approved by the president on an ex post facto—after the fact—basis. Lewis had given a great deal of thought to his assignment, and he believed that recruiting could be accomplished as he went from Washington, D.C. to St. Louis, Missouri.

Captain Lewis chose Lieutenant William Clark as his co-captain, a man of equal rank to himself. Captain Clark would run the organization, maintain discipline, and do the charting of their route. Captain Lewis would be in charge of collecting the scientific data. He would also be responsible for all astronomical readings and the scientific information that the Corps of Discovery would secure, record, and return to Washington, D.C. Captain

Lewis decided that he would keep a log of all the species of plants, birds, fish, insects, and mammals that they found along the route through the Northwest Passage. Settling disputes between the two leaders would be decided by a vote of the entire corps.

The members of the corps were to be paid at the end of the endeavor. Most would be paid $5 for each month and the non-commissioned officers $6. In addition to cash, a grant of land in the territory of the corps member choosing was to be given by the U.S. government. These wages were extraordinary according to the president.

Captain Meriwether Lewis was the expedition medical practitioner, and whether it was good fortune or not, only one person died at the hands of Captain Meriwether Lewis. It was Sergeant Floyd. The cause of death was a ruptured appendix. Even so, Captain Lewis blamed himself for not pulling Floyd through this illness.

The two Captains reviewed the abilities of each member of the corps, as they all had special skills. Captain Clark had given a great deal of thought and was determined that his corpsmen would be in place and trained for the exploration. In this way, the men so selected for the Corps of Discovery would be able to withstand the rigors of such a mission.

Among the skilled trades needed were a shoemaker, a map maker, and a person who could locate a position of the Corps of Discovery. There needed to be three or four skilled hunters to provide meat, and a sail maker was needed to mend sails and keep all the clothing in good repair.

So Captain Lewis made a log of all those characters and skills needed and deliberately sought them as his visit to Camp Dubois was proceeding. His method of operation would be to stop at a rest stop or provisional place along the river, contact the chief of a tribe or the owner of the rest stop and ask him the following questions:

"Do you know of any male under thirty who has the abilities to sew and is interested in an exploration of the unknown territory of the United States of America?"

Invariably, the chief of the tribe or the head person at the rest stop would advance names so that Captain Lewis could interview and hire them if they could agree to the monthly salary and promise of land.

Captain Lewis succeeded in finding three hunters, one shoemaker, and one tent maker who could sew canvas for a sail and repair the clothing. He gradually raised the fourteen or so men with special skills to make the Corps of Discovery whole.

———

Captain Lewis was in a quandary about when to start the Voyage of Discovery. Should the mission stay put until he, Captain Lewis, felt they had touched all the bases? Make the president happy and start on schedule? Get further instruction from the president himself?

So far Lewis had not been second guessed by the president. But this time it would be the president getting criticism from the American public and Congress, which had financed the expedition.

Would Lewis be able to justify the delay to get going?

After consulting with his friend and equal, Clark replied, "Meriwether, you know the president better than I do. He told us how important this expedition is to the nation. He wished us well. The men are already missing their loved ones at home. After I have been in charge of the corps for a longer time, I will help you decide. But now you are on your own on making the decision as to when to move. It is May 13. You have one day to make up your mind. I wish I could help you, but I can't! It is your call, Meriwether."

CHAPTER 7

Waiting for the "GO" Signal

CLUTCHING THE MESSAGE FROM THE president in his hand, Captain Lewis told Clark "The Louisiana Purchase is ours! This says that he is not ready to name the person to officially present the directions as to what we expect the French settlement's leader to do now. Why did he want me to deliver the message?"

Clark answered "Good question. To me, if I am asked to answer, it will conflict with his views. I am here. He is in D.C. How to do it and who should do it should be up to the leader on the field of action."

"President Jefferson told you to broadcast the news to everyone in Saint Louis. We had better do as he says because all its one thousand settlers need to be notified by an American official that the Louisiana Purchase is a reality. You are the official to do it for our country. Don't lollygag. Get a move on!"

These diplomatic formalities had to be performed in the French settlement of Saint Louis before the Lewis and Clark expedition could start. Captain Lewis finally agreed that the treaty was so important to the nation's mission that he would be the one to deliver it directly despite the disagreement of Captain Clark. Lewis took the bull by the horns and made the delivery.

Since this ceremony would take several days. Captain Lewis wanted time to have Straight Arrow, the Indian chief of the Missouri tribe, as well as Josh Smithers, the Saint Louis settlement leader, and a few other dignitaries to see the official ceremony.

As the president ordered, Captain Lewis made the presentation of "The Freedom Medal," the American flag, and a copy of the official treaty to the Missouri tribal chief. This ceremony was to be the beginning of the expedition. It was also a practice session for presentations that would take place as the trip progressed.

All was in readiness on May 14. It was a beautiful spring day on the Missouri river. Red-breasted robins pecked at the angle worms on the bank of the Mississippi. Seagulls circled overhead waiting to dive down to seize a dead minnow floating down the river. Captain Lewis laughed aloud at the sight. *A dead fish for breakfast—not much of a feast.*

At noon, Captain Clark blew a whistle to get attention and shouted so all could hear. "Sergeant Ordway, cast off! Sergeant Floyd, look to the ten boatmen we hired to row. Let's hear them pole the boat to the ditty *Row, row, row our boat swiftly up the stream. Merrily, merrily, merrily, merrily. Life is but a dream."*

The small crowd of interested people stared at the captains as Captain Clark seemed indifferent and ignored those from the Mizzou Indian reservation who had come out of their tepees and waved goodbye. The other people who had gathered for the sailing were singing *Nearer to my God than thee* as the white canvas sail ballooned out catching the afternoon breeze. It was a strange sight with the forty-foot keelboat in the lead, the barge being poled up the Missouri River, and the two man canoes in single file behind.

Fortunately, President Jefferson had sent a dispatch by official courier that had been received on May 13, 1804, which said, *"Gentlemen, you are directed to begin the Corps of Discovery's mission when this is placed in your hands. It is 'the Kickoff' of a trip that can never to be duplicated. You must find The Northwest Passage to the Pacific Ocean. May my prayers for your success reach the good Lord's ears."*

It was signed and sealed with the Shield and Arrow Eagle signet found on all official documents sent by the president. Captain Clark looked at the message after Captain Lewis had read it aloud. He said, "Wonderful. Wonderful."

Captain Lewis said, "William, you are always the practical soldier. I am always glad that I picked you for my leadership partner. We're in this together. I, too, hope for good luck and God speed."

As they prepared for bed that night each of the co-captains had remembrances about the other. Captains Lewis and Clark had met in the United States Army. Though they had become fast friends while serving in the frontier forces in years gone by, each man thought life had different challenges.

Captain William Clark felt he had to prove to the world he could organize and direct the Corps of Discovery. While his promotion to Captaincy had been at the insistence of Meriwether Lewis this act alone left a bitter taste in Clark's mouth. He felt that this promotion should have been as a result of his army service in the territory of Ohio rather than an act of the president's private secretary Captain Meriwether Lewis and his political pull with Congress.

On the other hand, Captain Lewis felt that the exploration and cataloging of man and beast was the purpose of this national endeavor. He sensed that the personal service he was providing to his country would be recognized forever by future generations of Americans. He wanted to succeed for those reasons.

Meanwhile, the three boats and a barge were docked and waiting near the hamlet called Saint Charles. The Corps of Discovery had disembarked and pitched their tents in a campground near the Missouri River. The Voyage of Discovery was meeting one of the president's demands: leave by May 14, 1804.

The entire group was anxious to get started up the Missouri River. Four months of army training had weighed heavily on their spirits. Lewis and Clark had wanted to start their voyage when the time was right. If the wind changed direction and blew from the east it was a signal from above that the weather was right. Yes, today was start day.

The corps boarded the keelboat, laughingly called the tub, and moved it several hundred yards up river so that the start of the expedition kept to the president's set schedule.

During the weeklong trip up river from St. Charles, both Captains had felt that it was wise to spend every day productively. Captain Clark said he would see that the boats and all the gear was in apple pie order. Captain

Lewis had business to take care as they met with the tribes of Indians in the Indian camps. He would spend his free time reading about the unknown land they were about to enter.

St Charles was a beginning point of the unknown. The river flowed from the northwest direction and only the Lord knew how many miles, as it had never been explored.

CHAPTER 8

Gassing Up

PATRICK GASS, QUARTERMASTER, WAS LOOKING to increase the wheat supply for the expedition. He told Captain Lewis, "We are in wheat country. I have been talking to the dock master here. He thought that he could bargain with local farmers and buy 100 sacks of wheat loaded on board for $40 because it is May 1804 and the winter wheat was sitting on the dock. I offered him half and it is O.K. I will tell the seller that it is C.O.D, and will say he must get the sacks loaded on the barge for the $20 gold piece."

The captain was impressed about the forethought of Gass. He pulled out a twenty-dollar gold piece and said to Gass, "Private Gass the Fort Pitt price is three times what the farmers here are asking. I actually paid three times more than you did. Go back to St. Charles and buy it provided they will deliver by tomorrow. Buy it but don't give the man his money until it is on board the barge. You will pay the man after that."

Gass saluted and left the deck. He felt the amount of wheat on board was not even a month's supply for the twenty-five privates and the rest of the boat's compliment—thirty-four hungry people including officers and staff. He knew how vital the need for energy was and that the farming of wheat was being done in the area. The cook could bake bread every day. Gass knew that this would make him a hero when Captain Lewis saw the bags of wheat being loaded on the barge.

Besides, he wanted to get away from the men in the corps. He was not concerned with being alone, as he was unmarried, about thirty, loved the freedom permitted with the ladies of the evening when he was away serving his country in the Frontier Forces before he was recruited by captains. He considered himself a cut above the rest of the corps because he came from the Pennsylvania area where he learned the trade of carpentry while in Boston and therefore had a better education than most of the others.

The weather was favorable. It was not too hot during the day and the nights were pleasant. This benefited the entire Corps of Discovery but especially the quartermaster, Sergeant Patrick Gass. He was in charge of the barge on which all the supplies and equipment that Captain Meriwether Lewis had received.

Captain Lewis and William Clark started up the river with high hopes and having been told by President Jefferson that the Voyage of Discovery should start by May 14th, he met his request by steaming from St. Charles, pulling their muddy way in the Missouri, and went off shore two hundred and fifty yards around a bend where they would not be seen, but would be able to comply with the request of Thomas Jefferson, the president of the United States. It was accomplished by five o'clock in the afternoon.

As the sun set in the west, the complement of the corps proceeded to bed down for the night on the keelboat and barge. This was to be done by laying out blankets and doing the best they could to make themselves comfortable.

Grouped around the fire, the men had pulled out tobacco and proceeded either to chew it or smoke it. As they watched the smoke curl up in the air they contemplated life in the 19th century.

The moon was shining brightly and reflecting off the water. It was very quiet as they were so far off the bank that they could not hear the crickets chirping.

Fields commented to the group, starting the conversation noting, "What a night. It is so balmy and pleasant. It's early in the season so the mosquitoes aren't a problem and tomorrow we start poling up the river. This will be the adventure of my life and my brother Reuben. We will certainly enjoy the experience of trying to find the Northwest Passage."

Reuben, the older brother nodded his head. "I do think that the two of us will guide our way. I sure hope the captains keep us brothers together as we are extremely close. We have been since I can remember."

Captains Lewis and Clark met the next night. They decided to explain the whys of the Missouri Expedition to the corps

Clark told Lewis, "We will compromise regarding lunch and that if that was unsatisfactory, the voyage would return to St. Louis and the crew would be replaced. In other words, I'll hire another crew."

After getting the Captains final offer, the boatmen held their own meeting and decided to peacefully arrive at a compromise, which was to row for a half an hour before sunset and eat lunch as they were working. The crew would attempt to get forty miles up the river every day wherever possible. If trying was not good enough, the crew would quit now and be replaced in St. Louis where they were hired. The two sides the Corps of Discovery and the crew agreed to stay. "Let's sign and go up the river together."

The corps was relieved because they wanted to go as far up the Missouri as they possibly could before the Missouri froze over. The shaking of the hands took place and the tacit agreement was concluded without a strike or termination by either party.

This was the first sign of a conflict that Captain Lewis and Clark had encountered and it proved to them that disputes could be settled peacefully. However, Captain Clark was much sterner in his position of "We are right, and you are wrong." Captain Lewis felt any difference of opinion could be solved by reasonable people in a reasonable negotiation. Flexibility was Captain Lewis's guiding principle, and this attitude could lead to trouble between the leadership. This was the first inkling that the two captains were playing with fire.

CHAPTER 9

Goodbye and Good Luck

IT WAS GO-TIME. IT WAS all the bells and whistles. It was several days of waiting for a change in the weather. The wind had swung around so that it was blowing from the south. Captain Clark talked the matter over with Lewis as he opined, "The delays in starting to travel up the river are over."

The tiny settlement was agog with excitement along with the two captains who were to begin an exploration of the century. It would rival the accomplishment of Columbus.

The word being bandied about was, "The departure was to be mid-May,1804. It was to start at the mouth of the Missouri River. It would involve all thirty members of the corps, who were waiting impatiently." They were pleased when the messenger arrived authorizing the start of the exploration date of the expedition.

Captain Lewis knew why the president wanted to get the Corps of Discovery underway. It was his re-election in the fall of 1804 and President Thomas Jefferson had very little to show for his time in office. The voters needed to see results, not promises. How fast time flies and how much there is to accomplish.

The crowd of settlers, Indians, and well-wishers went to the shore to watch. The public officials heard Governor General Blaine of the Missouri territory make a *Good Luck and Goodbye* speech as the keelboat and all supplies and armaments left the docks to travel west along the Missouri

River into virgin territory. Though now owned by the United States of America, it was inhabited principally by Indian tribes and animals.

Captain Lewis, a co-leader by choice was concerned as the Corps of Discovery left St. Charles. *"Have I forgotten to do anything that would cause failure?"* was in his thoughts. Captain William Clark on the other hand was optimistic. He felt his enthusiasm surge and much joy in his heart as the voyage of exploration was on its way.

The sun was going down in the west and the wind had changed so now it came from the east. The sail of the keelboat blossomed white like a cumulus cloud in the afternoon sky. An eagle flew overhead looking for small fish to eat. It was up the river, with the hope of the president sailing along, in the hearts and minds of the crew of the exploration.

The Missouri Territory, having been French for several years, was chafing at the bit while the Louisiana Purchase was finalized. In this time frame, Captain Lewis suggested to his co-leader Clark that he visit the French official for the territory. He could be contacted in the St. Louis settlement and he was the politico to see. Lewis should present the documents confirming the Northwest Territory was American.

"I respectfully request that you proceed. Please get going and May God Be Your Master." This instruction came by messenger from the president. Thomas Jefferson had it delivered the first week in April but the Corps of Discovery had moved from Camp Dubois.

Captains Lewis told Clark that protocol required him to officially present the instruction from the president to the settlement leader in the Missouri territory across the river. Only thirty miles away, St. Louis and its one thousand settlers needed to be notified by an American official that the Louisiana Purchase was a reality and Captain Meriwether Lewis was delivering the treaty

This ceremony would take several days. Captain Lewis wanted to have the Indian chief of the Missouri tribe, the St. Louis settlement leader, and other settlers to see the official ceremony. Lewis spent three days in the transfer of control. Captain Lewis made the presentation of the Medal of

Friendship, the American flag, and official treaty to the Missouri tribal chief. This was the beginning of the expedition.

Leaving St. Louis, Captain Lewis saw a beautiful spring day on the Missouri river. The robins were pecking at the angle worms on the St. Charles green and the seagulls were circling overhead. The two pirogues and the keelboat with their thirty-four members aboard were eager to start the expedition. President Jefferson had sent a dispatch that was received on May 14, 1804. It said, "Gentlemen, you are directed to begin the Corps of Discovery's mission. It is the beginning of a never to be duplicated journey. Never falter in searching for The Northwest Passage to the Pacific Ocean."

The two officers in the United States Army, though they were fast friends while serving in the frontier forces, had a different motivation.

Captain William Clark felt he had to prove to the world he could organize and direct the Corps of Discovery.

Captain Meriwether Lewis felt that the exploration and cataloging of man and beast was the end all of the presidential expedition. It was the *what, where, when, and why* of the adventure into the unknown.

Both Captains disembarked and looked for a campground from which on the morrow, they would begin their Journey. The four months of army training had weighed heavily on their spirit. Now it was outwait the weather which had a head wind from the Northwest

Captains Lewis and Clark felt it was wise to spend the time productively. Captain Clark said he would see that the boats and all the gear were in ship-shape order. Captain Lewis had business to take care of in St. Louis, Missouri.

The co-captains Clark and Lewis had met during the Revolutionary War, and they became friends. But they were completely opposite in appearance and demeanor.

Captain Lewis was twenty-nine years old. He was slender, had a tan complexion, a quiet voice, darting eyes, and was withdrawn in nature. As the private secretary of Thomas Jefferson, he thought he had found his niche in life, monitoring Jefferson's correspondence, maintaining the office of the president, and being important in helping the progress of the United States.

Captain William Clark had shocking red hair with a complexion to match. His voice was loud and commanding, his manner abrupt, and his spirit uncontained. He had an athletic built, he was meant to give orders, and see to it that they were followed.

The first platoon was to be run by Captain Clark. It included all of the organization and corps operations. It was army style with its rigid discipline and methods used. The second platoon would collect specimens and recorded scientific information. Captain Lewis would be in charge of the exploratory route, the collection of data of various animals, the forestry, and other physical aspects of the environment.

Major decisions of the expedition were to be decided by a vote. These included punishment and change of course to be followed. When, or if, to return to civilization would be jointly decided. The greeting and other Indian tribal matters were to be done jointly. Presenting the Presidential Medals of Friendship would be done by both Lewis and Clark.

Captain Meriwether Lewis was pleased that he had found his co-leader. He sent a letter by Pony Express saying, "I have the honor of letting you know that the compliment of the Corps of Discovery has been filled if you agree."

This became a reality and the proposed co-captains proceeded down the Ohio River to Camp Dubois on the eastern side of the Mississippi River. The integration and training of the Corps of Discovery was about to begin.

There was some concern in the mind of Captain Lewis that everything was tentatively selected, discussed, and would be the subject of co-leader William Clark's training and organizational abilities. There was joy at Camp Walton that night and the newly formed Corps of Discovery proceeded down the Ohio River to Fort Dubois, an abandoned fort at the juncture of the Mississippi and Ohio Rivers in a tiny corner of Illinois territory.

The two Captains of the Corps of Discovery set up the plans together and had nightly conversations about the four-month training period to be handled by Captain Clark and the completion of the study requirements to be supervised by Captain Lewis.

During one of these conversations Captain Lewis talked about his plans for the balance of the four-month training period in that he would return to the Fort Pitt area and pick up the keelboat, which should be finished. While there, Captain Lewis would purchase the necessary provisions.

During the first four months of 1804 the Corps of Discovery knew that this was extremely important to the country and as such especially to President Jefferson. He was facing re-election and would need the progress in the Corps of Discovery and its venture into the wilderness to bring to the citizens of the United States. In Captain Clark's mind, he was confident he could organize and operate the Corps of Discovery as to all the functions that would have to be accomplished except the ones jointly responsible to take on by the two co-captains and their reporting to the president and to the operations.

CHAPTER 10

I Can't Get Them Up in the Morning

DEAD MEN CAN TELL TALES was the story in the life of Sergeant Charles Floyd. This June morning Floyd was given the duty of giving the wakeup call. He looked around the compound and saw many of the men still asleep. The men had been sleeping by the fire, which had died down during the night. Some of the men had gone ashore at dawn just as Sergeant Floyd had started to sing, "I can't get them up, I can't get them up in the morning." It was this song that had greeted the corps on the seventh day of the trip.

Sergeant Floyd was standing on the deck of the keelboat. It was before daybreak, and Floyd seem to enjoy making the men in his platoon miserable. He thrived on the misery of others. Floyd prided himself in being a killjoy. The corps' daily duties, as were many of the menial tasks, were made more so by the way the work was assigned.

Sergeant Floyd had said, "Those of you who think you can get the easy work by kissin' the ass of your leaders, forget about it . . .it won't work with me." He knew he had the reputation of being a lousy noncommissioned officer, but that was the way it was going to be.

He thought to himself, *The corps hates to get ready to work hard, and I am the one to make it easier on them? No sir! That is the way it is! It's the way I like it, and so do the leaders.* He shouted to the men, "I say get up you loafers. Rise and shine!"

Captain Clark wished he could get Nathan Pryor, or any other man, in exchange for Floyd. Someone like Nathan Pryor would make Clark's disciplinary problems decline.

The keelboat, named Voyager, pulling a barge, meandered up the silty ribbon of the Missouri River, nicknamed the Big Mo. The water was such a dirty brown that the crew could not see the rocks that scratched the bottom of the keelboat. The two vessels, the barge and the keelboat, stayed in the middle of the river as the men walked along on the shore. Boatmen hired in St. Louis used twenty-foot poles to push the keelboat in a zigzag fashion against the current up the Missouri. Waterfowl swooped in and out welcoming the corpsmen to their river.

A sail on board could be used when the wind came from the right direction. At the moment the wind was coming from the southeast helping the boatmen's efforts.

Seaman, Captain Lewis's dog, ran around the decks of both the keelboat and the barge. He barked at the mallard ducks that flew in formation above the river.

The boatmen had been hired for the first part of the trip or until the keelboat was unable to travel any farther up the Missouri River. The river moved at about four miles per hour and the men could not walk that fast on the bank or while wading in shallow water. The helmsman would keep the Corps of Discovery away from any brush, rocks, trees, or other impediments stopping them from going up the river.

Captain Lewis came from the quarterdeck below to Captain Clark. "Good morning William. It is great to be underway. The wind is coming from the southeast."

William Clark said, "Aye, aye, Captain Lewis. It is great that the boatmen are being helped by the winds. We knew it wasn't going to be easy."

Neither of the leaders knew how far up the river they would be able to have the boatmen assist them.

Captain Clark continued, "We are moving at three miles per hour, zigzagging back and forth. It will take us several days, perhaps a week, to go to our first landing at the Kansa Indian Reservation. We will stop at the Nebraska Tribe along the way. You know that this will be an indoctrination to notify the tribes that they owe their allegiance to the United States now and forever. They are subject to all the laws of the land."

Captain Lewis replied, "As I understand, there are almost one hundred of such tribes who are now American subjects."

Captain Clark answered. "I think so, and I have to tell you that I am excited to be chosen by you to be the operation officer of this voyage and exploration."

The keelboat and barge, with crew, continued to the Kansa Reservation. Here the Kansa River joined the Missouri and that they would pass the White Islands but would not land there. Sergeant Pryor would scout the island to see if there were any Indian tribes or settlers there and report if he saw signs of life there.

Lewis and Clark had discussed the presentation of the friendship medal, the meeting of the chief, and the other council braves. A conflict arose between Clark and Lewis as to who should be in the presentation group. Captain Clark felt that it should be Captain Lewis along with someone to present the flag.

Captain Lewis thought both he and Clark should head up the presentation group, followed by four sergeants, and York, Clark's former slave, carrying the flag.

"It should be much more formal. We are leaders appointed by the president himself. We are to invite the chief to visit Washington, D.C. to meet with the president."

Because of the conflict between the two leaders, a vote was called the day before the presentation would take place. Captain Clark called the meeting to order. He asked Captain Lewis to present the issues to be voted upon.

Captain Lewis said, "Aye, aye sir," and he read the issues. "Should the presentation ceremony be held with only Captain Lewis and the presenter of the American flag? Should the presenters be a group of seven people with both leaders, four sergeants, and a presenter of the flag? Should the presentation be formal or informal?"

The vote was held and Captain Clark and twenty of the thirty-one voted in favor of having a larger group present the American flag and the order from the president. The remaining eleven decided that it was a fair vote and wanted to get on with it.

After the vote the corps reassembled. The seven people involved in the presentation ceremony would go on shore. The others would stay aboard the keelboat. The ceremony would be visible from the boat.

At three o'clock in the afternoon the official ceremony took place with the presentation of the Presidential Medal of Friendship, the American Flag, and the executive orders from President Jefferson welcoming the Kansa tribe and its territory into the United States of America.

After the ceremony the corps had a powwow with the Kansa tribe and Chief Amber Jack, including a war dance around the fire and a celebration with kickapoo joy juice—a native concoction containing alcohol and several special additives. The celebration was attended by braves, squaws, and the Corps of Discovery. Captain Clark indulged in a battle of drink-it-down. Before the night was over Clark had the privilege of helping the chief stagger to his tepee.

In the evening the corps returned to the keelboat and hit the sack. Those who wished to stay ashore were allowed, provided they reported in at eight o'clock in the morning.

This first encounter with the Indian tribes was to become the pattern for many ceremonies after that. Captain Lewis chided Captain Clark by wagging his finger and saying, "Thank you very much for your gracious welcoming ceremony. I feel that you should continue this type of ceremony at each of the tribal ceremonies. You sand bagged the chief and poured him into his bed."

Captain Clark responded with a smile "Aw shucks it wasn't such a much!"

It would seem that the Voyage of Discovery was off to a great start, greeting the tribes and ushering them into the new nation in such a fashion. It was hard to predict the problems that lay ahead. Failure in the coming days and weeks was a possibility. It was impossible for the two leaders to know if their mission would end in success or failure.

CHAPTER 11

Discipline Personified

"**D**ISCIPLINE BE DAMNED" GRUMBLED CAPTAIN Clark as his men slaved while they poled the keelboat upstream. Who hadn't heard of an army corps being wild and wooly? This was the question that was being bandied about by the crew in the keelboat as the crew struggled to fight the current tugging them downstream. The water flowing in the Missouri River was pulling Captain Clark and the others in the opposite direction they wanted to go.

Sergeant Charles Floyd, learning of the formation of the corps, wanted to be in the corps but as a small cog in the machine not the motor running it. Floyd knew he could handle details perfectly. He said, "Tell Captain Lewis that I have great ability to help him as quartermaster of the operation. Just give me a shot and I'll show him how to make the organization go army style." Through his presentation, follow up and pull, Charles Floyd became Sergeant of Discipline.

Soon after his appointment, his disciplinary prowess came to the fore. Two of Captain Lewis's men serving as advance scouts, John Shields and George Shannon, managed to scout their way into the liquor supply of the expedition. While on nighttime guard duty both were found in a drunken stupor. They were lying face down in a bed of clover each with empty flagon in his hand. As two of the scouts for the corps, they were unable to perform their jobs, which was to find the way up the Missouri River.

After rousing them with a kick in the ribs, Sergeant Floyd got them on their feet. He reported the incident to Captain Clark. Receiving Sergeant Floyd's account of the incident both captains had a hearing. After an hour the two leaders, acting as judge and jury, watched as Sergeant Floyd gave each man a tongue lashing as well as backlashing. It was so intense that neither man would forget it.

This was discipline personified. It was the beginning of the persona of the two Captains. Clark's was *the right way is the only way.* And his counterpart, Lewis, the scientist was, *don't do anything that will rock the boat.* Captain Lewis, whose main duty would be to collect information and continue to let the world know that the Northwest Territory made the United States of America a key player on the North American Continent.

Private John Shields was a Virginian, and at thirty-five, the oldest member of the expedition. He had joined the Corps of Discovery in August 1803 as one of the three men from Fort Pitt recruited by Lewis.

The other scout, Shannon, got lost on two occasions. On August 26, 1804, he was sent to retrieve two packhorses. He was separated from the party for sixteen days and nearly starved going without food for twelve days except for some crab apples, grapes, and rabbits he shot.

At first he thought he was behind the expedition so he sped up the river thinking he could catch up. Then, getting hungry, he went downstream to join some fur traders going down the Ohio River. Finally, John Colter was sent to find him.

Shannon got lost for a second time when the expedition was at the Three Forks. This time he rejoined the corps by backtracking to the forks near the Shoshone Indian Tribe. It seemed to the captains that scouting was not Shannon's forte.

The discipline meted out to Shannon and Shields as harsh as it was, became an object lesson for the others men of the Corps of Discovery. Captain Clark felt he had shown his resolve.

CHAPTER 12

Cliques

SERGEANT ORDWAY BARKED, "ATTENTION PRIVATES!" The group of men from Captain Lewis recruiting trip hopped to attention.

Captain Lewis told Co-Captain Clark "These are yours Clark. It is your duty to supervise the boatmen."

Nathaniel Pryor became a sergeant at Clark's request because Sergeant Floyd was ill and could not continue his job as leader of the boatmen. This was the corps' first replacement, and it concerned the two leaders because they could forecast cliques forming, and this would destroy the good attitude the corps had.

Sergeant Charles Floyd became ill in the middle of the summer. Co-captains Clark and Lewis met to make a decision. What to do about the fact that Sergeant Floyd, Captain Clark's operations officer, was unable to perform his duties because of a mysterious illness.

Captain Clark, though he was equal in rank, did not want to make decisions of such magnitude unilaterally without Captain Lewis's help. They met and agreed that both Charles Floyd and his substitute Nathaniel Pryor would be sergeants.

If small groups of dissident privates formed the workload of the menial members of the expedition might occur. Captain Clark told Captain Lewis that he wanted Nathaniel Pryor to be Floyd's replacement until Floyd recuperated from his sickness.

Sergeant Nathaniel Pryor assumed his promotion as the corps stopped in the Nebraska area. It was a hot summer evening, and the white chalk hills contrasted with the black of the night. Captain Lewis talked to Pryor before the corps retired.

Clark said, "Nate, I wanted to talk to you before I make the announcement to you. You are my suggested replacement for Sergeant Floyd. You and I are close enough that you could be my cousin. This could ruin the good fellowship in our corps. Even York, my black manservant, is accepted as an equal member of our corps. You were born in Virginia and are a cousin of fellow expedition member Charles Floyd. The two of you moved to Kentucky when you were eleven. Am I correct?"

Pryor saluted as he said respectfully, "Yes, sir."

Captain Clark continued, "Now Sergeant Pryor, assemble the corps on the river bank so that I can tell them of your appointment. I will tell Sergeant Floyd of your promotion."

With that Captain Clark returned to the officers' quarters on the keelboat and told Captain Lewis that Pryor was made sergeant. The new Sergeant Pryor and six of the men were assigned to Captain Clark. They were put in the first squad consisting of six privates who were assigned the toughest job on the expedition—poling the boat up the Missouri. Captain Lewis and Clark considered Pryor a man of character and ability. They felt that Nathaniel Pryor could handle his summertime appointment well.

It was not long in coming. Sergeant Pryor presided over a court-martial of Privates John Collins and Hugh Hall who were accused of stealing whiskey and drinking on duty. The men were found guilty and sentenced to a flogging. This became the duty of Sergeant Pryor. The punishment of fifty lashes with a bullwhip was watched by the crew.

As the entire expedition viewed the flogging in silence, the men who observed the criminals being punished came to realize that the stores of food and equipment of the expedition were sacrosanct. Any violation of the rules and regulation aboard or ashore would quickly result in the culprit being tried and punished. It did not matter if the culprit was caught in the act by one of the captains or was reported. Such an act would be viewed as the commission of a crime and would result in swift punishment.

This choice bothered Captain Lewis, and though he was not happy about the new sergeant's appointment, he had agreed. This was the start of a problem. It was to restore the Chief Sheheke to his tribe when they passed through the Dakota Territory. The two captains agreed such an action should be done on the return trip from finding the shortest way to the west coast of North America, after the expedition was finished--even if President Jefferson's term had been completed.

George Drouillard was conscripted by Captain Meriwether Lewis as he was bringing the keelboat down the Ohio River to start the voyage up the Missouri. Captain Lewis stayed overnight on the way to rejoin Captain Clark. It was at this chance meeting Captain Lewis sat next to George at dinner in a hostel.

As they were smoking a pipe of tobacco after dining, the two travelers one born at the start of the Revolutionary War the other at the end of it, shared backgrounds

George and his family roamed the French Canadian countryside finally settling in a small community raising sheep. George had a little schooling but was a talented student in language skills.

So at age sixteen George left the Huron area of the Great Lakes. He joined the U.S. Army and was stationed in the Ohio River Valley. His mother knit wool sweaters to shield young and old from the bitter cold of the Lake Huron winters. It was a skimpy living for the family as the wool she used was from the sheep they grew.

George volunteered to enter the army and was stationed near the Ohio River. It was there Captain Lewis found him. George's language skills were unusual to say the least. He learned sign language from his mother. He learned to speak French and English while going to school near Quebec. His father spoke the Huron language and moved his family to a Canadian settlement where both English and French were spoken. It was little wonder that Captain Lewis could not believe his good luck. The interpreter to dream about.

Neither man was married. Both had government backgrounds of army service. Both were young enough to take a gamble with their lives--going from safety to the unknown. Captain Lewis leaving President Thomas Jefferson., George Drouillard leaving the U.S. Army where the regimental motto was "Don't shoot you, don't shoot me, shoot the man behind the tree."

The fact that these thirty-four men of diverse occupations were heading into who knows what and were willing to stay a long time searching for the golden grail, the shortest way to the orient. Just a few days on their way and already officers found trying circumstances facing them. Leadership tests, punishment meted out to keep the group in line, and incidents unexpected but normal. What will happen next on the voyage?

CHAPTER 13

Duty Comes a-Calling

"WATCH THE STORE WHEN I am not here with the corps. We have $500,000 dollars from the United States treasury to spend wisely. It is set aside for our expedition. You will be held accountable," cautioned Captain Meriwether Lewis, who was instructing Charles Floyd, quartermaster in the Lewis and Clark Expedition. Floyd, his junior in rank, was a corporal in the U.S. Army.

A native of Kentucky, Floyd was a relative of Captain Clark and the first man to join the expedition. He was chosen by the co-Captains to become the guardian of the supplies and equipment purchased by Captain Lewis while he was stocking up in the spring of 1804.

Charles Floyd was both lucky and unlucky at the same time. He was lucky enough to be related to leader Clark, but he was unlucky enough to be the only person to die on the expedition. His death was after less than a year of duty. The cause was non-violent and Captain Lewis, as the corps medical specialist, administered the miracle cure all, Dr. Benjamin Rush's Elixir of Life, but it failed to work.

Corporal Floyd wrote in his diary, *July 31. I am very sick and have been for some time, but have recovered my health again.* However, this recovery was temporary, and he wrote no more. Just before he died, Captain Clark heard him whisper, "I am going away. I want you to write me a letter."

The funeral was held, and Floyd was buried on a bluff overlooking the Missouri River. The expedition named the spot Floyd's Bluff in his honor. The corps spent the night after the funeral service on the river. The crickets chirped and the bats swooped down to snap up mosquitoes as they flew close to the water. It was a beautiful evening in the Iowa Territory. It was the middle of August, which saw thundershowers almost daily, often accompanied by hail as big as marbles.

Captain Lewis thought Floyd's death was likely to have been caused by a ruptured appendix or some kind of a sexual disorder, like gonorrhea, since rumor had it that Corporal Floyd played around with Indian maidens on many occasions.

In the fall of 1804 Private John Newman, another volunteer who hailed from Camp Wood and said that he had reached twenty years of age, was not only caught lying but also failed to obey orders. As punishment he was given a lesson taught by a lashing from Sergeant Patrick Gass. This was coupled by John Newman being expelled from the expedition. But because they were en route in the wilderness he continued to travel with them to Fort Mandan in the Dakota Territory.

Captain Clark adhered to the theory he learned early on: nip disciplinary problems early and often they disappear as fast as sandwiches at a free lunch. In this case John Newman was confined for having uttered repeated expressions of a highly criminal and mutinous nature.

Forgive and forget was not in Captain Clark's vocabulary. At Fort Mandan Newman received a court-martial and was sentenced to hard labor at the Fort. He was to be sent back to Saint Louis with the return party in April 1805.

Captain Lewis wanted leniency. Captain Clark wanted to adhere to the letter of the law. After the expedition Lewis recommended that Congress grant Newman his pay for his period of service up to his expulsion. Newman received some pay and a land warrant as a member of the expedition. He settled in the Missouri territory.

Failure to perform his duty was William Bratton's down fall. He joined the corps late in the fall of 1803. Of Scotch Irish bloodlines, his six-foot build, ruddy complexion, and square of build pleased the two captains because Bratton could pole them up the Missouri River without a whimper. Somewhat reserved, and of strictest morals, he pleased preachers and the ladies. William Bratton was a woodsman, a great buffalo hunter, and liked by most of the corps.

John Shields was praised as the expedition's blacksmith, and Bratton, who was also a blacksmith as well as a gunsmith and hunter, was number two man to Shields. They would have worked together, of course, and it may be this close association that led Shields to take such elaborate measures with the steam bath to relieve Bratton of crippling back pain.

Amazingly, Bratton's discharge from the expedition was signed by Meriwether Lewis and dated St. Louis, October 10, 1806. Bratton and Captain Lewis did not agree when duty came calling. This became a source of irritation for both captains. By the winter in Fort Mandan, Captain Clark told Captain Lewis, "I need Bratton for getting our gear together. He is a good smithy and a great hunter, and you are wasting his skills by having Bratton chase butterflies and smelling the flowers. Let him work on man's duty."

Rather than argue, Captain Lewis gave in grudgingly. He said, "I don't agree, but I want peace so I can get all the information together to send it back with the corps members. This will be after we find the spring bubbling up—the source of the Missouri River."

Captain Clark said, "Whatever you say Meriwether, but remember I run the operation and you collect the information. O.K.?"

Meriwether Lewis was a captain in rank but not in the eyes of the corps members. They could see the way the expedition was being run. They could see that when duty called it was Captain Clark who named the order.

CHAPTER 14

Hail and Farewell

THE BLACK CLOUDS TO THE north looked ominous. The wind had picked up. It was blowing leaves into the Missouri and it looked like bad weather was coming. Captain Clark signaled to the boatman that they should pull in their oars and lie down with their faces on the deck while the black cloud of the tornado passed overhead. It was the elements conflicting with man.

It was the bad weather syndrome that Captain Clark had always loathed because there was no escaping the high winds. The hail and the debris that was swirling in the air made visibility zero. The two captains followed their own orders and also hit the deck and waited for a half minute after the wind had passed. They signaled to the crew, "Stand up."

Captain Lewis shouted, "It's all over. We have made it through a windstorm that few men have seen and many who do, have perished. Thank God for delivering us safely."

Captain Clark raised his eyes to the heavens make the sign of the cross as he gave thanks for being spared the tortures of a tornado. Captain Lewis looked over the keelboat and saw that the thirty-four men and two animals were in great shape. The roar of the wind and the pounding of the hail had made the gusts of air a frightening event.

Captain Lewis said. "Thank God, it's over. Now let's get underway and continue upriver on our Voyage of Discovery. We must maintain our progress, and our next stop will be to visit the Kanza Tribe. They are located fifty miles to the west of us on the Missouri River.

This is an Indian Tribe that exists by raising corn for the winter season and to feed the pinto ponies they had rounded up during the summer. They farmed foodstuff to trade for other valuables that were needed in order to maintain the quality of life the Plains Indians had known for centuries.

Captain Lewis surveyed the countryside. He saw hills to the right and to the left that had vegetation. The bushes included willow branches for fishing poles. The corps expected to feast on the fish that were swimming on the Missouri River bottom.

Captain shouted, "Sergeant Ordway check the bow of the keelboat to be sure that nothing was damaged by the tornado in the last few minutes."

Captain Clark said, "Sergeant Pryor look lively and do as Captain Lewis has requested."

Both Sergeants said, "Aye, aye, sir."

In a few minutes both sergeants finished inspecting the damage that had occurred to the keelboat and found that the sail, which had been furled, was in good shape. The mast had been cracked and would have to be replaced. They could not do it without beaching the keelboat and it was too late in the day to do so.

The replacement of the twenty-foot mast needed a tree that was at least twenty feet high and four inches at the base.

Sergeant Pryor said, "Captain, we will have to spend at least one day locating the replacement. I do not think it's safe for us to head upriver without having a replacement mast. I buy your idea of doing it now. This is definitely a time to get our act together so prepare to pull into shore."

Captain Lewis said, "Captain Clark, I think that you have made a wise decision. Tomorrow is another day."

Sergeant Ordway shouted for Sergeant Pryor to give orders to head for the starboard shore and prepare to spend the night so to repair the mast tomorrow.

Without waiting for more instructions, Captain Clark proceeded to get the keelboat tied up and await the morrow. It was then that Sergeant Ordway called out the names of three of the privates—Willard, Newman, and Windsor—and told them to prepare to land and that they were a work party to repair the mast that fell to the corps and each would be assigned duties to prepare the Voyage of Discovery for travel up the Missouri.

In the meantime the crew assigned by Sergeant Pryor had gone ashore and located a white pine tree that was twenty feet high and six inches in diameter at the base. They cut it down and took the branches off so that they had the replacement mast. Sergeant Pryor was an expert carpenter and handled his men. His inspection showed that the new mast could be attached to the old mast and that the twenty-foot sail of canvas could be positioned immediately. He proceeded to have the three crewmembers finish their work.

Captain Lewis had taken Sergeant Floyd on the south side of the Missouri and proceeded to do a tour to view the Kanza countryside. After preparing the mast, the keelboat started up the Missouri and docked at several Kanza Indian reservations to award the President Jefferson's Medal to the chief of the Kanza Tribe.

The weather in July was hot and the men in the corps were tired of seeing the sun blazing down on the river even though it was a beautiful day on the Kanza Plains. The sky was covered with white clouds. The waves of grain were rippling in the light breeze. The Kanza Tribe had surrounded the keelboat and were chanting, "How, How, How," waving their hands up in the sky, palms faced forward as they did so. It was an impressive sight—one that Captain Lewis and Clark will remember all of their lives as it was the first greeting of an Indian Tribe that they met on the Voyage of Discovery. The gentle breeze of the yellow-framed waves in unison with the chanting that was happening was a sight and sound to hear. Crows were eating their fill of the winter wheat that was just maturing ready for harvest and the Indian tribe of Kanza had met for the harvest festival that would take place soon. The Corps of Discovery had never seen a sight such as this and two sergeants, two captains, and the twenty-five members of the Corps of Discovery would remember this as long as they lived.

CHAPTER 15

Conflicts

CONFLICTS AROSE IN THE VOYAGE of Discovery when the troops were in training and at Camp Dubois in the Illinois Territory on the Mississippi River near the junction with the Ohio River. It occurred when Private Hall was on guard duty at the fort and went over the wall of the stockade used for protection, down to a local pub near the Indian village, and proceeded to drink until he was staggering. On his way to return to climb back up the wall, he did not realize an Indian brave from the local tribe had followed him and climbed up the rope Hall had used to get up and over the twelve-foot wall.

The guard on duty saw the incident, went to Captain Clark, and reported, "Sir, I have two men, one Private Hall, the other an Indian brave from the local tribe. They had breached our security and I caught him attempting to return to his private quarters. He did not give me any resistance and is a waiting outside for me to finish my report."

Captain Clark thought for a minute. "Private, take Private Hall to the quarters, tie his hands and feet together so that he cannot move, and we will hold a court-martial tomorrow morning where this case will be heard."

The guard said, "Aye, aye sir," and the two men left.

The next morning at eleven o'clock the prisoner, Private Hall, was brought before a court-martial consisting of Captains Lewis and Clark. The case was reported by the private who had been on guard and it was an open and shut case. The security of the corps had been broken allowing the local Indian tribe, the Sioux, to come in and pilfer and steal the horses and anything else they could while the men were sleeping and nobody was on guard.

The case was concluded when Private Hall offered nothing in his defense, but begged for leniency. The two officers, Captain Lewis and Captain Clark, retired for five minutes and returned to report.

Captain Lewis said, "We have reached a judgment. The vote was unanimous. Private Hall broke the most serious of the rules we have established, which is that we will have a twenty-four seven guard observing the area around our fort, and if any activity is noticed, will report it directly to a sergeant, his superior. This was not done and Private Hall must run the gauntlet of this twenty-five people, ten times receiving two hundred and fifty blows as he does so. The penalty and punishment will take place this afternoon at two o'clock, after which Private Hall will be confined to quarters for the next ten days and will serve double duty during that period in the treatment of our latrines and assisting in the kitchen. Is there any other matter before this tribunal?"

Captain Clark dismissed the court-martial and the prisoner was taken out. The punishment was executed at two p.m. and once done; the men of the Corps of Discovery were released to take care of their regular duties.

That evening Captain Lewis said to Captain Clark, "William, I think that punishment was extreme and far more serious than the breach of duty required. Can you tell me your reason for that?"

Captain Clark cleared his throat and said, "Meriwether, I have been in the army and I have seen what the Indian Braves can do to a settler and/or prisoner and/or fellow tribesman. It is not pretty and is a serious offense, much more serious than it appears to you, but we must keep our guard up and prevent any breech of the rules and regulations. We must punish it immediately treating it as a serious offense. I'm sorry but that was my training in the Frontier Forces as a leader. Now we have given the other members of the Corps of Discovery, his fellow privates, a chance to see what happens if the rules and regulations are broken. Punishment is immediate and will fit the crime. I hope I've made myself clear."

This ended the discussion, but it was the first time such a disciplinary matter had come up and it showed that the two leaders, Captain Lewis and

Captain Clark, were not on the same wavelength regarding the punishment for the offenses.

This conflict was the first of two times the leaders did not see eye to eye. A couple of months later another, a conflict between a man and his duty, Private Moses Reed, who left the Corps of Discovery by telling Sergeant Ordway that he had lost his knife on the trail and would go and look for it because he did not want to be unarmed and felt that he could find it.

Sergeant Ordway referred this to Sergeant Floyd since it was an operational matter and within the purview of Captain Clark again. Captain Clark told Sergeant Reed to look for his knife, but to return to the Corps of Discovery that would be traveling up the river, that he would be able to catch up by nightfall. Private Moses Reed left to look for his knife, and in fact he was planning not to return to the work camp that night, but was going to start to return to St. Lewis, deserting the operation.

One of the hunting party who had been actively looking for game, had seen Private Reed untying one of the pirogues in order to start his journey back down the Missouri to freedom. Captain Clark sent out a search party immediately and they located Private Reed, captured him, and returned him to the Corps of Discovery, resting at a place on the river that night.

Again, Captain Clark did not want any of the other twenty-five privates to desert and as such dismissed Private Reed from the corps with the proviso that he stay with the corps until he finish and perform all duties, but have no benefits. His pay would be discontinued and he would be given latrine duty and other activities to punish his desertion—an object lesson to the rest of the corps. In this way, the punishment was made to fit the crime.

CHAPTER 16

The Misfits

A S IN ALL GROUPS, RICH or poor, organized or disorganized, regulated, or at sixes or sevens, the Corps of Discovery didn't explore the Missouri River for the fun of it. They wanted to be famous. They wanted the world to know they had found the Northwest Passage to the Pacific Ocean. However, there were three members of this select bunch who didn't give a damn. These three were ordered to go on this dangerous mission.

The first was York, a slave, whose owner was Captain William Clark. York followed his owner's wishes. Clark took his slave along on the Lewis and Clark Expedition as was the custom. York was over six feet tall, husky with a wonderfully muscled body, and as strong as an ox. Though he was a slave, he was an equal to anyone serving in the corps. This service was either the day-to-day operation of the exploration or special jobs.

York was a good hunter, guide, and cook as could be found. He followed Captain William Clark around like a puppy. He obeyed Clark's instructions to the letter. He was a misfit only because he was a black slave in a white world.

If needed, York assisted Captain Lewis in treating injuries that occurred on the expedition. York was given a musket to use in hunting for game such as deer and buffalo, as well as for his own safety.

The native Indians tribes treated York with respect, and he played a key role in diplomatic relations of the expedition. York shared and shared alike in the actions of the Corps of Discovery.

The second misfit was Seaman, the dog. He was a large Newfoundland. He was bred and owned by Captain Meriwether Lewis. Seaman joined the corps because of mutual devotion. This dog worshiped his owner and went on the expedition to guard his master. Captain Lewis treasured Seaman because he reminded him of his youth when he had more time for fun.

The third misfit was Toussaint Charbonneau, who joined the expedition on the way to Mandan, a settlement under the Dakota tribe's control. Charbonneau was an interpreter who spoke three languages. He offered his services to the two captains as they entered into the wilds of the Northwest Territory.

Though he was qualified as an interpreter, employing Toussaint Charbonneau had one major drawback, and it was a growing one. He had his thirteen-year-old pregnant paramour with him. Her name was Sacagawea, an Indian maiden. The couple wanted to join Captains Lewis and Clark because Charbonneau was greedy and a lecher who preyed on young girls. Money was his motivation. He had his wife who was with child. He was selfish and very timid as he joined the corps in the fall of 1804.

The corps faced the upcoming Montana winter. They found themselves in Dakota Indian Territory waiting for springtime to come and needing to build Fort Mandan for shelter. The misfits represent individuals who were vital to Captain Lewis and Clark, but they did not fit the mold of the Corps of Discovery. This goal had been set by President Jefferson. It was "Be true to the mission. Find a route to the Pacific Ocean or die trying."

Because Captain Clark was the ramrod, stiff and inflexible, and Captain Lewis was the scientist, a dreamer, who was reserved and stayed behind the action practically invisible until he sensed time is right, conflict between the leadership was inevitable.

Strangely enough, at every river stop for presentation of the American flag, the exchange of gifts and the presentation of the friendship medal, York was the star attraction. Even though a misfit, he shared the stage with the Indian Chief. Buckskin clothing could not compete with the brave's war paint, feathered headdress, beaded buckskins, and tomahawk.

Captain Lewis said, "We are also-rans in competing for attention by the Indian tribal officials. It looks like your man York has stolen the show. Such is life."

Captain Clark replied, "Meriwether you are too reserved to own your own slave, let alone give him orders. I enjoy the adulation occurring at each stop along the river. We have passed through the Missouri territory and the Kansas territory. Soon we shall reach the Topeka tribal hunting grounds. Our receptions have been loud and long, especially the dancing and good fellowship. Our men are fraternizing with the squaws. You know that York has been my personal bodyguard. He is to me, William Clark, what Seaman is to you. He is your little bit of home that keeps you going when the future looks the darkest. I say thank God for York and Seaman!"

It was so true. The trinkets and the friendship medals given to tribal chiefs, medicine men, and the braves made them pay attention to the Voyage of Discovery.

Each stop up the Missouri was a festival celebrating the new status of North America and the U.S. citizenship for all who lived nearby. It was important to the tribes who rode Indians ponies, wore headdresses, and smoked tobacco around the campfire.

The second misfit shown to the crowd was Captain Meriwether Lewis's dog, Seaman. A Newfoundland breed, he ate scraps of meat, fish, and anything else he could find. The captain often remarked, as all three of them ate dinner together, that the one thing Seaman didn't relish was whiskey. Clark had tried to introduce him to the crews evening *grog*, but the pleasure of a gill of rum every night did NOT fit into the dog's life. After sniffing its odor Seaman swore off the stuff. His enjoyment was servicing the Indian bitches whenever he could find one in heat. This animal entertainment caused Captain Lewis to say, "Seaman is a sexual dynamo. He keeps performing despite being over the hill."

Clark replied, "What a lover."

Despite his failings Seaman was worth his weight in gold. Every night at docking time, whether it was on the shore of to a small island or in the middle of the river itself, the dog kept the Indian braves from stealing food and whiskey. Seaman had a loud bark and a frightening growl. In addition, Seaman was big enough to scare away bull buffalos. Seaman at his middle-age survived the rigors of the trip much to the surprise of the crew. Living on the keelboat was tiring to all the corps including the misfits.

The final misfit, Sacagawea, the Indian maiden, unmarried and pregnant, was more sensational and received more attention than even the two Captains, Clark and Lewis. Her pregnancy was caused by a French Canadian guide, fur trader, and interpreter who was always interested in a toss in the hay. He knew how to say with a wink and in four languages, including Indian sign language, "How about playing house?" He said this in Indian sign language by elevating his middle finger.

Sacagawea never told her lover, Charbonneau, "Not tonight Toussaint, honey." To make matters worse, the interpreter had her friend Otter Woman, in his tepee just in case of a special erection.

Sacagawea gave birth to Jean Baptiste Charbonneau just after February 1805. It was in stockade where the corps wintered at Mandan Dakota territory. Both captains realized that they needed the interpreter, Toussaint Charbonneau desperately. Thus the misfits were added to the Corps of Discovery. In all circumstances, their Seaman showed that devotion to duty was important to the corps. Sacagawea was invaluable assuring the tribal chiefs of the peaceful purpose of the corps, and York showed that having a different appearance was an asset rather than a liability. This group of three misfits were vital to the continued success as they struggled to find the gold ring called the Northwest Passage.

CHAPTER 17

From the President with Love

IT WAS A BEAUTIFUL DAY in May. The afternoon sun sparkled and there wasn't a cloud in the sky. Captain Meriwether Lewis was going to deliver an important message from the president of the United States of America. This announcement was to notify the settlers in the Missouri Territory that the Louisiana Purchase had been made. Therefore, the people who lived in this frontier land stretching from the Mississippi River basin to the Pacific Ocean now owed their allegiance to the United Sates, and that the new country had more than doubled its size—overnight!

Captain Lewis was coming from the St. Charles settlement located on the south bank of the Missouri River. He was going to St. Louis to give the French officials notice that the juncture of the Mississippi and Missouri Rivers would be the starting point for two army captains, two sergeants and twenty-five privates to head into the wilderness. This group would explore the new land to look for the Northwest Passage to the Pacific Ocean. This expedition was named by President Jefferson as "The Voyage of Discovery".

Captain Lewis jumped into a canoe and headed out on the Missouri River toward St. Louis, the largest settlement in the Midwest. Five hours later Lewis arrived at the settlement of St. Louis. It was located on a meadow and had a landing where he could dock.

St Louis was settled in the 16th century by the French and became a mixed community composed of French Canadian fur traders, the Missouri Indian tribe, fur trappers, and other adventurers who loved the idea of going into unoccupied territory and living there.

The occupation ruled by the French was ended by Napoleon Bonaparte's sale of its territory called a Godsend by both the French who sold it and the United States who purchased it.

After a half-day's paddling the canoe down the Missouri and across the Mississippi to St. Louis, a town of slightly more than 1100 residents, Captain Lewis carefully turned the canoe so it faced up the Mississippi River. He threw a rope up to a dockhand and came ashore.

The landing he was using was the one that all river boat traffic used when they transported goods and people up and down the Mississippi. It was a busy place. A number of boats were tied up to the wharf.

As usual, the Missouri Indian tribe was excited about a stranger, Captain Lewis, tying up to their landing. Lewis saw Chief Broken Bow in full regalia waiting as if he was going on the warpath. The braves had accompanied their chief. The squaws and papooses were left at home in their tepees keeping the home fires burning.

It was the first meeting that Captain Meriwether Lewis had with an Indian chief while on the Lewis and Clark exploration of the Missouri River.

Captain Meriwether Lewis asked in English whether there was an English speaking brave so that the purpose of his coming could be told. Seeing no response, Captain Lewis turned toward town and commenced walking toward the settlement.

As he approached a meadow he saw the Missouri Indian tepees spread across the landscape He arrived in front of the largest tepee to see two Indian braves standing guard. Each was standing at attention with a spear in his right hand and a bow and arrows slung across his back.

Captain Lewis took the presidential Proclamation and handed it to the guard while pointing inside the tepee. The brave entered the tent and a few minutes later, the chief came out with two braves at his side. The chief had his feathered headdress on and a look of wonderment on his face. He pointed to the proclamation from President Jefferson. He turned to the meadow and ventured toward the central path lying between the tepees and the bank of the Missouri. He was looking for the Missouri Settlement leader that represented the French occupants in the St. Louis area.

After walking toward the settlement Captain Lewis saw a small sod hut that had the French flag on a pole next to the front entrance.

He went to the entrance and said, "Anyone here?" Hearing a grunt from inside he waited patiently until the person appeared at the front entrance and said, "Who are you? What are you doing here?"

"I represent the United States of America," Captain Lewis replied. "I am Captain Meriwether Lewis from Washington, D.C. I have been appointed as one of the co-leaders of the Corps of Discovery. I have been waiting for the official notice from Washington, D.C. And now I have it. It is the order from the president of the United States who asked me to start up the Missouri River. My small company is looking for the Northwest Passage to the Pacific Ocean. The president asked me to tell you and all the others of the Indian tribes and the settlers west of the Mississippi River that the Northwestern land area has been sold to the United States.

"This sale was completed two years ago. Now I am confirming the purchase and will explore it from one end to the other. Here is a copy of the treaty documenting the Louisiana Purchase." Captain Lewis handed the document to the settlement official.

With some difficulty, the French Canadian settlement leader said, "My name is Francois. Please call me Frankie. I lead this small settlement. We belong to France. We fly the French flag. I salute it to show who is my king!"

Frankie, pointing to his shabby structure, "The place we live. Not good, but it best we have."

Answering him, Meriwether Lewis handed him the treaty. "From this date forward the United States has control of all persons and inhabitants of the Missouri Territory. It is owned by the United States of America. The sale was signed sealed and I am delivering the treaty to you this 14th day of May 1804.

Then Captain Lewis returned to his canoe and took the Friendship Medal and the American flag and said "From your new Great White Father as he welcomes you and your people. Here is your American flag. Please fly it proudly from sunup to sundown only!"

Lewis looked around and saw the Indian braves as well as the squaws waiting in a circle in front of the settlement leader's hut. They waited while the conversation of the two was completed. In about an hour the settlement leader approached with Lewis at his side, and introduced him to the Indian chief.

The captain saluted and said to the chief, "Captain Lewis at your service. I will be here for a day or two. Please help me in any way that you can, to do what I have to do."

With that, Frankie said, "Until tomorrow" and returned to his home.

Captain Lewis took the arm of the Indian chief and said, "Show me a tepee that I can stay in for the night."

The Indian chief turned on his heel and walked toward a group of tepees, the largest of which had a fire in the center of it. The tepee poles were tied together at the top and covered with deer skin sewn together with rawhide. It was much larger than the typical Indian tepee.

After introductions in English, what little French Captain Lewis knew, and sign language he had learned at William and Mary College, Captain Lewis indicated he would remain there for a day or two and stay with his Indian tribe called the Missouri. The chief knew no English but had an interpreter who did and could indicate in sign language what had been said by Lewis and could reply from the chief's conversation back to him.

Lewis saw that the St. Louis settlement was over fifty percent Indian. The families each had a tepee and all seemed occupied. By that time, it was early evening and the Indian chief had his medicine man take Captain Lewis and show him the tepee in which Lewis was to live for the next day or so.

Captain Lewis saw that there were Indian squaws doing family chores while the Indian braves were away hunting for food and protecting the tribe from danger.

He started wandering around the settlement. Captain Lewis noticed that the Indian squaws were looking at him with his fur cap and buckskin garb. A couple of the squaws approached him and felt the buckskin to see how it was made. They looked at the moccasins Lewis had on. Lewis thought to himself "They are giving me the once over. I am intrigued. What should I do?"

Captain Lewis looked at the squaws and was attracted to one who was youngish, in her teens, and had no papoose or any children around her. He beckoned to her as he said to the interpreter, "Me interested. Me Captain

Lewis." As he approached her she shook her head and indicated that she did not understand by cupping her hand behind her ear.

Captain Lewis then pointed to her and to himself and crossed his fingers. This indicated that he was interested in staying with her for the evening.

She nodded in agreement and proceeded to lead Captain Lewis to a tepee, open its flap, and took him by the hand into the tepee.

Lewis really got the idea she wanted to sleep with him that evening. Lewis thought that it would solve his worldly worries but quickly put away the notion of their being together by shaking his head negatively. He did not want to cause an incident. He smiled at her but again shook his head, telling her by his action "Thanks but no thanks" letting her know emphatically that he was not going to have a pleasant interlude sleeping with her.

She raised her eyebrows in amazement and proceeded to make a separate bed for Captain Lewis of a buffalo skin that was big enough for Lewis to fold over him for the night. Without further ado, she did the same for herself on the other side of the tepee and they spent the night together, but there was no sex involved.

This act alone showed Lewis that he had common sense. Captain Lewis knew that discretion was the better part valor. He sensed that it could cause an international incident if it was known in Washington, D.C. The politicos would censure him for disgracing the country. President Jefferson might even court-martial him.

The young squaw in offering herself to him, but being turned away would disgrace her in the eyes of her tribe because her offer was rejected. Even though she did not know that it would not be proper for him to accept. She knew by his actions that no meant no. Thus Captain Lewis rejected her approach by shaking his head negatively and placed his hands palm out as if pushing her away.

Lewis went to bed, and as he was about to go to sleep, he thought dreamily how nice it would be to have someone to gratify desires. He closed his eyes exhausted by the day's activities and went to sleep.

The next morning at daybreak, he looked around and the young maiden was gone as was her buffalo blanket. Lewis guessed she returned to the tribe, perhaps shamed by not having sex, but at least he felt no obligation to her or to the Missouri tribe.

A day of activity followed. Captain Lewis noted that the Missouri River flowed lazily in front of the settlement, that there were wild geese flying overhead in the morning sun, and that the Indian tribe was up and active. He went to the chief and indicated that he would like to look around. The chief nodded in understanding and went to a young brave, took him by the arm, and brought him over to Captain Lewis using sign language to tell him that he would be Captain Lewis' guide for the day.

Lewis left to look at the landscape The rolling hills behind the encampment were lightly covered with tall Lombardy poplar trees pointing to the heavens, and the summer grass on the meadowland was emerald green as it pushed through the patches of snow. There were birds aplenty, including the ever present red-headed blackbirds, and meadow larks singing with their yellow breasts puffed out and gray feathers shining. The dogs in the camp were many and scruffy looking as they wandered aimlessly around looking for scraps of food.

Captain Lewis indicated to the Indian guide that he wanted to walk out in the forest and along the banks of the Mississippi River. He pointed downriver. The young brave followed and they saw the flowers of May including buttercups, Oregon grape, and Oriental poppies, crimson in color and with dusty black centers. There were rabbits scampering as the two approached, and there was a deer or two munching the greenery on the low hills rising to the east.

The two explored the bank walking the first mile side by side. Captain Lewis studied the countryside detail and ended the day returning to the largest tepee of the camp where he was invited by the settlement leader to partake of dinner prior to retiring for the evening.

Lewis made notes on a pad of the happenings of both the previous day, where he conducted the president's business, and the day of exploration that he had. It was almost ten o'clock when he found his tepee and went to sleep.

At dawn the captain thanked the tribal members as well as the chief. He climbed into his canoe, swung his canoe into the current, and silently thanked the good Lord for the ten mile an hour tail wind that was blowing from the southeast offsetting the river's current. He paddled the few miles across the slow moving Mississippi and up the Missouri arriving at St. Charles camp late in the afternoon.

After talking to the longshoremen hanging around the dock for a couple minutes he returned to the keelboat and looked for Captain Clark. He found him smoking a stogie and then talked with him regarding the previous day and the incidents that happened during his stay away from the corps

Captain Clark asked, 'Well Meriwether you are back. How did it go?" He had a tone in his voice that indicated he thought that Meriwether Lewis his co-captain had a ball. Captain Lewis kept his conversation centered on his seeing people at a distance and did not discuss the young squaw's advances made and his rejecting it.

He wrote his daily diary and also discussed the goings on in the keelboat, the schedule, and reported to Clark the incidents that had happened, about objects he had seen, and what he written in his diary. He replied to any questions Clark asked. The two agreed to discuss each day about new and unusual flowers, birds, animals, and fish.

Captain Lewis' diary told of scientific and cultural information. His notes were general in nature. He had written about those Missouri Indians that he had seen classified by sex, physical characteristics, and other details.

Captain Clark asked to see them. Captain Clark was amazed at the detail that Captain Lewis had made in his notes. ·But thought to himself, *No sex, hmmm.*

Clark told Captain Lewis, "You will be a big addition to the bureaucrats in Washington, D.C. and a hit as the luncheon speaker at congressional hearings, but I think the Senators and Congressmen like it down and dirty. I am a little disappointed in you, Meriwether. You have a chance to do fun things away from straight-laced society functions. You are a wonderful cohort, but as a matinee idol I don't know if you will pass the test. I reserve judgment about that."

Captain Lewis ended the daily summary by bringing up the conflicting nature of the two parts of America. The European culture involving a more educated, or as Lewis put it, "with it" societies, the "dandies" of the Parisians.

Captain William Clark said that he represented the other end of the culture scale. It was what Clark called the backwoods and frontiersmen personality. This class of American were the adventurers who came from Europe to escape tradition and seek their fortune and adventure. Their attire was buckskin and fur hats, raccoon tails attached. They had chewing tobacco stains on their teeth, wore ragged trousers, and liked wild women and song.

This was a conflict of personality types. It would be a factor during the entire "Voyage of Discovery". Neither Meriwether Lewis nor William Clark knew which captain would prevail.

CHAPTER 18

Illicit Love

SACAGAWEA, AN INDIAN MAIDEN WAS pregnant. Her Shoshone tribal name meant *bird woman*. She and her sister, *Otter Moon*, became the mystery women of the Voyage of Discovery. During the years of 1805 and 1806, these two squaws had become more notorious than Captains Lewis or Clark could believe.

Sacagawea's common law husband, Toussaint Charbonneau, lived in the Pacific Northwest. Her husband had met the captains in a December snowstorm while seeking shelter from the elements.

The Charbonneau's, a soon to be family of three, wanted to return to Sacagawea's tribal reservation in Idaho where Sacagawea had been raised. She, though young, could provide guide services for the corps by joining up with them and becoming the captain's atlas. She knew the mountains and about the Northwest Passage to the Pacific.

Toussaint's interview showed that Sacagawea could help show them the way. He could act as interpreter who knew the language.

But first Charbonneau must lead them to the source of the Missouri River, after which he would be able to boast, "My son Pompeii was the first United States citizen child to be born in my wife's Shoshone territory."

Captain Clark interviewed the interpreter to find out if he was the man to lead them in their search. In broken English with a French accent Charbonneau said, "I am a French Canadian. I trap animals for their furs.

My coming up zee river is good for you. I know zee way through Indian country, beginning to end. If you go on, I go over zee Rocky Mountains and finally down zee beeg river. It is called zee Columbia. It runs into zee Pacific Ocean. After you find Zee ocean, I take my family back and live with zee Shoshones."

When asked by Clark, "Why should we hire you rather than any other interpreter from the Shoshone Tribe? What makes you so special? You are a French Canadian. There aren't any French or Canadians where we are going."

Toussaint Charbonneau drew himself up to his full height and said, "I am zee best fur trader and my wife is the best Indian interpreter in this neck of zee woods. I am zee only one you know that can guide you. As one married to a Shoshone squaw and who is always interested in a toss in zee hay, I know how to say 'Your teepee or mine?' And most of all I can do so in three languages."

As he finished he turned and faced the captains. He looked Clark straight in the eye and said, "N'est pas"? He said this with a wink and a knowing smile on his face.

Lewis turned to Clark and said, "Since this is an operational matter, you decide. I'll do what you want to regarding this."

Captain Clark thought for a moment and said to Charbonneau, "As long as you and your women behave yourselves, you can be our interpreter of the Shoshone lingo. The corps needs one. I see your so-called wife is having a baby. When is it due?"

Toussaint Charbonneau, said, "In February I think." He continued, "If you will help me, we will stay in zee camp's sleeping quarters and keep out of zee way. My wife knows zee lay of zee land. We will help with chores. Any interpreting we do will be from Shoshone to French and from French to English. It will be tedious, but we can do it. It can be done."

Captain Clark said. "Congratulations, you must start immediately if not sooner."

Captain Lewis said slowly, "I hope you can help me, too. Getting there will be great, but recording what we did and where we did it is our mission, too!"

This tale of illicit love occurred in Indian tribal territory. It was just a stone's throw from the spot chosen for the Corps of Discovery's winter quarters on the north side of the Missouri River and a few hundred miles south of the Canadian Border.

It was while he was trapping near the Mandan reservation that Charbonneau, the interpreter, found this thirteen-year-old, a Shoshone maiden. She had been kidnapped from the Idaho tribe's territory near the Snake River basin. She, her younger sister, and several other squaws, had been stolen and sold to fur trappers who were on their way up the Missouri river.

Coincidentally, Charbonneau was on his way up the river in 1803 on his annual fur-trapping mission. He stopped to overnight in The Travelers Rest Tavern. After dinner he went into the lodge and joined men gambling in the table stakes Whist game. The story he tells is not unusual.

Sacagawea's former owner was losing heavily and wanted to call the pot. He had no money left for making his bet. He was positive he had the winning hand.

He said, "I have too little money. This is the last hand, and I have no money left. I own these two young squaws. I will put my two girls as my stake to cover my bet. Both are young. Especially that one," as he pointed at Sacagawea. "She is young, beautiful, and a virgin."

He waited for Charbonneau to answer. Sweat was on the gambler's brow and his hand was trembling. The silence was deafening. Her father turned to look at his young maidens.

At this point Charbonneau got up, walked over to the girls, and inspected both from head to toe. As he did so he was shaking his head and said, "I am not interested, but if they will spend the night with me, I will let you call the bet for this last hand."

The owner took the two girls by the hand walked them over beside the table and said, "These are my bet. I call. Let the best man win. If I win I keep the girls and take the money."

Then Sacagawea's owner pointed to the two girls and said, "It is double or nothing." He sent this message loud and clear using the elevation of the middle finger of his right hand pointing to the sky to emphasize his action.

Sacagawea's face paled as she thought of what this meant. If the man who had been her owner lost she would have a new master who could do as he desired. Her sister, Otter Moon, did not know she was part of the bet so she smiled sweetly.

Charbonneau said, "I am making a mistake but I can't resist a good gamble. I take your bet. Turn the card."

The dealer slowly turned the card and said to Charbonneau," Mon Dieu, you win, Monsieur, not one but two young virgins."

Charbonneau led the two girls to his teepee and proceeded to make love to both before the night was out.

From that night forward it was the same routine. Sacagawea never told her lover, Charbonneau, "Not tonight Toussaint honey." To make matters worse her sister, Otter Women, slept in his teepee just in case Sacagawea did not perform to his liking.

It was nine months later that Sacagawea gave birth to Jean Baptiste Charbonneau before February 1805 was over.

Captain Meriwether Lewis being the corps medical officer officiated. Lewis realized that they needed a place to birth the child and that the officers' quarters was the only place in Fort Mandan that would be available.

Captain Lewis was the only one in the corps who had had any medical training. The interpreter and father, Toussaint Charbonneau, was helplessly looking on.

Captain Clark, the operations officer counted how the corps had grown while at Fort Mandan. He reflected that sometimes more is better.

The first addition was Seaman, Captain Lewis's dog. He showed that devotion to duty was important to the corps. The second was Sacagawea, invaluable in assuring the tribal chiefs of the peaceful purpose of the visiting corps. The third was York. He showed that having a different appearance was an asset rather than being a liability. His ebony skin color that did not wash off was valuable. This became a plus to the Voyage of Discovery in meetings with the tribes. The next was Otter Moon who ended up being the corps whore, the good time girl.

Two other add-ons were vital to the continued success of the corps. The new baby boy was insurance because the Indian tribes felt the corps had no warlike intent if it was making the journey with Sacagawea and her baby boy. Otter Moon, a young squaw and sister of Sacagawea, made the nights shorter for all the privates in the Corps of Discovery as they struggled to find the gold ring called the Northwest Passage and had found personal pleasure while doing so.

The conflicts created by the addition of two adolescent women, Sacagawea and Otter Moon, to the Voyage of Discovery were often and serious. The conflicts between the twenty plus men vying for Otter Moon's favors was not conducive to tranquility in the corps. This was true even though stops along the way found that Captain Lewis gave the corps their choices of getting part of their pay in baubles, silks, and table salt or to trade for sexual favors. These unique goods were as not available away from the seashore or the Great Salt Lake.

It was like Captain Clark said at the end of every month, "It is pay day. We have kept a record for each and every one of you. You can draw down ten percent of your pay for the month that is four bits. You can take it out in rum, baubles, silks, or tobacco. You can give it away, smoke it away, or piss it away. The balance of your account plus the land grant you'll get will make you the envy of every girl in your home town when and if you fulfill the gig you signed on for. Sergeant Floyd is paymaster. See him for any questions you may have."

Captain Lewis said, "I am sure that President Jefferson, our fearless leader, will see to it that all commitments promised you are met promptly. But first let us do our jobs—find our way to the sea. The Indian tribes have been distraught by the action of the Caucasians and most are hostile to us. We must get Jefferson's message across. He told us that we explorers want peace and prosperity, not killing and devastation. Our citizens of the United States of America have a Constitution with its bill of rights. All the new territory we have bought from France has cost a pretty penny, but our expedition will show that the United States of America is worth much more than we paid for it." Lewis ended with, "The winter cold is bone-chilling, but we are safely tucked away in Fort Mandan awaiting the arrival of spring. Then we will be on our way."

After Jean Charbonneau was born, the challenge resulting from this expected but unusual situation became difficult and dangerous to manage. The resulting stress was not anticipated. The Corps of Discovery was in the wilderness. The men were jammed together at night, in eight stacks of four bunks each, one man to a bunk. The blazing fire-pit in the center reminded the corps of home, and caused friends to be testy, and strangers to want to fight each other. The captains did not know the answer to this conundrum, and so the winter boredom grated on the nerves of all members of the expedition. What would the thirty plus members of the expedition do as the short days of the Christmas season passed?

Little did Lewis and Clark know what 1805 had in store for the Voyage of Discovery. Captain Lewis said as he raised his new year's mug of Jamaican rum, "William, the past eight months are like the Black Hills of the Dakotas forever cast in stone; the future is like the morning mist, fading away before your very eyes; but the present is like the sun--it is always there and it is up to you to take advantage of the opportunity it provides!"

Captain Clark's reply. "I hear you, Meriwether, Happy New Year and many more."

CHAPTER 19

Wintering in Dakota Country

F AR UP THE BIG MO, the Corps of Discovery was faced with a momentous choice. It was late in the fall of 1804. Winter weather was approaching. The thirty-four-man corps was unhappy. The maple trees were red, and brown leaves littered the ground. The unanswered question the corps faced was "What to do next?"

The choice was hunker down where they were throughout the winter and wait for spring weather, or continue on as far as they could before stopping to wait for good weather to come.

In any event, it was decision time! Soon it would be freezing cold and what should the corps do about it? The two leaders had a major disagreement as to what action to take.

Captain Lewis favored waiting until spring. Since the Mandan Indian village was nearby, the corps could spend the winter in a stockade isolated but with peaceful Indians, the Mandans, just across the river. This Indian tribe had been wintering there for centuries and appeared to be hale and hearty.

Lewis felt that President Jefferson wanted to get as much information about the land purchase as could be collected in order to show Congress and the nation what a great deal the United States of America had made in purchasing the land.

Captain Clark wanted to keep on going even though the Missouri was frozen over and would make the journey more hazardous. Clark thought the sooner the value of the Louisiana Purchase was made known to the citizens of the country and the world at large the better it would be. He thought the expedition should continue to move toward the Pacific Ocean until forced by the weather to wait for spring.

Clark felt that his leading the parade would keep it moving ahead despite the elements. His mantra was *keep moving* toward the Northwest on the Missouri at all cost, despite the winter weather.

The two captains got into a heated discussion. Captain Lewis favored the first alternative, stay put, build a stockade, and move forward again in spring time. Captain Clark wanted to keep on moving.

Captain Clark said, "I have been in the military most of my career-- giving orders, not taking them. My order is keep moving toward the Pacific despite the fact that winter is upon us."

Captain Lewis answered with a question. "William, how can you move on without scouting the trail ahead of us?" He added, "The Missouri River is freezing over. Soon it will be difficult for us to follow it."

Captain Clark replied, "The army rule that I go by is, 'keep moving forward until the enemy stops you. And then you stand your ground.' We have not been stopped by weather yet, and so we should keep moving up the river. Then, if stopped by bad weather, we will camp until weather permits us to move on."

Captain Lewis thought for a minute, and said in measured tones, "I call for a vote. We'll have Sergeants Gass and Ordway assemble their men for a meeting."

"By all means take a vote," said Captain Lewis. "If you win, we move. If I win, we stay put!"

Within fifteen minutes the corps was assembled

Captain Clark told the men, "We have a decision facing us. The choice is to keep going forward until the winter snows force us to make winter camp or stay here in Mandan until spring. I say we continue on, following the Missouri River. It makes a path that we can follow until the snow gets too deep. It will shorten the time we are away from our families. I want to move on and get our job done in the shortest possible time." He added, "I have had my say. Now Captain Lewis, why are you anxious to stop here now?"

Captain Lewis said, "I am a scientist on this voyage. I have been gathering information and have collected enough to keep me busy to get it ready to send it back to the president. This preparation will take several months for me to get it ready. I operate in the basis that it is better to be safe than sorry. We need to get ready for the unknown. We need to build a stockade now. We can store the supplies and the equipment. We can beach the barge, tie up the keelboat, and wait for spring."

The two Sergeants, Gass and Ordway, huddled with the men and then Ordway said, "Sir, before you take our vote, there are two questions that the men have asked. Will you tell us how long you think we will be looking for the Northwest Passage? We were told when we signed on that we would get $5 per month and land of our own. Will our pay continue even though it might take several years to finish our exploration? Can we get more money since it will be more dangerous if we are away from home more than thirty six months?"

Now the two Captains talked quietly. Captain Lewis smiled as he turned to talk to the men. "All of you in the corps are grown men. The money increase will have to be budgeted by congress and both of us leaders can say we'll try our best. Now I call for the vote."

Captain Clark promptly said as he raised his hand, "My hand goes up for let's keep moving as far and as fast as we can. I think we can beat old man winter. Who stands by me?"

Three others raised their hands with Captain Clark. Captain Clark was clearly unhappy.

Then Captain Lewis said, "Those of you who want to wait for spring before we move on, please raise your hands."

Lewis maintained his composure as he and twenty of the corps who agreed with him raised their right hands high.

This vote dampened Captain Clark's feelings that his word would be taken over Captain Lewis. Captain Clark said, "Twenty-one to four--against me. The majority of you want to sit the winter out. You are voting the wrong way, but I accept your decision." He turned to Captain Lewis with, "This ends the meeting."

The growing difference between the two captains' attitudes surfaced. Captain Lewis was reserved and thoughtful. Captain Clark was more straightforward. Shorter is better. Clark felt the longer the corps spent in reaching the Northwest Passage, the greater the chance for bad things to happen. A longer trip would provide a failure of the effort. Thus, the first crisis of joint leadership had been averted—or had it?

The answer to this enigma of what to do and when to do it was delayed until the following month, January 1805.

Captain Lewis called the corps together. He said, "President Jefferson himself told us what to do. We want to find a land route to the sea. Captain Clark and I will stay in the Dakota's territory till the ice breaks up We now plan to winter here. We will explore our surroundings and profile the area. When spring comes and the daffodils and crocuses poke their heads through the snow, we will continue our journey to the Northwest."

The next day Captain Clark stood up walked over to the charcoal brazier and said, "By Jesus it's cold out there, but according to my experience we are better off getting out of here than sitting around. What a waste of travel time when the corps could be finding our way to the Northwest Passage. It is within our grasp. My experience has shown that keeping on the move is the best answer. Again as the operation officer I think it is time to move on."

Clearing his throat, Captain Lewis said in his low measured voice, "Thank you for your expert advice, but President Jefferson gave us a send-off message, 'when in doubt, stay put.' I am in doubt so we saw the members vote. The majority said let's wait till spring comes. It is freezing cold!"

CHAPTER 20

Who Turned on the Cold?

CAPTAIN CLARK LOOKED AT THE calendar and said to himself *Christmas is but two weeks away. I will listen to any requests you all have regarding our stay here. We're here until the weather is bearable and permits us to continue moving west.*

He then faced Sergeant Patrick Gass, looked him in the eye, and commented, "Christmas is nearly here. I will talk to Captain Lewis about the holiday season. Within a week or so the New Year will be coming. Plans should be made. Yes, the corps should celebrate. Tell Captain Lewis I need to talk with him. That'll be all, Sergeant Gass."

Clark sat down at his desk and resumed working on the maps he had been drawing as the expedition followed the river. It was tedious work and required patience. He recorded his observations and wrote notes in his diary. He recorded magnetic compass readings, telescope sightings, and talks with Lewis. His goal was to create a record of where the corps had been and what they had observed.

Both the captains kept a diary. Clark recorded geographic data. Lewis recorded surroundings, specimens, native people, and habitat. Each officer made entries at noon each day, recording the longitude, the latitude, and weather conditions.

Clark told Lewis. "Do call a meeting of the corps. Christmas is upon us. Have them consider this matter and refer it through the sergeants. We will consider it and, if proper, will issue an order to comply. You can confirm that you will comply."

At a hastily called meeting the men nodded their heads in agreement. The twenty-five privates followed the two sergeants, Ordway and Gass, to discuss the matter further and came back with two requests. The first was that the contract with the United States Government and the Corps of Discovery be approved and would cover the Army Frontier Forces after they return to their homes. Second that the corps receive the monies they've earned so far. Training started on January 1804 and it was December 1804. That would be $60 for each of the twenty-five privates. The non-commissioned officers Sergeants Ordway, Pryor, and Gass would get $12 more. This would enable the corps to send money to their families or use it for any purpose they want.

As an afterthought, Captain Clark said, "Our cause is clear. We are claiming this Northwest Territory as part of the U S A. We are telling the Indian tribes they are United States Citizens. We will find a land route connecting the Atlantic and Pacific Oceans. Our goal is clear. Find the Northwest Passage. We can make the song that America extends *from Sea to Shining Sea* a reality. We will concentrate on performing our mission as quickly as possible."

Then it was Captain Lewis' turn. He looked at the men and said, "You flatter me that you would make such a request as you know you are already part of the U.S. Army, a part called the Corps of Discovery and, as far as your compensation is concerned, you will have to get the Congress of the United States to approve your request. All I can say is that I will do my best to have the compensation you are to receive not only paid but increased by the president and the Congress. If you have nothing else, this meeting is dismissed."

"Hip, Hip, Hooray!" was shouted by all the members of the corps. As those assembled started to leave Captain Lewis added, "Those of you who wish to go along come outside with me, and we will plan for tomorrow and explore the territory immediately surrounding Fort Mandan. I will be more than happy to have you accompany me. It will be by snowshoe. It will be cold but we will return here to Fort Mandan every evening. The information we have discovered can be recorded in your personal diaries if you're keeping one, or I will include it in the record that President Jefferson wanted maintained."

At this point the men left the area to have a smoke and talk with each other about this new venture of the morrow. About half the men wanted to go with Captain Lewis and said so as a group. But Captain Lewis said, "Anything else bring up while we are snowshoeing. Goodnight!"

The next morning, the sun was a golden dollar in the sky. The English sparrows that did not fly south to warmer climes were nesting in the blue spruce trees. Captain Lewis had chosen a path in the frozen meadow. There were jackrabbit tracks that led to the frozen river, but the wind was blowing and drifting the snow. The corps would wait till the next day before they would cross the river.

Looking south toward the Indian village Captain Lewis saw two Indian braves ice fishing the south side of the Missouri. He got out his telescope and saw that the braves were by an open fire with coonskin hats and wolf fur outer garments They had cut some willow branches that they used for a pole and had it rigged so that they did not have to hold the poles but that the fish would catch themselves. The proof of the pudding was that they had a dozen fish which looked like perch and catfish that were freezing on the ice.

Captain Lewis said, "I can take three to five of you and we'll alternate days so that we do not have too many of us leaving the fort at any one time. This fishing would be entertaining and a different food from the venison, raccoon, or rabbit stew."

Robert Frazier said, "Cappen Lewis sir, I comes from Kentucky, and I knows how to fish. If we stop on the way back to the fort so I can cut some willow branches for poles Cap'n Clark and his men can hunt and fish tomorrow. You have made snowshoes so that we can travel on snow. Be sure that the snow is packed solid so that you don't fall through the top of it."

By three o'clock in the afternoon the freezing weather had taken its toll. It was time for the frozen corpsmen to call it a day primed for game and with excitement in their hearts they would bring home fish the following day and maybe kill a couple of doe.

The next day Captain Clark turned to Sergeant Gass and said, "Sergeant, will you instruct these men as to how to use snowshoes. You had this experience when you were back East in the New England States. And please get my pair as well as your own so that we can travel without getting frozen feet."

Sergeant Gass said "Aye, aye, sir"

That being said the men waddled out of the stockade with Sergeant Gass and he proceeded to show them how to ski overland. It took several days to make ready for the exploration away from Fort Mandan. The rest of the corps that were not going outside the stockade were at leisure.

The first leg of venturing to visit the Mandan Settlement, located across the Missouri River on the southwest side, might be horrific. Captain Clark told Lewis of his meeting with the Indian fishermen and the fact that the men were going to use snow shoes and that he, Lewis, also would be visiting the Mandan Indian Settlement to view it in the flesh.

Captain Lewis asked of Captain Clark, "Do you have any information you want me to collect from the Indians for our diary."

Clark was very serious when he said, "I want you, my co-captain, to be careful. It is very cold and we do not wish to lose part of our corps as well as you, my co-leader and co-captain."

Captain Lewis said, "You know I'm much more careful than you are because of my natural instincts, and I am much more a loner than you, but these men that we're taking are some of the best. They have volunteered and we will do as the president has asked: collect information, catalogue it, and any specimens we can find we will bring back so that we can return these when we send the group back to civilization."

At the end of the week the snowshoes were ready, the group had prepared and got on as much clothing as they could, including fur caps, buckskin jackets, sweaters, and the snow boots they had received, which were waterproof but made of leather and would withstand the cold.

The men assembled outside around eight in the morning. Captain Lewis had Sergeant Gass demonstrate the use of his snowshoes which Gass had made. This creative skill to make the snowshoes in the middle of nowhere had been learned when he had lived in New England. The cold here at Mandan was far greater any of the volunteers had ever experienced. The temperature reading was twenty-two degrees below zero centigrade. The wind registered twenty miles per hour,

The grumbling included John Newman saying, "Yes it is a cold day in winter. However, if the corpsmen keep moving, I am prepared for just such a day."

After lunch the men started the visit with Captain Lewis explaining what they were doing, pointing out to the men, "Those of you who took muskets with you don't forget shot and powder, and be prepared to protect yourselves from the many bears and other wild animals that might attack you."

The party took off using their snowshoes for the trip and they followed the path toward the Hidatsa Indian Tribe who had been camped at their winter camp on the other side of the river. It was cold. They saw no bear because the marsupials were hibernating and could not be seen. Many of the jackrabbits they saw were able to elude their fate and did not become dinner that night. However, they were able to shoot two of them: one as a specimen for the National Museum. Both of the hares provided meat for rabbit stew. A doe was shot and gutted ready for cooking. This was a typical visit to see the winter wonderland and do the president's bidding.

A solo visit outside the stockade was a typical day for Meriwether Lewis, observing unusual geology and recording as well seeing the natural fauna of the countryside. He often covered an exploration within a twenty-five-mile radius of Fort Mandan. The winter weather forced him to return to the stockade. The exhibits and specimens would be preserved and sent back to Washington, D.C.

They saw a few snowy egrets and tracks of the ground squirrels called prairie dogs. They lived in colonies of several hundred underground most of the time. They fed themselves with nuts that they had collected in the summer and buried in their caches. Captain Lewis wanted to catch one and send it back to Washington, D.C. Seaman tried to dig the gopher out of his burrow but gave up after reaching eight feet underground. At the end of the afternoon the exploration party returned to Fort Mandan exhausted but pleased with their day away from the fort.

The next morning they assembled at eight o'clock and started on snowshoes on the path by the outside of the stockade. They traveled down the ravine in which the river flowed and crossed the river to the Mandan Indian Reservation. Captain Lewis went to the large mud lodge house that was occupied and with one of the interpreters, who knew the sign language, told the chief and other elders the purpose of their visit and how the president of the United States was wishing them good luck and friendship and had a medal to give the chief. It was the Friendship Medal as Captain Lewis said, "From our Great White Father in Washington, D.C. to you. Welcome to our United States." The chief smiled as the interpreter translated the words.

Captain Lewis had an interpreter use sign language to explain what it meant to become citizens of the U S A. Captain Lewis smiled while the exchange of the medal took place. It was climaxed with a handshake

The chief said, "The only thing I have to give you is a tomahawk to present to the Great White Father of your nation and now our nation." So saying, the Indian chief gave one of the brave's very ornate tomahawks that had been handmade and presented it directly to Captain Lewis. Both men shook hands and said "how" as they raised their right hand high and proceeded to eat lunch together.

After lunch, Captain Lewis indicated he would be returning to Fort Mandan and he would like to reciprocate with the Indian chief and have him attend Fort Mandan after the end of 1804. He added that his men had shot some deer and that it would be deer meat and other food that was available that the Corps of Discovery had.

The rest of the afternoon was spent looking at the Indian Village and some of the Indian braves exchanging trinkets that had been bought and brought by Lewis. The trip back was easier and they returned long before the sun went down.

Captain Lewis dismissed his crew and said, "I will take the other members on an exploratory visit up the river and see what we can see." This was possible because the river was frozen over. While there were snowdrifts on it they would be able to catalogue the type of trees that they saw with which Meriwether Lewis was familiar and take back items of scientific interest he could find. This was his modus operandi subsequently followed every day the weather permitted.

The group with which Captain Lewis took a trip the next day went up the Missouri River. The river had frozen over and the ice was approximately a foot thick and the wind had blown the snow from the ice as it was blowing very hard during the daytime at least twenty-five miles per hour.

The interpreter, George Drouillard, was a great hunter, had a lot of experience with cartography, and was distinguished. He was actually involved with interpreting those men who spoke French Canadian such as Toussaint Charbonneau.

When he found out that they were going on the ice and that it was possible to drill a hole through the ice, he talked to Captain Lewis and told him that he would like to try ice fishing as he had done this in his travels when he was involved in interpreting in the eastern part of Canada.

George Drouillard was born in France and he had taken up residence in the Canadian city of Quebec. He had been extremely handy in not only interpreting French but also the Indian language from eastern Canada. Captain Lewis was extremely grateful to Drouillard. He would be useful in the Shoshone country where the Corps of Discovery would soon be dealing with different Indian tribes. Drouillard had a way about him that was acceptable to the Mandan Indian Chief.

He was commissioned to go on this expedition into unknown territory. He knew what he was doing and while the men continued to go up the river, he practiced his favorite hobby—fishing. He drilled a hole through the ice, tied a line to the pole and a hook to the line. Drouillard took the liver from a deer that had been shot and baited his hook.

Sheltering himself from the wind, he sat on a log and tried his hand at fishing. On the return down the frozen river Captain Lewis saw Drouillard hold up a large trout and then flashed five fingers. He caught five trout and several large catfish through a hole in the ice. He was a hero because his catch fed the corps for dinner. Drouillard said, "Zee rivaire loves Geeorge, I must speeek fish talk." He was hailed after dinner was served.

After dinner Captain Clark asked if there was any more trout. Drouillard said, "Where there are catfish usually there are no trout. But here the catfish can't eat the trout because the trout are too big. If you want I go again. But . . . ," he added with a laugh, "you will have to bait your own hook."

Captain Lewis said, "You have made a believer out of me George. You will be crowned king of the sea. You will take these back to the stockade and we will eat them. A channel fish, when they grow up, are four or five feet. You have a small one that will be delicious and since we are in camp for several months, it seems to me that you can take some of the corps with you and catch enough fish to fry for at least a meal or two. Does that seem possible?"

Interpreter Drouillard said, "Yes Captain Lewis sir it will be possible. I will try tomorrow to return and with the other lines we make we should not only have enjoyment catching the fish but also eating it."

George Drouillard had been one of the Indian language specialists hired in St. Charles as an interpreter: however, when Captain Lewis found that he had a lot of experience in hunting, doing cartography, and language capabilities to deal with the French including Toussaint Charbonneau, the arrangement had been wonderful. He had helped the three hunters track the game and shoot them down for food. He was familiar with the musket and the pistol. He had been doing this since he'd been twenty years old.

The captains were pleased with the Mandan winter layover. The corps would have nearly three months to get ready for the next leg of the trip leaving the eastern plain country and finding their way through the Rocky Mountains. The primary goal for the Voyage of Discovery was the Northwest Passage to the Pacific. According to the bold Captain Clark, "So far the adventure has been a piece of cake."

According to the cautious Captain Lewis, "The future is cloudy and gray."

Clark thought the waiting would destroy the great attitude the Voyage of Discovery had demonstrated during 1804.

Would the rest of the trip be a cup of tea or a bitter pill to swallow?

CHAPTER 21

You Bet Your Wife

THE DEADLY SILENCE WAS SHATTERED by a steady tattoo of drum beats coming from the opposite side of the Missouri River. It was the Mandan Indian ceremony giving thanks to the gods for a great fall harvest. This peaceful band of natives were having a pow wow. All the Mandan tribesmen had a chance to show their leader, Chief Blackfoot, how pleased they were in having a successful hunting season. The ceremony continued until the campfire burned low.

As in every other year since time began, the meadow around the fort was covered in snow. The Voyage of Discovery was to be snowed in until the weather warmed up.

Captain Clark told his co-captain, "The Mandan Medicine man says last year it was a very late spring. The baby lambs were not born until the end of May. The snow is too deep now and the ice did not break up in the Big Mo till April. This was a very bad sign for us."

Then Captain Lewis came down with a familiar illness. It was a raspy voice and a hacking cough. He could not get out of his bed in the officer quarters which he shared with Clark. Even so the compound was being spruced up. A big Christmas wreath was being made by Nathaniel Hale Pryor, George Gibson, and Joseph Whitehouse. The three privates braved the cold and the frozen river to pick holly, shiny green leaves with bright red berries. Sergeant Gass volunteered to make plum pudding if Captain Clark would give him some rum to flavor it with. Finally the hunters went out to shoot deer for the Christmas dinner since the duck and geese had flown south for the winter.

The Mandans would prepare for the New Year. The braves would form hunting parties and shoot deer, antelope, and buffalo as they protected their land from the Sioux and other tribes from poaching on the sly.

The year of 1804 was the same as any other year. Late fall gave the tribe time to rest up for the next year's effort to live in the Northwest. Many of the other Indian tribes in the Louisiana Purchase lands roamed the plains. The Mandan tribe being less nomadic than most of the other American Indian tribes had found that the lush meadows adjacent to sections of the Missouri were ideal. They had provided pasture for their livestock and the range had vast expanses of land available to allow for their Indian ponies to roam. Hunting had been good. All was well with the world.

Coincidence changes lives and as so often is the case, the Corps of Discovery proved this theory. The two captains were approached by a French Canadian raconteur who was traveling up the Missouri to get back to the Shoshone tribe's reservation in the Northwestern territory. His name was Toussaint Charbonneau, a sometimes gambler

While he was in St. Louis he had a run of good luck gambling. This nondescript man had sex appeal. Almost every night he played Whist. He had learned this card game while he was growing up in Montreal, Quebec, Canada. He had gone down the Mississippi to become a fur trader in the Northwest Territories.

Staying in a Travelers Rest before going up the Missouri River, he joined the nightly Whist game. He became a regular so much so that anytime someone wanted a high stakes game they would get Charbonneau out of bed and a crowd would surround the table to watch the game.

One evening found the Chief Blackfoot of the Otto tribe with Sacagawea (Bird Woman) and her sister (Otter Moon) watching him play poker. The game was nearing its end and Chief Blackfoot was losing heavily to Charbonneau.

Finally, when Chief Blackfoot ran out of wampum, he turned to Toussaint Charbonneau and pointed to the two young squaws and said, "I will call your bet using my two squaws as wampum."

The chief added, "The winner gets ownership of these lovely Indian maidens, Sacagawea and Otter Moon. If I win, I keep the squaws and win the gold. If you win, you get the squaws and all the gold wampum on the table."

Toussaint Charbonneau eyed the squaws carefully. They were young, in their early teens with braided hair, wearing buckskins and moccasins. They looked unhappy and bedraggled, but did come forward and turn around so that Charbonneau would be able to see their bodies. Charbonneau said, "Well the one you call Sacagawea is okay, the other one, Otter Moon does not appeal to me but as a pair I will gamble my taking the girls if I win and you taking the pot if you win. Agreed?"

The silence was deafening After what seemed an eternity, Chief Blackfoot, the owner of Sacagawea and Otter Moon nodded his head and said, "Deal 'em." Ever so slowly the card was turned over and with a flick of the wrist the gamble was done. Charbonneau had won the gold the young squaws and the plaudits of the small crowd watching the game

The Indian chief got up in disgust and started out of the room in anger. He turned to Charbonneau and said in Shoshone, "You will be sorry you won."

Charbonneau, seeing the game was over, took his pot of gold along with the two girls. He went to his room to spend the night. The girls could speak Shoshone and no English. He was a French Canadian fur trader from the Montreal area of Canada and could speak very little Shoshone Mandan. He had come by way of the St. Lawrence River through the Huron Territory and down the Mississippi to St. Louis and was going up the Missouri to do fur trading in the back country.

He was looking for a temporary position as an interpreter and wanted to return up the Missouri river to the Rocky Mountain area where the Shoshone Tribe lived. His delay in Mandan was caused by a change in the weather and a blizzard so intense that he was forced to wait for relief from the cold.

Charbonneau talked to the Mandan Chief who had welcomed him. Chief Blackfoot told the two Shoshone maidens to attend to his every wish of trapper Charbonneau.

Toussaint was a frontier interpreter and fur trader who had lived farther up the Missouri near the Snake River—Shoshone Reservation. The tribe of

Shoshones were industrious but often were raided by other tribes capturing squaws both young and old who worked for their new masters.

It was in early December as Charbonneau had crossed the Missouri near Mandan and saw the stockade that Captain Lewis and Captain Clark had constructed in order to wait out the snowy cold and high winds. For Charbonneau it was hole-up until spring came and then go back to the Shoshone area.

Charbonneau came to see Captain Lewis and said, "The situation that I find myself I am many miles away from my Shoshone tribe. I can do a great job of interpreting. I know Shoshone and French. I can help you to cross Montana. You need to hire me."

Captain Lewis told Charbonneau, "I do not hire any of the Corps of Discovery but would talk it over with my partner, Captain Clark, who does."

The two Captains argued. This discussion was heated. Captain Clark said, "Meriwether, you know that we have limited foodstuffs to eat and that we will rely on our hunters to provide us venison, buffalo, and rabbits to provide the major portion of our diet and that it will be a long cold winter."

"We do have flour and some potatoes for our bread, but our vegetable requirements are necessary and we will not have more until the spring when we can head toward greener pastures."

Captain Lewis said, "I understand that William. We are on short rations and do not need to add another mouth to feed. But we do need an interpreter who can take us farther up the Missouri to where the Shoshone live. They will be able to lead us toward the Northwest Passage to the Pacific Ocean. I say they stay on if they work for their keep."

So it was that a group of three joined the corps—an interpreter who would have additional assigned jobs and the two girls as guides knowing the Shoshone area farther west toward the Pacific. The deal was struck and the fact that Sacagawea was seven months pregnant was ignored. The only concession made by the two captains is that they would move out of their officer's quarters and make room for the three new additions to their party. They did not make them members of the Corps of Discovery, but it made the corps now thirty-four members.

Sacagawea was seven months pregnant and the baby would be born before the end of winter. The only persons who could help deliver the new baby was her twelve-year-old sister, Otter Moon, and Captain Lewis whose activities included providing all medical care needed at the fort. BUT he had never delivered a child!

The Captain's quarters were to be used when the baby came and Captain Lewis talked to Toussaint Charbonneau. Lewis explained to the new members of the expedition, "I have limited knowledge of such things as pregnancy, delivering a baby and the care of the child during the ensuing months." He added, "I will give it a go!" The conflict was between man's hopes and nature's demands, which the Captain admitted was in the hands of God! Captain Clark said to himself, *We shall see. We shall see.*

CHAPTER 22

The Losers

THE WORLD IS FLOODED WITH people who are born losers. Why? No one knows. It just happens. The old folks called it getting up on the wrong side of the bed. This occurred on a gorgeous spring day at Fort Mandan and the two captains were excited as they were about to embark on the second leg of the Voyage of Discovery.

The two officers, Lewis and Clark, realized that it must be done as spring had sprung.

Clark said, "Meriwether, we must decide today who goes and who stays with us on our great adventure. No matter how often the cards fall, it is not their way. I am in charge of operations. I make the choice, don't I?"

Lewis replied, "Not necessarily. I will scan your list and will cross out those in it and give it back to you."

Dead silence.

Here was a conflict in the making, Clark versus Lewis operations, deciding who will continue on and who will be sent back to St. Louis in the keelboat with the work that Captain Lewis had done during the first nine months of the trip.

The day was beautiful and the spring flowers were sprouting from the Plains of the Dakota Territory and the forests that surround the Fort Mandan that was built in two months utilizing the efforts of all thirty-one members of the corps. The plan that the two captains were discussing was what the second leg of the voyage would be like as they attempted to find the Northwest Passage during the delay of wintertime and the inability to travel up the Missouri River by keelboat. The ice was gone and the keelboat couldn't be taken up any farther.

Captain Clark and Captain Lewis were in agreement again as far as continuing the exploration. The Mandan Indians had been helpful and their chief had been back into the interior and during the Christmas powwow, had met with Captain Clark and Captain Lewis and told them that the next portion of their trip would be much more difficult than the first coming up the river on the keelboat.

The two captains talked over how many and what type of crew they needed. They had talked during the hiatus of winter and had come to the conclusion that they would send back to St. Louis everyone except the twenty-five privates, the four sergeants, one corporal, and the three new members of the expedition.

Captain Clark continued, "Meriwether, we better get underway as quickly as we can. We cannot take the keelboat farther up the river because of its size and the fact that the barge full of goods is empty and we promised the chief of the Kanza Tribe that we would send it back to him in return for their return in getting us going in the right direction and in the right way."

Captain Lewis said, "Well, I am sending back the scientific information I have collected regarding the Northwest Passage, the trip called the Voyage of Discovery, and the tribes we have visited. We are following President Jefferson's order to tell him about the Louisiana Purchase and what it means to their becoming citizens of the United States under the big White Father in Washington, D.C. I will have to talk to the head of the return trip and explain what to do with the materials I am sending back, how to get them back to the National Museum in Washington, D.C., and specifically to deliver a message to President Jefferson as to the first eleven months of our Voyage of Discovery."

Captain Clark said. "I can understand your picking Corporal Richard Warfington as he will get the president plugged in and he wants to get home and resume his position in life. "

This would give an update about progress. It would tell him how much they had accomplished and send back a record of what they did and when they did it going up the Missouri to build their winter quarters. It was very important because the corps were asked to collect all the information about people, activities, and *The Squaring of the Triangle*.

Each of the sides of the triangle represented President Jefferson, Captain Clark, and Meriwether Lewis also as Captain. The fact that there had been dissension among the troops and internal conflicts had developed involving the permanent members numbering twenty-five and the six leaders and specialists.

This conflict between the thirty-one of the Corps of Discovery was to continue until its success. With that as a preamble Captain Lewis called out his list of the permanent party and referring to the Captain who has been in charge of operations said that he had none.

The twelve boatmen hired in St. Louis had been hired for a specific purpose of going up the Missouri River and that they did. They were done and sent home.

Toussaint Charbonneau the guide was to stay. Charbonneau spoke French, knew a little bit of sign language, and his mistress Sacagawea who came from the Shoshone Tribe with her older sister Otter Moon, not able to do anything but entertain the corps members at night and with abandon. The corps had traveled at least a thousand miles and tested only mettle of the corps. This action would unload all the losers

CHAPTER 23

Taking the Right Fork in the Road

WHICH WAY IS THE RIGHT way to go? Sergeant Patrick Gass had stopped on the way back to the corps. He said to himself, *I have an even chance of choosing the right way back.* Walking down the path he saw a small black animal ambling along in the same direction he was going. It had a white stripe running from nose to tail. The animal was moving away from him tail in the air.

As the Sergeant walked over to get a closer look he was overpowered by a smell that he had never smelled before. It was horrible and it was issuing from the rear end of this small animal. This creature was a skunk.

A skunk uses as his protection, a scent that is so horrible that it won't go away by itself for several days. Gass couldn't believe he had been odorized by a skunk. He had been sprayed by its liquid spray. It stung his eye. He tried to wash it off with water from a spring he found close by but to no avail.

Gass thought, *Now it's too late. I have been skunked. I can't stand myself. What will the corps say when I get back?* He had never known anyone that had been sprayed. Gass hoped it would be gone in a couple of days. He would be shunned by anyone getting closer to him than ten feet because of this odor.

The effect on Gass was immediate. He had left the keelboat to scout for food such as beaver, deer, and wild turkey. He was the noncom in charge of the party from the Corps of Discovery looking for game. It was Captain Clark's order to find enough food not only for the next two days but also for more if he could do so. As the best shot he often led the search party who foraged for meat, fish, or anything else that could satisfy the appetite of thirty-four hungry explorers. After being sprayed Gass could not continue to lead his party of five up the Yellowstone River hunting for game.

Sergeant Gass hollered to the five, "I've been skunked! Stay away! I will return to the boat. Pryor you take over. We need game food. Come back by dark loaded."

Rubbing his eyes and sitting down on the ground by the riverbank Gass was washing his buckskins to rid himself of the fluid he had been sprayed with. To no avail, he thought, maybe the lye in soap would help.

Later in the day his fellow corpsmen returned and started to approach Sergeant Gass but the odor was so offensive that they hollered to each other, "No way! We'll wait until this smell goes away. Walk back by yourself. "

The next morning the Corps of Discovery sent a rescue party who stayed their distance and escorted Gass back to the boat.

Captain Clark getting on the deck hailed the returning Gass saying with a laugh, "Sergeant Gass, you stink. We will tow you behind in a canoe until you smell better."

Having traveled some one hundred miles toward the West the corps came to the fork in the river where sand on the river bottom had the tones of yellow and brown. The other branch had water that ran clean and clear.

At the joining of Missouri and Yellowstone Rivers, the corps docked to let Gass off the barge to take a cold bath. Sergeant Pryor told Gass, "According to Cap'n Lewis you will have to get sand and scrub where you were sprayed. The stench should be gone in a couple of days."

The water was cold. Gass climbed down the bank and picked up sand from the bottom and rubbed the sandy water over his entire body. He shivered from the cold, and the smell he later found out, was still overpowering. He wondered as he laid out his clothes in the sun if the smell would go away. He did this for an hour and noticed no decrease in the odor.

Sergeant Gass figured that he should talk to Captain Lewis, who was the closest thing to a medical doctor they had, and get his advice as to what could be done.

But without special knowledge of an antidote, since washing it away did not seem to help, Gass was not allowed on the keelboat where the Captain would be able to reexamine him, refer to his medical text he had brought with him from Philadelphia, and find out what besides Benjamin Rush's tonic could work.

Captain Lewis cornered Captain Clark and said that he had to go ashore. "Our search party we sent to get food has had an accident. Its leader, Gass, has been disabled. He's one of the best hunters we have. If I can't cure the situation there will be hell to pay. I will hasten to look at our wounded corps member."

So saying he got in a canoe, and with the Private Goodrich, started to go up the Yellowstone River. It was approximately a mile and a half against the current and it took Captain Lewis two hours, both men in the boat rowing furiously to come within hailing distance of Private Gass. Resting on the sandy bank, he was trying to rid himself of the skunk smell.

Captain Lewis reached Gass on foot. He walked up to him, held his nose, and inspected the damage. He asked, "How did it happen to our best hunter? What happened?"

Gass said, "I've been ruined forever! I can't stand my own smell. It won't wash off and I've been using the sand to scrub my skin until it is raw from rubbing, but I still stink up to high heaven!"

Captain Lewis retreated and said, "You have been attacked by a woods skunk even though you said you had approached carefully and did nothing. You must stay far enough away from the skunk or kill him in his tracks so that he cannot release his spray and immobilize you."

"You have to help me. Captain Lewis, please, please help me. What can I do?"

Captain Lewis turned slowly away and said, "Gass, you'll have to walk back along the bank until reaching the keelboat. I will follow you in my canoe keeping you in sight. Stinking the way you do you do not have to worry about being attacked by anyone from a bison or buffalo to the smallest titmouse. You will be immune as long as the smell remains."

The other corpsmen rowed down the river except two men, Howard and Hall, who stayed at a distance and continued foraging for food. They stood by the bank of the Missouri and caught some thirty-plus catfish using bacon rind for bait.

Captain Lewis put a clothespin on his nose so he could stand the smell of odiferous Patrick Gass as he was towed back to the keelboat. Captain Lewis yelled to Patrick Gass, "Get in the water, keep washing yourself over and over again and I will consult with Captain Clark as to any remedy we could use. My only advice might be to bathe yourself in Dr. Rush Golden Elixir and wait for the smell to go away."

Patrick Gass said, "Hopefully I can live on the barge until I am deskunked." He hollered to Privates Hall and Howard, "You fish from the shore. When you have caught and cleaned enough fish come back to the keelboat and give them a chance to roast the fish for chow."

Patrick Gass continued to try to remove odor from his body. He washed his clothes several times with lye soap and water, but to no avail. The scent of the skunk was all-pervading and was like rotten garbage and spoiled meat mixed together and left to disintegrate in the sun.

The skunk escaped into the brush adjacent to the river and was not seen. Of course the private that Captain Lewis had sent with Patrick Gass, the Sergeant, was extremely upset by this accident. He had delayed the Voyage of Discovery for a day and a half.

Such was the effect on the crew. Patrick Gass had attempted to remove the smell, had waited to approach the keelboat and his fellow explorers from the corps until he passed the smell test. The privates in his squad could tell him, "You stink," and get away with it.

The principle that Sergeant Gass had applied to himself as well as to others was that unexpected events result in accidental results. Many are not fatal but most are unpleasant.

This accident occurred in exploring the territory between Fort Mandan and the Pacific Ocean. It seemed that every time something unexpected happened it was under Captain Clark's watch and made his directing operations of travel more difficult. The possibility of finding the Northwest Passage was decreasing by the day. The Missouri River had been very turbulent and difficult to conquer during the first spring. It was slowing down the exploration. Captain Lewis was spending much more time doing the scientific work that was his principal activity.

Now that spring had come the hope of the two captains was that the rest of the travel to the Pacific would be direct and not very difficult with one exception—the mountains were snow covered to the west of the Corps of

Discovery. Captain Lewis and Captain Clark did not need physical accidents such as coming upon a skunk in the wild and later having scouts being overcome by being sprayed by the skunk.

The Mandan tribe had warned the corps and its captains of the possibility of being attacked by wild animal, but had not dreamed it would be a skunk. The Indians knew that the scent would take a week to go away. In the meantime, soap, water, and bathing in the Missouri River seemed the only way to attack this problem. Patrick Gass was aghast when he heard skunk stories of those serving in this band of explorers and the Indian Braves who spent lots of time in the forests of Montana. It seemed that the only balm was time and living in the fresh air.

Patrick Gass was involved in outside activities on shore and away from the corps. The weather was favorable. It was not too hot during the day and the nights were pleasant. This benefited the entire Corps of Discovery but especially the quartermaster and Sergeant Patrick Gass.

Sergeant Gass was able to sleep at night after the scent diminished noticeably. In the meantime the sergeant was able to get his notes in order so that his diary was current—including information useful to the nation and those hearty settlers that would follow him.

Looking ahead at what was in store was the prime objective of Patrick Gass as he recovered from his situation, which was not only medical in scope but obnoxious to all others—the fact that skunks were to be found in the New World and up the Missouri River close to the Rocky Mountains.

Patrick Gass told the two captains that he understood his being assigned to outside duty but would do his best to find the answer to being skunked.

Obnoxious animals with obnoxious odors certainly qualified as conflicts of environment verses man. It is timeless. It pertains to living in the current day world where the future of the corps was not to be jeopardized. This conflict of man versus beast is as old as time. Gass guessed that his tracking skills would be questioned by Captain Lewis or would they?

CHAPTER 24

Hip-Hip-Hooray

THE CONFLICTING ATTITUDES OF THE two leaders became apparent the last week of 1804. Captain Clark was a religious man. He started the day facing east toward the Holy Land and said a prayer asking Jesus, "Another day. May the lord forgive the sins of yesterday give me strength to face my future trials and tribulations. Amen."

Captain Lewis was a pessimist. He looked down at the ground and said to himself *we are here in the middle of nowhere. I don't believe in God and have not felt cared for since I became a man. I think evil thoughts and have great trouble sleeping at night. I am a lost soul.*

The twenty-five privates were scattered around the room with homemade pine bough mats shielding them from the winter cold. The fire in its pit had burned down to glowing coals. Each morning the sun moved from east to west with the rays interrupted by the western pine forest.

Each day of Christmas week was dull and the same. The captains updated their records as prescribed by the president. The corps did the housekeeping and after the sun disappeared played whist or read by firelight.

The year 1805 started with the boom of the cannon of the Voyager. The two captains had decided to celebrate January 1, 1805. This was a chance for the corps to let off steam since the winter snows had struck at Fort Mandan. This was the opportunity for the group of explorers to let their hair down and have a rollicking good time. The captains and crew came to the realization that it was going to be cold and lonely. It happened in the stockade where the Corps of Discovery had holed up for the winter.

The scene was set. A roaring fire, a roast deer dinner using the four doe shot by Jean Batiste Le Page, a private who had been apprenticed to a gun smith while in his native state of Virginia.

It was a joyous time and rum was poured as a special treat. It was hot and buttered and tickled the palates of the twenty-five privates who were being incarcerated by the winter weather. The prison was Fort Mandan itself. It had taken two months to build and had sleeping quarters for Captain Lewis and Captain Clark.

The two officers faced each other and said as one, "Happy New Year." A few moments later Captain Clark said, "If the New Year is as good as the old one was we will be in great shape, Meriwether."

Captain Lewis answered, "You optimist you."

The problem that Captain Lewis envisioned was getting on with the trip. It was hoped that they would discover the Pacific Ocean and locate the Northwest Passage at the instruction of the president.

The mission was clear. The first leg up the Missouri River from St. Louis had been reached by November 1,and the ensuing two months had resulted in the meadow on which the Corps of Discovery were camped giving up its logs so that a stockade could be built.

The Missouri River was too small for the keelboat to pass any further as it was too shallow. The territory was Indian country. The natives, who had never seen a white man, lived across the river. It was the tribal area of the Mandan and Hidatsu Indian tribes.

Captain Lewis had said, "William you must be responsible for the mapping of our route and I will be responsible for keeping records and specimens of the territory we are traversing. The environment and Indian tribal conditions will be my cup of tea."

Captain Lewis replied, "Where we are wintering is our base camp for 1805. I have the exact position marked down from using the Adelaide, the air temperature, and the readings taken by both of us."

Clark agreed to do it during daylight and Lewis by night. Lewis had acquired the skills while studying at the University of Pennsylvania.

The week after New Year's Day passed by quickly. Captain Clark took Sergeants Gass and Pryor with him as he hunted for game to provide food to eat during the cold winter. The Missouri River was frozen solid and the two Indian tribes lived in igloo-style mud huts several miles south of the frozen river.

The Indian chiefs and braves planned a celebration of the new year. Activities involved a dance and dinner with the Mandan Indians across the Missouri. The two cultures had intermingled since the day the Missouri froze over and could be the bridge of exchanging niceties.

The two captains, Lewis and Clark, had made a New Year's resolution. Clark made a toast, he said, "Here's to the United States of America and our corps. Our goal is good. Our spirits high and our progress tolerable."

Lewis realized that the social structure of the tribe was composed of a chief, his medicine man, advisor, and a tribal structure much different than that of the Discovery corps.

Therefore, Captain Lewis spent a great deal of time interfacing with Chief Littlefoot of the Crow Tribe located above the Platt River from the south banks of the Missouri. He also talked with the Mandan tribe. It was three miles south of the Missouri. It was within walking distance of the corps. At the first meeting of the two groups Captain Clark wanted to have snowshoes available for use by the Corps of Discovery. He traded some needles and thread for them.

The snows of late December had impeded any outside activity of the men with the exception of taking a walk to relieve themselves. The walk to the pit, though short, meant leaving the stockade several times each day.

Captain Clark and his two Sergeants, Patrick Gass and George Juilliard, who was also an interpreter, left the camp to explore on snowshoes. The weather was below zero and a man would perish in the cold in less than an hour. Thus, the desire to intermingle was limited by the weather.

The Mandan Indian Tribe who lived across the Missouri was very interested in seeing what the Corps of Discovery was doing at the Fort. Twenty-five members of the Mandan tribe snowshoed across the frozen Missouri and entered the compound of the fort.

The visitors arranged a powwow celebration of the two groups. It was an event that Captain Lewis recorded in his memoirs. Lewis recorded the powwow as an Indian celebration of their community life. It set forth the ceremony and the attitude of the Indians toward their tribe and its life style. It showed the captains that the two groups were different but compatible. It made the captains realize that the two races could learn to live with each other and were not inherently antagonists.

The potential of both the Americans and Mandan braves not tolerating the other was great. It was the ancient custom of the Indians versus. the let's-see-if-it-will-work of the explorers. It was the new versus the old. It was democracy pitted against plutocracy.

The two captains knew that the winter break would seem endless, but it was the only course of action. It was a cheer heard by the corps, "Hip, hip, hooray saves the day!"

CHAPTER 25

And Baby Makes Three

THREE SHIVERING STRANGERS ENTERED THE stockade. The guard realizing that the below zero temperature would kill the three said, "I will tell you what to do as soon as I find out from the watch officer." He went to get instructions from Sergeant Pryor. The guard ran from the gate to the sergeant's desk. Out of breath, he explained, "Sergeant, three strangers from the Mandan Indian Tribe need shelter before they die in the snow."

The sergeant asked, "Are they armed?"

The guard said, "Not as far as I could see. But it is so cold. I'll let them in and take any guns they have away from them. O.K.?"

The Sergeant replied, "Private White, I'll go with you." He grabbed his pistol. "You lead, I'll follow."

Seeing the three on snowshoes the Sergeant said, "If you two have guns throw them on the ground."

Charbonneau complied tossing his pistol on the ground. He said, "You have saved us. As you can see," as he pointed to Sacagawea, "she is with child."

The sergeant said to the private guarding the gate, "You can let them stay inside and after you do, return to your post. "

At this point in time, Sergeant Pryor hustled the three into the living quarters. As he did the fur trader, Charbonneau said pointing to the pregnant girl, "We are going up the river to her family tribe, the Sioux. As you can see my wife Sacagawea is very pregnant. She is a month away and we can't get any farther. The other girl is my sister-in-law Otter Moon."

Captain Clark said, "I will check with Captain Lewis in the morning. In the meantime, we will let you stay the night."

The following morning Captain Clark met with Captain Lewis saying, "Meriwether the arrangement we can make with our visitors will not please them. If we leave Fort Mandan and continue west they will have to work as the rest of the members of the corps do. But such a drastic step should be voted on just as President Jefferson has wanted us to do. This is a case of an unexpected event and this sure qualifies as unusual."

Clark said, "If you say so. You are the man who dealt with President Jefferson."

Clark and Lewis held a meeting with Sergeants Ordway, Pryor, and Gass and raised the matter of the three unwanted visitors and how this intrusion would require approval by a vote of the members in the expedition.

The situation facing the Voyage of Discovery was explained to all of those aboard and the men voted to allow the new members of the expedition to join the Voyage of Discovery.

The one person who did not like the arrangement was Toussaint Charbonneau, the interpreter-fur trader who said, "We have no other choice but to accept your terms. We preserve our right to leave the corps at any time with one day's notice. Is that understood? We have no other choice but to say we agree. I have talked it over with my wife and her sister."

There was a murmur in the compound as Captain Clark stood up and looked the two visitors standing before the group and said, "This seems to have conflicted our main plan to find a way to the sea. We want to continue this, but the problem has arisen where three uninvited guests have come to our fort and have asked for help. They want to go along for a free ride. I say no work no stay. This is strictly against our plan, but we have no other alternative. They stay, they work, they continue with us to their eventual goal, which is their Shoshone Tribe near the Yellowstone River and its source Yellowstone Lake."

Captain Lewis added, "We present this to you as Toussaint Charbonneau will be attached to our corps and hired on as an interpreter since he does understand both English and French and Shoshone. The young woman is named Sacagawea. She is about to bear Charbonneau's first child and she and her sister, Otter Moon, who both are capable of cooking and locating food that we would have difficulty finding in the wild of the Northwest Territory, and therefore they will be employed to provide these services in return for their being transported along with Charbonneau to their Shoshone Reservation."

He turned to Captain Clarks and said, "Is there anything you wish to add Captain Clark?" Captain Lewis in hearing no response said to the men, "We have a decision to make. We do it by raising of hands. Would you please listen to Captain Lewis and his presentation of the following?"

Captain Lewis said, "I am pleased to follow the procedure required by our president, namely, that we have three uninvited guests who will leave with us and they have requested the right to join the Corps of Discovery and this search for the Northwest Passage. They wish to go to the Shoshone Indian Tribal Reservation approximately a thousand miles west of here along the Missouri River or they would be asked to leave and return across the Missouri River to the Mandan tribe. In this freezing weather that would be sentencing them to certain death."

The question being raised was moot. It was unanimous. All thirty-one members of the corps raised their hands and there was jubilation amongst the men who gathered around Charbonneau, Sacagawea, and Otter Moon shouting, "Welcome, welcome, welcome."

Having no need for further attention by the Corps of Discovery, Captain Clark said. "Sergeant, please dismiss your men." Thus, the three strangers were allowed to become part of the Corps of Discovery and had agreed to provide work in return for their journey.

This conflict was evident from the time that the three came out of the cold and their deportment had been fine. The transition from guest to worker remained to be seen. It went smoothly. The corps members talked and felt that Charbonneau and the two women were given privileges that were not available to the corps as a whole. Captain Lewis did not like to have his policies ignored, but the spring weather was just a couple of months away.

Captain Clark and Captain Lewis lived together ate together and slept in the same room. It was probable that they would discuss this closeness during the hiatus of the winter. The next conflict had to do with Otter Moon and her sister, Sacagawea. Otter Moon was a year older, Sacagawea was the one that appealed to Charbonneau and with her he had sex. He always kept

Otter Moon at a different teepee. If Sacagawea refused his sexual overtures, he would call for her sister and tell Otter Moon, who was more than willing to comply. Thus he had the conflict of this threesome in having sexual needs as the husband and to play around.

This conflict came only after Toussaint Charbonneau had his fun and games with both sisters. He asked for a chance to join the corps and was taking them from the Mandan tribe back up to the Shoshone Village on the Snake River. It would be foolish to claim that such a family love triangle would be possible. However in the middle of nowhere and the availability of women to twenty-five privates, all in their early twenties, seemed probable.

In the spring of 1805, the twenty-five privates were young and were seeking the favors of two women, actually young girls, not yet in their teens. The triangle would rear its ugly head periodically as the Voyage of Discovery continued looking for the Northwest Passage. It was a case of conflicts on of the oldest professions in the world being plied where demand was the ruling force.

CHAPTER 26

Isolation

IT WAS IN LATE IN the afternoon. There was a spring breeze from the east. Captain Lewis and Captain Clark met on deck, facing the small crowd they had and saluted the American flag as they left the dock. The sail on the keelboat had caught the wind. It was allowing the keelboat barge and pirogues to make progress moving up the river. The tiny armadas dodged rocks and sand bars in the river as well as the limbs and other debris floating down the river. To do so, the helmsman turned the keelboat to the starboard or larboard as the channel of the Missouri River demanded.

The barge was trailing behind the keelboat and the two pirogues dutifully acted as scouts on either side. It was a hurried departure because of President Jefferson's reminder that had been received while Captain Lewis was following his presidential instructions sent to him in St. Louis. It was that the Louisiana Purchase was a done deal. The rest of the corps from sergeants to privates and non-military personnel had been told to go to their quarters unless they had assigned duties to perform.

This think time gave Captain Lewis a chance to mull over what the prospects were for the morrow. Today, as usual, he had his pipe in hand unlit to save smoking precious tobacco he had had sent from home. Many times he had his eyes closed deep in thought. He planned his next days' activity. He wrote his plans down in a diary leaving room for changes as they would come to mind. He envied Captain Clark who had scheduled responsibilities that were often repeated daily, weekly, or monthly. Clark did most of the cartography. He did it after the sun went down.

Lewis activities were often vague. A typical example was to record all breeds of birds, animals, fish crustaceans, snakes, humans, plants, flora and fauna observed on the voyage. Specimens were to be captured and those most unusual brought back to civilization live, if possible. Lewis's activities were limited by time only and were continuous. Lewis soon found that the fact that he had over half of the privates assigned to him, he could designate what these corpsmen were to do and which of his platoon was to do it.

The division of activities was to be an ever-increasing source of conflict. One of them happened when the corps was entering the Montana territories wide-open spaces. The timing occurred one morning just after sun up and Captain Lewis had taken Seamen out for his morning walk along the bank of the river. Seamen earned his keep by being the corps' night watchman.

After the dog relieved himself on the shore he jumped off the barge, swam to the riverbank, and climbed up to the level desert. Once there he started barking up a storm. Captain Lewis being the great owner of the corps' watchdog went on deck, got to the shore, and walked over to see what the problem was.

It was a catfish sunning himself on the top of the water. Lewis sketched the fish, whiskers and all, noted its common name, size, estimated weight, time of year, where it was found, and then would send the information back to the National Museum in Washington, D.C. The sketch was named "Whisker Fish" as Captain Lewis described its distinctive markings and gave it a descriptive name, its common name.

Conflicting work schedules was apparent from the start of the expedition. Captain Lewis was able to alleviate the conflicting time of the nature of his duties because it was set up so that the two were in the captains' quarters, either on the keelboat, or ashore before Sergeant Floyd had the craft anchored in the middle of the river for the safety of the corps. Watch was always posted with pistols at hand to fend off any Indian marauders till the corps could defend itself. Fortunately Seaman would bark if the keelboat was approached during the night when the corps were asleep.

The candles would burn down and the captains would have to make written notes by candlelight. Captain Lewis was much more introspective and treated their isolation differently. Captain Clark had military training thus his character was formed such that he handled things on a top/down basis. He headed the corps military style organization and at least once a week the two Sergeants, Ordway and Floyd Gass, would attend the meeting to pass on "the poop" from the privates and other non-army persons who made up Corps of Discovery members.

Captain Clark and Captain Lewis met daily in the evening and discussed what happened during the day, made notes, and planned the next day's operation. Thus, this expedition covering three calendar years was to be a voyage to collect information about the Northwest Territory and to meet with the Indian tribes and other settlers in this vast area.

The nightly meetings were informal and both Captains kept diaries in pen and ink, recording activities of the day. Lewis' diary reported environmental information as well as the powwows held with the Indian chiefs and tribal members. They were meetings held ashore and afterwards the Indian leaders were shown the keelboat and the swivel gun was demonstrated by the gun crew. The corps stood at attention for the presentation of the friendship medal designed by President Jefferson.

After the ceremony the Indian braves danced around the fire and the trading and exchanging of gifts by the two separate cultures took place. It was a festive event with the squaws serving dinner featuring venison steaks, Buffalo tenders, duck, quail, geese and of course yellow ears of Indian corn. Captains Lewis and Clark had never eaten ears of corn before and after meeting the Kanza Tribe, asked for it at every greeting ceremonial dinner celebration.

Lewis was in charge of a collection of data, the recording of the same, and the investigation of the various elements of the trip. He had studied at the College of University of Williamsburg to get the basis information about the proposed trip to the Northwestern Territories. Now the Corps of Discovery was on the Voyage of Discovery. It would be a lonely trip as no one other than a few fur trappers, adventurous settlers, and Indian tribes were residents in the vast area.

CHAPTER 27

Gates of the Mountains

T HE TRIP UP THE MISSOURI proceeded. The group reached Great Falls and heard that they would encounter an impassible area where they would have to portage and go by boat, as it was impractical to attempt to traverse the area of twenty-five miles of the Missouri without having everything on the boat.

The men reloaded the boat and took the balance of the merchandise, supplies, gunpowder, and left the gunpowder and lead and other products for protection, including muskets and those items needed to portage and go by boat through section of the Missouri. The captains agreed that they would portage the boat and if they could not get through, they would come back up the river and pick up the stragglers.

It was a dangerous time and the captain of choice was Clark. He said to Captain Lewis, "This is my time to shine. I will take the first group down the river and at the end of the first day, we'll come up the river to pick up the rest of the Corps of Discovery."

They were able to take the pirogues having three men each, leaving twenty-four taken up river. This would be Clark's time to show his ability to solve a transportation situation. He told his men, "Don't worry, we will get around this. We're supposed to see some amazing features but it can only be done by water."

He proceeded to load the pirogues and by taking the men, they would be able to navigate the river ever so slowly by staying in the channel and away from the shore so that the only time they had to beach their boat the sun was going down. It was summer time and the sun stayed up thirteen and one half hours so they would be able to make this portage within two to three days if everything went right.

Captain Clark selected half of the men and told them to put any belongings they had in a sack and strap the sack onto their backs so they would be able to wade if necessary and help move the keelboat down river with a lightened load.

They started down the river. The first thing they saw was the white chalk of the mountains, which one of the crew said had to be calcium carbonate, and it must have been laid up there when the lake was found centuries before, then a river started and the carbon showed on the hillside. Captain Clark sent some scouts up the mountain to see if this was true and to bring back a sample. It was calcium carbonate and Captain Lewis verified the fact. A small pile of acid in a medical kit was removed to make a test to see.

The first day ended when the white mountains disappeared and on the opposite side of the river was the settlement, so-called where the mountains had formed blocks that looked like a house piled on another house and it continued in that fashion along the tops of the hills so that it looked like a settlement of square houses looking down over the river. Captain Clark sent a group of three men up the side of the hill and sought the structure at the side of the hill and found that the shale formation was such that it terminated due to earthquake or some other means and that the lift of the earthquake had made a different section of this several-mile stretch appear like there were structures looking down over the river.

The men returned with some samples of the shale for Captain Lewis and said that there was no need for him to go up and personally look at it because he would get the same impression that they had. He disagreed with that and asked Captain Clark to spend the night on the north shore and he would arise early in the morning and take the climb to verify the situation reported by the three explorers. This happened as scheduled and by twelve o'clock the following day the men had eaten breakfast and lunch and Captain

Lewis turned along with Sergeant Gass, who had indicated that he knew how to call the mountains and had demonstrated his ability.

On the side of the river, those who left early in the morning, and the Corps of Discovery considered going down the channel to the center of the river and avoid the rocks that were periodically sticking up out of the water. With great care they came to a vantage point and saw a spire that the Indians had told him to look for called *the eye of the needle.* They saw the hole that had been blasted by wind through the rock so that you could see a true hit. This was it. It was a needle with its eye available. The size of this was approximately one hundred-fifty feet high with the eye estimated to be ten feet high and three feet wide so that you had a sensation of a needle being held up to the sky.

After this had been seen, the men agreed to go down river and they saw one of the strange events that occurred due to the structure of the river. The river spread out and then narrowed again, so that there was a promontory extending out into the center of the river. Approximately two thousand feet further downstream there was a promontory on the opposite side of the river sticking out into the river, leaving the effect of the gate of the mountain.

As the keelboat proceeded downriver it came around a curve and as it rounded the curve the promontory on the north side of the river appeared to close on the promontory on the south side of the river so it looked like the two points were closing—as if this was a gate being closed. This impression was so real that Captain Clark drew a sketch in his diary.

After several days and thirty miles down the Missouri River, the Gates of the Mountain, the Eye of the Needle, Chalk Hills, and the Lake City Houses were the talk of the Corps of Discovery as they prepared to return to Great Falls and traverse them or portage around them. They had been told by the local Indians that this was a dangerous effort and that they should scout the Great Falls before attempting to continue going up river around this danger.

CHAPTER 28

Mercy vs. Hunger

DURING THE WINTERING IN THE Mandan stockade the Voyage of Discovery was suspended. February 14 had seen the birth of Pomp, Sacagawea's baby boy. The three new members of the expedition had filled a gap in the group of thirty-four. The two captains had followed the plan advanced by Captain Lewis. They had been snowed in since the middle of December. The Christmas week holiday parties, Indian pow wows, and holidays had been a pleasant interlude. But the corps was getting restive. Captain Lewis had been reorganizing the corps.

The co-captains had decided the night before that one of them should take one-half of the corps and portage around this stockade with Captain Lewis making a visit to the Hidatsa tribe.

After crossing the Missouri River Captain Lewis had a day to remember. The ice covering was a foot thick. It truly was one of the many miracles found in the interior of Montana. The buffalo herd was grazing on the frozen alfalfa, wild oats, and other luxurious grasses found under the snow.

The sun had peeked over the horizon. The wind was blowing mightily and the ospreys were sailing in the blue sky wanting to dive into the water if they could find any pools of water not covered with ice.

Captain Lewis had crossed the Missouri River to explore the south bank of the river. His primary aim was to collect information about the territory including the river and any flora and fauna not covered with snow.

It was morning and the mountains were painted a deep purple by the yellow sunlight. The rays of the sun cast shadows on the men of the Corps of Discovery that were with Captain Lewis.

This was an epic moment of the Voyage of Discovery. The two captains had agreed that Lewis would take some of the corps to assist him. The temperature was below zero and the men struggled for air as it burned their lungs when they inhaled. The stretch of frozen meadowland that they were traversing was causing the buffalo to band as close together as they could for warmth.

Captain Lewis wished to see any buffalo so that he could observe their calves and the male guards that stood at the end of the herd so that they would not be disturbed as they searched for food. It was a peaceful site and Captain Lewis estimated there were over a thousand buffalo in this herd and they were able to get enough forage that their hunger would be satisfied. Here again was a conflict of nature: man versus beast, and the fact that once a buffalo herd had grazed an area, it was barren and the plants were eaten to the height of less than one inch. Thus, the herd would trample the snow and it would take several years before it was green and lush again.

The Hidatsas and the Mandans were in the process of getting buffalo meat. The buffalo was tough and almost inedible except by the wolves that fed upon the buffalo calves that strayed too far from the mares. Lewis and the corps walked around the herd and stayed one hundred yards away.

Captain Lewis marveled at the buffalo and their habits of grazing. This herd would travel several miles a day eating their way towards water. It was a peaceful sight. The buffalo were in abundance, and since it was wintertime, the calves and cows were tending to stay in the center of the herd. Normally, buffalo drop their calves in the late fall and manage to feed them buffalo milk, carrying them through the winter.

Captain Lewis marveled at the physical structure of a buffalo—large head with horns on the male, big eyes recessed in a crown of fur around its head, and neck area and teeth that were set in their jaws at the front so that they could graze the greenery and plants found on the plains.

It was a peaceful site, and Captain Lewis talked to the Indian tribes surrounding the Missouri area that they were exploring. Captain Lewis asked the Indian braves, who were at the rear of the herd, what they were doing there and was told by the brave at the head of the tribe that they were preparing to stampede the herd and drive them over a cliff nearby. The herd was moving in that direction, so that Captain Lewis being on the edge near the Missouri River was able to observe the movement of the herd and estimated that it would take several hours before the herd would pass him by.

Captain Lewis noticed that there were wolves that did not seem real that moved as the buffalo moved at the rear. On closer look he found that these were Indian braves that had wolf skins draped over them for camouflage and so they could be as peaceful as the natural wolves.

The wolf pack continued to capture and eat any of the buffalo calves that strayed too far away from their mothers at the rear of the herd. The three Indians were concealed behind a clump of bushes and had wolf skins thrown over them so that they would be thought to be wolves and the buffalo would be scared to wander too far away from the herd.

The purpose of this scheme was to get the buffalo to stampede and it was a conflict of man and beast, very difficult to predict, but usually occurred when the herd has the Indians closing in from the rear.

This was a day to remember for Captain Lewis. He had never been on a buffalo hunt before. It was a great adventure since the beautiful weather, though freezing cold, was a new event in his life. The wolves were at his back and the herd was at the front. Lewis felt he was between a rock and a hard place.

The rest of the Indian tribe was collected about a thousand yards behind the scouts in wolf skins. The signal was given by one of the men in the vanguard in front. He stood up and whistled so that not only would the buffalo hear him, but also the vanguard of Indians mounted on horseback. The buffalo turned around in the rear, and seeing the approach of the Indian braves, turned and started to bellow signaling to the others in the herd.

Danger was in the offing. The buffalo in the head of the herd turned to face the Missouri River and started to stampede toward it. The river was in a draw approximately seventy feet above the riverbed on the cliff. Buffalo rushed toward the river, and the herd behind the front-runners pushed them over the cliff. They fell to their death and the herd just kept coming until there were approximately a hundred dead bison, buffalo, and calves.

It was a gory scene—a massacre that greeted the Indian tribe. They were able to descend on a path to the frozen riverbank. The dead buffalo were still twitching from their fall and the weight of their compatriots on top of them. What a mess.

Meriwether Lewis could not believe his eyes. The two men that were on the flanks, Privates George Shannon and John Potts, had taken up their position on the flanks and were racing toward the cliff at the back of the buffalo pack. The scene was over in a minute. The twitching animals had breathed their last.

Captain Lewis said, "It's our turn. Find three calves and we will help each other to strap them behind our saddles and go back to the stockade. If we hurry, we will have enough meat for a week or two in this freezing weather."

It was a time of taking eats back for the rest of the corps on the part of the three men from the Corps of Discovery. They proceeded to load the buffalo steaks, tongue, and testicles into saddlebags on each side of their saddles. After a few minutes, they had filled up their saddlebags and proceeded to go back up to the top of the riverbank and head for the stockade.

The attitude of the two members of the corps was very astounding to Meriwether Lewis. They were amazed at the amount of meat and food they were securing for the diet needs of the corps. It would last for several weeks during the middle of winter when food was hard to find.

Captain Lewis thought to himself *It will be a month or more before we push on. The weather is our enemy. The buffalos are grazing eating the clumps of grass that are under the snow pack. The herds of these mammoth animals are so large that I wonder how they managed to survive,*

The spring of 1805 has shown me that the frozen Missouri has made an icy surface very difficult to cross to say the least.

It will be a couple of months before we can look for the Northwest Passage. I hope that President Jefferson's dream becomes a reality. I expect to see the ocean hundreds of miles away, go over the Rocky Mountains, the Continental Divide, and go down the river which was flowing to the Pacific, the beautiful Columbia.

It was a feeling of elation that success would be a conflict of man and beast and the men had won the battle. The Corps of Discovery could take credit for meeting one of the conflicts head on and they had prevailed over their buffalo opponents.

CHAPTER 29

The Missouri River Begins

CAPTAIN CLARK BENT OVER, CUPPED his hand, dipped it in the spring that was puddling in a ten-foot pool running to the northeast. The water tasted so sweet and he knew it was a source of the Missouri River and it was tumbling down the hill from the path they had been following.

Looking ahead Captain Clark hailed Sergeant Pryor to have the men assemble. "We will eat lunch here and then get on our way. Tell Captain Lewis I would like to meet with him and discuss our being able to tell President Jefferson that we have found the source of the Missouri River."

The watercress that surrounded the pool was bright and clean and Captain Clark pulled a handful, dipped it in the water, and tasted it. It was definitely watercress. He hadn't had anything like that since he had been in the Adirondacks several years before.

It was a joyous meeting and the Corps of Discovery tied up the two pack mules they had purchased from Indian tribes along the way. The two captains sat down apart from the group and said to each other that it looked like they'd found what the president was looking for, but had not reached the saddle ahead of them dividing the two peaks that were snow covered and a thousand to two thousand feet above them.

"I am sure that this is the Continental Divide." Captain Lewis opined. "It's flowing east northeast and any snowfall or rainfall will drain west down into the little river that heads north below."

The surroundings were bleak. The snowline above which there was no vegetation that would grow and the rocky shale, was yellow and red in color with layers exposed to the elements. It was the Continental Divide according to Captain Lewis, and although they would have to wait 'til night fall to check their location with the stars, the most prudent thing to do was to record their location and try to climb to the top of the peaks.

Captain Clark said, "I'll take one on the east, northeast. You take one on the south, southwest. We'll take a couple of men with each of us. Have the other men set up camp for the evening. In this barren territory we don't have to be afraid of bear. We may see some bighorn sheep, antelope, or other wild animals that could live off the bushes that we found."

Lewis said, "These are scrub and will green up in the spring and stay green in the summer as we see them now and will turn various shades of red and yellow and brown when the cold and snows come. I need to take some samples for my specimens."

Clark added, "Well, Meriwether, while you're collecting the information and specimens for the National Museum in Washington, D. C. I will talk to the men," Captain Clark continued, "and explain what the next few days will hold. However, we must continue westward, and I'm sure this news will please each and every one of the corps."

Captain Lewis went to the guide Charbonneau and said, "Ask Sacagawea if she has ever been here before and if she knows which direction the Shoshone Tribe, in which she was captured by, lies."

Captain Clark said, "I'll do this right away." He went back and assembled the men and told them that they will head over the saddle and down into the valley below where a small stream was running, evidently fed by the snow-covered mountains climbing the veldt.

That evening he made camp some two miles in the valley below. The river was running northwest and represented what Captain Clark called Clear Water. The name was given as it appeared to be fresh and heading in the right direction, their major concern.

They had that night around the campfire. Captain Clark said, "This is a day to remember, and we shall give each and every one of you corpsmen a dram of rum and toast a victory over the elements and our finding the source of the Missouri River. We will continue on to find a route to the Pacific Ocean so that we will make America whole. It will be a feather in our cap and I'm sure the people of the United States will receive this news with great pleasure."

The next morning the corps sent the sergeant down toward the river with scouts to look for animals such as antelope or big horn sheep or any other warm blooded animal. The men were instructed to bring back specimens they thought would be interesting and Captain Lewis would select those he wanted to use in his collection.

Captain Lewis looked at the rock strata and saw that they were composed of slate, schist, and granite gravel so that at one time these mountains and the path had been thrust up from earthquake activity during the eons before.

It was cold at night and the men wanted to continue down to the Clearwater River and head towards its northwesterly course and hopefully the shores of the Pacific. The night was clear and moonless so that the observations made by Captain Lewis would give them the exact location within a couple of hundred yards to commemorate their find at two-thirty in the afternoon and the two captains said, "We'll camp here for the night. The Clearwater River has trout in it, as Captain Lewis saw some yellow eggs that had been produced and that our fishing for them should provide fresh fish for dinner."

The fishing group shared their equipment. That evening around the campfire, the cooks prepared fresh trout and baked some potatoes. This went well with the dried beans and hominy grits.

Captain Clark wrote in his diary: *The specimens found were igneous rock, hard, and formed volcanically. The fish we had for dinner were trout, but of a different kind than we get in the east. They have a rainbow running from head to tail on both sides of their body that sparkles when they are pulled from the water but dissipates within a half hour. We will call these rainbow trout and I will take some of their eggs back with us to see if we can introduce them to our eastern naturalists. We have found the Continental Divide. While the Corps of Discovery is small in number, it has great achievements and we are barely half way to our mission. We anticipate continuing to the Pacific and spending the New Year there.*

CHAPTER 30

The Needle's Eye in the Sky

IT WAS A CONFLICT OF the beauty and the beastly sky where a sapphire blue sky was the back drop for the red rock needle pointing upward. The white tiny cumulus clouds looked like sheep scattered on the blue canvas. The orange yellow sun was just above the horizon. It was a panorama that confirmed Lewis' opinion that the sun was climbing up to its zenith and would complete its daily trip from east to west overlooking the Missouri River. The river was moving lazily downstream on the Montana Plains.

Captain Lewis was leading his squad of pioneers. They were the first explorers to see the Missouri River running over this rocky river bed. He gathered his platoon around him and said, "You will never see a battle of the elements more unusual than this as you travel life's pathway to the great beyond."

The mighty Missouri River had battled its way between the red sandstone cliffs on its way downstream. Lewis marveled as he saw the white blocks of limestone looking much like an Arabian City climbing to the Montana plain above. He said to himself, *It is a conflict of the geographic features the mountain ridges that we should explore before we go on, toward the Northwest Passage.*

Captain Lewis continued, "I must tell Clark about this geographic find on our exploration. It is a panorama that we should describe to President Jefferson as to the wonders this presidential purchase has provided our country. The Rocky Mountains on our west provide a barrier as to what we seek, but I will make a rough sketch of our route and the geographic features we have found. It is too bad that Sergeant Floyd met his maker before we discovered this picture of conflicting features of the Northwest."

Richard Windsor spoke up, "Although you are with us and I came from Captain Clark's platoon, let's investigate the white cliffs and find out if there are any animals we have not yet seen on our journey so far. We can camp out here on the grassy meadow found next to the Missouri. Can't we?"

Seeing a nod meaning *yes*, Richard Windsor said, "Aye, aye, Captain." He saluted and left to get the supplies he needed for a two-day trip into the Limestone hills.

Captain Lewis was looking for his latest discovery. It was told to him by Chief Thunderhead of the Chippewa Tribe. The chief was very descriptive. George Drouillard was careful in translating every word about the valley leading to the great falls.

The chief said, "This experience should be a heart-stopper."

Captain Lewis prepared himself for a two-day trip down the Missouri to observe the beauty of the landscape and collect specimens of a canyon. Coming between the two giant rocks he saw what he called the gates of the mountains.

He stopped to make a mental picture of the scene. This image would be of prime importance to Captain Clark. He would later tell him, "As I was viewing the wonders of the Missouri River and walking toward the mountains, I seemed to be walking into a valley with vertical walls extending up into the clouds. I walked slowly downstream into this valley looking ahead. At the time I was walking, the mammoth cliffs on each side appeared to be moving together as if a giant in the sky was moving them together closing, closing, closing until they were shutting together. It was an optical illusion to be sure but so real that walking back upstream a couple of hundred yards, the two walls seemed to open up."

Lewis' solo look at the natural exploration was lasting several days. He prepared to return toward the base camp with a tale to tell. It would take him a few days to return to the rest of his platoon and have some of them explore the wonderland with him.

The men would see the white cliffs and red rocked mountains. He proceeded to pack the canoe with all the necessaries. A bedroll and flint and steel to start a fire to cook some deer jerky that he could fry. He would soak it overnight and add some rice that they had carefully kept for just such an occasion.

As usual, Jefferson's instruction was to be careful and, above all things, to return safely with the information regarding the birds, the flora, and the fauna, and of course, any fish that they caught or were able to observe.

The object of this mission was to explore the most interesting park-like canyons, lakes, and connecting river that had not been seen on the voyage. The morning that Captain Lewis had selected was a day in June, the longest day in the year, and the man he chose was William Werner who had experience in scouting and training in first aid so that if anything happened to Captain Lewis, he would be able to take care of him, and return to pick up help. The excitement of the day took over as the three men started down the Missouri to see wonders that had never been seen by any white men before.

According to the Indian chief the first things they would see as they traveled by canoe were the white cliffs of the Missouri and the red mountains there. The white cliffs appeared on the right as they approached the entrance to the *Canyons of the Gods,* as the Indians called it. The opposite, or north side of the river Missouri, was a structure of slate-like rocks that rose some hundred feet above the river, and when looked on the panoramic view from the south side, it looked like an Arabian town with square houses piled next to each other of varying heights and these, rather than being white, were the yellow that the Yellowstone River so portrayed. It was with wonder that their trip was without incident. Few rapids were encountered and the river had spread approximately one hundred feet wide and was relatively shallow. The two men could see trout heading with noses upstream waiting for tasty worms or other food to float by.

Captain Lewis had already caught several trout and had their basic statistics recorded. These fish were sketched, cleaned, and eaten for lunch. The two noted that fish hawks were nesting in the cliffs. Lewis climbed to the top finding various bird nests on the way to the top. All this information was noted by Captain Lewis before returning with data he had already collected. He stopped to have dinner with Werner on a grassy meadow that led down from the mountains and provided a place to rest up and have lunch and walk the territory taking notes. They did this and Captain Lewis told

Werner and Wiser, "I think we should stop here for the night. We'll continue on tomorrow at daybreak. The surroundings are pleasant and safe; however, keep your musket handy in case a bear or Indian appears."

Captain Lewis was not joking when he said, "I have my musket at the ready at all times." The observation of the green canyon with sumac bushes, quaking aspen, and sycamore trees were found in patches along the grassy bank. This morning at dawn they looked to the east and saw the gates of the mountains, which they had been told about, and after a hasty breakfast in their canoe they headed down towards the east. As they rounded a bend in the river they saw the gates of the mountain and as the natives had said, the two mountains seemed to close together and obscure the view of the sun coming up. It looked as if the two mountains were closing together as of two doors were being shut. It was an optical illusion but impressive never the less.

After this experience the three looked up at the sky and saw fish hawks circling overhead looking for an unwary trout or other food to come near the surface and be plucked from it with their claws. A couple of deer at the water's edge were so peaceful that Captain Lewis did not want to scare them, but no matter how carefully they approached, the deer looked up and bounded up the side of the hill as fast as their legs would carry them. Captain Lewis did not want them killed. It was not necessary. Then big horn sheep appeared in dirty white coats blowing in the breeze. They had large twisted horns that were used to pound their prey into the ground. The big horn sheep stood silhouetted on top of the mountains

Lewis said, "Let's keep moving," as there was no way to get close to them. It was so hazardous that Captain Lewis said, "We can report that we have seen them, but as far as killing one, it is too dangerous for us to do that."

Back into their canoe they went and proceeded further down the river. They saw what the Indian Otto Chief Running Bull had said. "It is the eye of the needle," as he pointed up to the rock formation, the needle in the sky with a hole in the top, so slim and so unusual Lewis wanted to have Werner climb up and see how tall it was by comparing his height with the height of the object. Lewis sketched it and showed the dimensions that Werner had seen and the needle itself was eighteen feet high. The hole in it was oblong and it was a four feet long and two feet wide so that Captain Lewis could see why the Indians called this the *needle in the sky*.

The adventure continued until the evening sun was obscured by the cliffs in the west and Captain Lewis said, "We will stay here tonight and return to the corps tomorrow and see how their efforts to portage around the Great Falls of Missouri is coming."

Setting up camp under the eye of the needle seemed a fitting end to this adventure and exploration and the wonders of the Missouri. The next two days Captain Lewis and Privates Werner and Wiser spent rowing and paddling their canoe up the river. They rested every hour and then proceeded, the trip took three days as opposed to two. They saw again the white cliffs that Lewis described as an *Arabian town in the sky*. The white cliffs appeared and the visit to the needle in the sky was almost over.

They saw some jackrabbits bounding in the fields adjoining the Missouri. There were wild horses that had escaped from Indian Tribes. Once saddle broken, they were ridden by the braves. Captain Lewis marveled at the wild ponies which were trained for use in hunting deer and other native animals such as antelope and big horn sheep. No bear were seen nor had any buffalo had been seen, although they had been told by Indian guides that they were in evidence but preferred the vast plains to roam than the Rocky Mountains.

At the end of the three days they approached Captain Clark's platoon getting ready to go around the Great Falls of the Missouri. Thus a needle in the sky viewing had proved to the corps that man's significance pales when compared to the wonders of the world.

CHAPTER 31

Yellowstone

"THERE SHE BLOWS." THE INDIAN chief turned his eyes to the sky and watched a stream of boiling water four feet in diameter cascade over the cone of a geyser that became famous throughout the world known as Old Faithful.

The proud Chief Broken Bow raised his two arms as if he was reaching for the heavens and said so that all could hear, "The Great Spirit in the sky shoots boiling bath water up to himself, but it never comes high enough to reach him. He tries again and again, but only the clouds can take a bath. Sometimes the lightning and thunder roar in anger and drip tears of rain. We your children gaze in wonder. So be it, Great One."

His Shoshone followers watched as tons of water shot up to a height of ninety feet and returned to earth. It splashed anyone within twenty feet of the geyser action. The Indian chief had turned to his medicine man and said, "Ugh, strong medicine. Oh Wise One, will it ever happen?"

His medicine man assured his chief that it would occur again every hour of the day and night. This daily ceremony had the Indian chief turning to the crowd, raising his hand in the welcome greeting as he walked away going to his teepee followed by the crowd of Shoshone braves and squaws.

The band of Shoshone Indians entered the front of the great lodge where the chief presided with his Indian coterie of braves and the squaws prepared all of the household needs. The braves who stayed outside the great teepee were mounted on horseback preparing to forage for the food in the surrounding hills and valleys of pine tree forests.

The geyser jets erupted adjacent to a mountainous area where a steaming stream of hot water drained into the Yellowstone River. The discolored water flowed through the ochre colored landscape. It had a yellow cast to it reflecting the yellow sandstone of the mountains nearby. The green-headed Mallard ducks blasted off the river. Captain Lewis shivered in the spring breeze. He did not know if it was caused by the wind out of the north or perhaps nostalgia at the thought that he was following in the biblical footsteps of Moses who had led his followers to the Promised Land. Captain Lewis looked across at the far shore of the large lake and wondered if the previous four months of stocking up for the expedition was a precursor to the actions recently made by President Thomas Jefferson. The question remained, "Were my own actions foolish or fantastic?"

Captain Meriwether Lewis believed that the mountains themselves held the answer covered with blue spruce, fir, and pine trees. Yellow pines abounded the area and came down to the shore.

This natural animal kingdom was over about a hundred miles from the Missouri River and had been cherished by the Shoshone Tribe. It was just a two-day hike from the Teton Indian tribe's habitat. Yellowstone Lake was the largest body of water in two hundred miles.

The lake itself had a number of islands scattered over its twenty square mile surface with pine-covered islets where the osprey raised their young. The brown bears competed with the eagles in catching trout as food. This is the place Captain Lewis had heard about from the Shoshone interpreter Drouillard. Lewis wanted to investigate and study the surrounding shore with Sergeant Ordway and Private François Labiche. Captain Lewis gathered his small group of explorers around him as he explained what each would do during the two-day stand in God's Country

Lewis said, "Bratton, you will record the birds you see: name, colors, size, and whether it was part of a flock."

Bratton acknowledged with a nod of his head and said, "Yes, Captain."

Then turning to the Field brothers, Lewis said, "You two will gather rocks, plants, flowers, and stones and record unusual rock features. Please record location of hot pools and whether or not they are steaming."

Facing Charbonneau, Lewis said, "You will stay with me. You know Shoshone language and you will interpret the Shoshone talk as this is Indian Territory. See y'all at sundown back here at the lake. Now get on with it."

Lewis himself took his portable desk and wrote notes about what he saw. He thought that Lake Yellowstone was one of the largest lakes he had seen in his life. He walked a mile along the shore and saw some gulls and a couple of moose with their mammoth antlers ignoring the smaller deer grazing nearby. A peaceful scene to be sure.

Lewis reviewed the area and surmised why it was named the Yellowstone River basin. This river was twenty feet wide and had tons of water trying to reach the Missouri River as one of the main suppliers of water to the Missouri.

He started to go down the stream and found some bear dung. The large pools in the meadows had large trout guarding the orange trout eggs to keep scavengers from eating them. He had been told that once the trout spawned they died after burying their eggs in the sandy bottom.

As he rounded a bend in the river he thought to himself this is brown bear country. Then Lewis came upon a frightening scene—a brown bear with two cubs eating on a downed doe with relish. He carefully went around the clearing and resumed his inspection of the Yellowstone River.

Captain Lewis heard a roaring noise as he followed the path that overlooked the river and he saw the flowing water rushing over a waterfall. It was falling down a deep gorge with steep walls about one hundred feet high. He named these the Upper Yellowstone Falls. About two miles along the rim and farther downstream another falls of lesser height he recorded as the Lower Yellowstone falls.

That evening the local Indian guide told Lewis, "This area was a gift from the Great Spirit in the sky and it has almost a religious significance to the Shoshone Tribe who treasure its beauty and importance. The flow of this wondrous river and Yellowstone Lake itself is the center of this green wonderland. It has several small rivers and streams going immediately south to the Tetons with snowcaps on the peaks. These patches of snow are there the year round and supposedly are the Indian gods guarding the three lakes below."

The area was forested and the Shoshone braves caught any trout of great size with three gold stripes running down their side and swimming in schools in Yellowstone Lake. The flock of pelicans with big beaks competed with black bears for the dead trout. It was spring and the females laid eggs on the bottom of the River. Bears waded and ate the trout, which were easy to catch after they had spawned and were about ready to die.

Lewis marveled at the peace of the area while he took lunch. He gathered up the dead trout floating down stream, a natural source of food during the spring and summer. Because the Yellowstone Lake froze over, the resource of food was not available to the Shoshone Tribe.

Captain Lewis wanted to record his observation. Writing his thoughts, he noted that the Voyage of Discovery would be a major economic success of the 19th Century. The forests alone were worth millions of dollars more than France had been paid.

Each of these Indian tribes supported itself by killing herds of buffalo for their hides. These mammoth animals roaming the flat lands of the Missouri Territory weighed half a ton and Captain Lewis sketched one for his scientific artifacts.

There were so many interesting discoveries that Meriwether Lewis was making that the time raced by. Three days and nights in the area after sundown and associating in the Shoshone area was not enough, but the exploration, observing, and describing Yellowstone was right up Lewis's alley. He thought to himself that Captain Clark would be interested in seeing this amazing area, but would have to wait until they returned from seeing the Pacific Ocean if the corps survived the trip.

The following three days were spent by Lewis on his horse with Indians guiding him to all the interesting spots. One of the most interesting other than the Yellowstone Lake itself was the Northern Gateway where the Shoshone had an encampment called Red Lodge. This was a large enclosed structure whose name was derived from the red logs used to build it.

The corpsmen were excited when the Shoshone invited Captain Lewis and his warrior explorers to an Indian war dance held in his honor whereby the Indians would beat the drums and dance in a circle around the bonfire in the center. This was done at Red Lodge since Captain Lewis was there for three days and two nights.

The celebration was in his honor and a feast was held. The Indians danced until late in the evening not with the squaws, but with their fellow braves raising their tomahawks high, singing out their chants in unison, and encircling the fire. They were honoring Meriwether Lewis in the one way they knew how.

The members of the corps reciprocated by presenting the President's Friendship Medal and trading trinkets and trade goods with the chief in exchange for both information and for his needs as well as those of the Corps of Discovery.

During the evening after the dinner hour the group of explorers helping Captain Lewis gathered around the campfire, talked, and smoked a pipe of tobacco with the Indian squaws. The Shoshone tribe was friendly. The Shoshone braves were on a hunting trip so the squaws would attend to the corps members with their every wish including bedding down with them.

The Shoshone could not fathom why a white man entering their territory would waste his efforts in distant travels and collecting items such as flowers, fish, and other small animals such as ground squirrels, red squirrels, and gray squirrels, which were so easily found in the territory.

The animals seen by the Lewis Yellowstone side trip gave the Voyage of Discovery exposure to the American Indian culture and would be a tale told not only to his fellow members of the Corps of Discovery but also to the President Jefferson upon their return.

The amount of information and specimens that Captain Lewis collected was limited by the saddlebags he had on the horses they rode. He tried to see if the Indian chiefs knew and understood the few words of Shoshone sign language that Sacagawea had taught him during the winter at Mandan. He was able to ask questions about the surrounding area, the size of the Lake, the animals that were abounding in the area, and the Teton Mountains.

Meriwether Lewis would remember visiting the lodge of the Shoshone tribe, how red the logs were, and the ceremonial dance his men had enjoyed. It was a wonderful powwow as the Indian leader of this tribe was more than happy to greet a stranger who brought word from the Great White Father in Washington, D.C. and who had gifts to give and to trade.

The inquisitiveness of Captain Lewis made the evening pass by. He arranged to partake of a feast given in his honor with Indian dances and he had his eye on some of the squaws, but thought that discretion was the better part of valor and that he should enjoy smoking the peace pipe using an Indian version of tobacco from a plant that they grew called the tobacco plant. It was brown in color but not related at all to the tobacco plants of the South with which Meriwether Lewis was familiar.

Such goings on enhanced his diary and made it a thing of beauty. He sketched beauty, trout, the bushy tailed squirrels, gray squirrels, and the red squirrels that were scampering up and down the yellow pine trees surrounding the Yellowstone River and area.

Furthermore, the Indians had given him some information as to how to cross the Rocky Mountains and what time of the year was the best time to continue to journey. The chief said, "Oh Wise One, take care when crossing the mountains in the sky. The snow is deep, the wind cuts your breath short, and the treacherous Great Falls cannot be forded or passed by boat."

The Great Falls was a hundred miles west of Yellowstone and the Great Falls of the Missouri. Captain Lewis had agreed to meet Captain Clark to discuss the three days at Yellowstone. The side visit by his co-captain ended with talking about the major concern of Captain Clark. It was Clark's opinion that the Great Falls was too massive in width and too rocky for them to get the keelboat down the falls. They had to go around the falls.

Captain Lewis asked, "Bill, I know nothing when it comes to getting down the falls. What should we do?"

Captain Clark said, "While you were having fun surveying the Yellowstone area, I was figuring out what I think is the only way for us to go. If you agree, I will lead a portage around the Great Falls we are facing. I will continue leading the Corps of Discovery and command the corps operation as I have done for over a year.

You, your corps squad, and the Yellowstone trip have been bothering me. To me following the Missouri River to its source and finding the Northwest Passage is number one goal. To you, getting scientific information about the birds and the bees, et cetera, is number one. I don't mind managing and running the corps except discipline, crew problems, and greeting the Indian chiefs and presenting the Jefferson Medals.

I have a plan, but I want to mull it over before I go over it with you. Let's discuss it tomorrow, first thing. Ok?"

Captain Lewis was somewhat shocked. He nodded and said, "Yes, Goodnight."

CHAPTER 32

Jealousy

AFTER THE FIRST HUSBAND BOLD Warrior had died the widowed American Indian mother of the two maidens remarried and raised the two adolescents. In doing so the family shared the same teepee. The two sisters were compatible, but Sacagawea having been one year older was the decision maker. She was prettier and a favorite of the young braves in her Shoshone tribe.

Otter Moon had mixed feelings about Sacagawea. At eleven she was second fiddle to her more attractive sister. In the tribal pecking order being number two is a bummer. At every social event Otter Moon was the one who cleaned up the mess. It is a demeaning situation.

Her sister, Sacagawea, was known as Bird Woman. She was special. Otter Moon was the outsider at any tribal affair at Mandan reservation. She sat in the corner dressed in rags with a dirty face and lonely. Otter Moon looked at her half-sister with envy. Such jealousy often happens when two siblings are born with either the father or mother being different.

As most of the Indian tribes in North America were nomadic and raided each other as a matter of self-protection, so it was in the case of the Shoshone tribe. The Shoshones had fought the Sioux for territory in the Northwest for centuries. Being the number one tribe meant having the best hunting grounds on the continent. Thus there was tribal warfare and the Northern Sioux had raided the Shoshone tribe in their mountain territory. This attack destroyed Sacagawea's Shoshone village. The Sioux stole many of the Shoshone horses and kidnapped twelve women including the two young girls, Sacagawea and Otter Moon.

This raid became a battle to determine which Indian tribe would be dominant in North America. Sacagawea and Otter Moon were two of the young girls captured and abducted by the Sioux during this raid.

A year later, Captains Lewis and Clark met Toussaint Charbonneau, a fur trader from Canada. It was during the construction of Fort Mandan in the fall of 1804. At that time, Sacagawea and Otter Moon were owned as slaves by the French Canadian, Charbonneau.

Charbonneau not only had married twelve year old Sacagawea, but also was saddled with her younger sister who had no teepee of her own. The three lived with the Mandan Indians on the opposite side of the Missouri River from Fort Mandan, which was under construction by the Americans.

Sacagawea did not realize it at the time, but the Mandan tribe considered that her marriage to the white man was an honor even if it was no pleasure. Being with child in the wilds of the mountains of Montana was not an experience she would remember as being a blast. It was at this time Charbonneau relocated, going up the Missouri River some 800 miles to the Mandan Indian tribe's reservation.

It was during the fall of 1803 that Sacagawea had been taken as a common law wife by the fur trader. They moved and joined the Mandan tribe. She was only twelve years old, six months pregnant, and wanted to return to her Shoshone parents before the baby was due in February of 1805.

For the previous two years, Sacagawea had done her utmost to make her familial relationship bearable but to no avail. Her becoming pregnant strained the sisterly feeling, to say the least!

To make matters worse February 14, 1805, was Saint Valentine's Day and the Captains Lewis and Clark awoke to groaning issuing from their former quarters. Charbonneau came out of the room and said, "It's time. It's time. The baby is coming. How can I help? It is my child. What can I do to help?"

Captain Lewis said in a subdued voice, "Just take it easy. Labor is just starting. I will get someone in. Sergeant Ordway will do."

Turning to Captain Clark he said, "This is a new one for me. I have never delivered a baby before. Would you tell Ordway to hurry up? He must get to the Mandan tribe and ask chief to send a squaw over here to midwife a child. I didn't learn this while I was in training at William and Mary College!"

While the two Captains were awaiting help they discussed with the father-to-be, Charbonneau, how the two half-sisters were raised together, the close relationship of the two, and how it was strained with jealousy; one being more loved, more beautiful, and older. So it was with Sacagawea and Otter Moon.

Two young girls were born a year and a half apart. They were of the highest rank of the Shoshone tribe. They were squaws that were fathered by a brave who was part of a group of hunters; a band that went hunting all the time to provide food and to protect the Shoshone Territory from invaders.

The tribe wandered the plains of Montana. Sacagawea and Otter Moon were raised as squaws to marry and bear children. Such women did not usually have a long life expectancy and so it was with the two maidens.

Sacagawea was the older and had the features that all Indian braves loved. She had long shiny black hair she kept in a ponytail and brown eyes and high cheekbones with a svelte figure and an easy pleasant way about her. Her sister, Otter Moon, on the other hand was thinner, taller, had pimples on her face, and her hair was especially hard to braid. In height she was slightly taller than her sister, Sacagawea. Otter Moon did not make a good impression when she was introduced; she was shy, hesitant, and unappealing to the Shoshone braves.

Before they were in their teens these two Shoshone maidens were kidnapped by roaming Indian braves from the East Plains and taken to their tribal area and territory adjacent to the Missouri River. Once kidnapped the two maidens were sold to the Mandan tribe roaming near Yellowstone in the Wyoming area

The Mandan tribe were not nomadic but had made a reservation of mud-shaped teepees that looked like igloos with a small Indian teepee perched on top. In the summer, the tribe maintained themselves by growing corn over the summer, storing it, and grinding it up to make maize. This flour was used for baking corn bread or selling as corn meal or trading it with Indians of other tribes. In the winter they stayed close to home.

The tribe enjoyed raising their Indian ponies especially their Canadian American interpreter. Charbonneau was one of the experts in bartering furs for the tribal needs such as cloth purchased in St. Louis. These fur pelts of otter, beaver, deer, and buffalo were sold to the various buyers in St. Louis and all points east as far as the Atlantic Coast.

Charbonneau, though only twenty-nine years old, was an aging handsome man. He looked older than he was because of living in the wild west. He had a French Canadian background. He had come to the Mandan tribal area and was staying with the Mandan tribe waiting for the snows to melt so that he could go back with his Shoshone bride Sacagawea and her new baby son, Pomp.

The girls were in Saint Louis to watch the Shoshone chief sell the summer's hunt of fur pelts. Toussaint Charbonneau, a trapper, was a gambling aficionado and loved the game whist. Charbonneau met with the Indian chief of the Mandan tribe named Le Gros Blanc.

After smoking the peace pipe he approached the chief by saying, "How. I want to go up river to hunt fox and may I stay a day or two at your reservation before I go to my fur trapping area farther up the Missouri River?"

The chief said, "Have you come here before, Charbonneau?"

"No," said Charbonneau, "I'm here for the first time, but I have gone to the Shoshone Territory before."

The chief said, "You can stay until you have rested up and then continue your trip up river to the Idaho Territory."

The Shoshone then turned and reached for his pipe. As he did so, he put Indian tobacco into his peace pipe, lit it, took several puffs, and said "Smoke peace pipe before you go to tell your people the Mandan and Hidatsu tribes are peaceful and want to always be friends."

Charbonneau took the peace pipe and took a puff. It was strong and he said, "I will tell the tribe about our good smoke." He handed back the pipe turned and said, "Where is my teepee?

The chief pointed out a teepee and said, "Stay in that one"

As Charbonneau entered the teepee, the fire was burning brightly and he said, "I am hungry."

The two young squaws, Sacagawea and Otter Moon said in unison, "Sit down, eat, while we prepare your bed."

Charbonneau followed the two girls and went into the teepee. He saw a buffalo robe lying on the dirt floor where he would be able to sleep. He was tired and blew the candle out. He sat up the next morning and rubbed his eyes, realizing that he was still a virgin as far as the two Shoshone maidens were concerned.

Charbonneau went to greet the chief and asked him if he had furs to trade. The chief had none. He would have to get them from the Blackfeet or Shoshone tribes farther up the river in Idaho Territory. The meeting was concluded and Charbonneau went out to walk around the reservation of the Mandan Indians. He thought to arrange for his sexual satisfaction after talking with the regular braves and squaws.

After dinner he went into the chief's teepee and said to his medicine man "Do you arrange for my evening entertainment? If not take me to the brave that does."

Without saying a word, the Medicine man clapped his hands and sat down waiting. In an instant the two sisters entered the teepee and started to do the mating dance before the medicine man. He took the two maidens by the hand and walked them over in front of the waiting Charbonneau.

Otter Moon and Sacagawea did the mating dance and watched the medicine man back out and leave the two young girls writhing before a smiling Charbonneau. The show was over and the two innocents waited to see which he would choose. After glancing at each Charbonneau took Sacagawea's hand and pulled her toward him. Otter Moon realized that she was number two and retired, shamed to be number two.

Despite the choice of the more voluptuous Sacagawea, Otter Moon knew that she also would be summoned to the bridal couch to display her lovemaking. The conflicting passion flowers showed that choice could be a matter of luck, skill, or the efforts of a higher being. In the case of jealousy it involved the nature of the lover, Charbonneau, and not the beauty of Sacagawea or the wild abandon of her half-sister Otter Moon, the jealous one.

CHAPTER 33

Pessimistically Optimistic

CAPTAIN CLARK EXPLODED. THROUGH CLENCHED teeth he hissed, "Meriwether, I have given you my opinion once and I repeat it. My opinion is the corps is going the wrong way. It has chosen the wrong branch of the Missouri River. It is NOT the Northwest Passage to the Pacific Ocean."

Clark was talking to Lewis as they stood on a bluff one hundred and fifty feet high overlooking the Missouri River. The two men had to make a vital decision—to backtrack and lose a week of discovery time or to return to St. Louis a failed exploration. What should they do?

William Clark got up the next morning and shaved as usual. Being optimistic he had thought of an alternative that would work—split the corps into three exploratory parties led by Lewis, Sergeant Gass, and himself. Each would explore one of the three river branches. The entire corps would decide by a vote of the officers and privates what action to take.

Captain Lewis had pessimistic thoughts. He felt that the river branch chosen would have to be correct. All the negatives that raced before him seemed insurmountable. The snowcapped Rockies were barriers to success. The winter weather of 1805 and 1806 was an unknown. Lewis would make up his mind after the short explorations were reviewed by the corps.

The Missouri had reached a point in the Rockies where two other branches had joined with the Jefferson to become a much larger single river. The three smaller tributaries joined each other to become the Missouri.

Sergeant Ordway stood a respectful fifty feet from the two captains as they heatedly exchanged views about the potential mistake they might make by choosing the wrong branch of the Missouri River as the northwest gate to the sea.

The Captains were at another turning point and had to make a decision. This looked to be critical. Captain Lewis specifically chose the route. The fact was that they had reached the overlook of three rivers. It was a saddle in the mountains at least a quarter of a mile above the river valley where the Marias, the Jefferson, and the Gallatin Rivers came together and formed the Missouri.

Captain Clark called it the mystery of the source because it was unexpected and made continuing ahead a divided decision. In fact, Sergeant Nathaniel Pryor overheard three of the privates discussing the standoff. John Potts from Captain Lewis' platoon said, 'I don't like the way this mission is being handled."

Joseph Whitehouse, nicknamed Mansion, opined "You got to be kidding. The captains have made the right choices so far. I say let them keep on doing it."

Thomas Hall said, "When I signed up, Captain Lewis told me that if there was a hung up decision, put it to a vote. The side with the most votes wins the day."

All of a sudden, the entire corps would be able to cast a vote. Sergeant Ordway would count the votes. Everyone would be given a ballot.

Realizing a mistaken choice could be fatal to the Corps of Discovery Captain Lewis was pessimistic as to which of the three would lead to the Northwest Passage. It looked like they were at the end of the road.

Captain Clark was silent because he felt if he opened his mouth and vented his thoughts he would lose his temper. The captains did not want to appear indecisive and felt that a day's rest would benefit the whole mission.

It was about noon and the corps wanted to have lunch so Captain Clark returned to the main corps waiting below the overlook and told them "We are taking our noon break and the noon sun is hot. There is a ledge providing shade. Stop here and we'll continue on at three o'clock."

The men proceeded to follow orders. Captain Clark returned to where Sergeant Ordway was gazing out to the south. Captain Lewis was the first to speak, "Captain Clark, we might as well admit we are blocked no matter which alternative we choose. It is not promising. The way back is discouraging and the men in the corps will not be happy to retreat."

Captain Lewis answered, "It has been a difficult climb for the corps. All of us are dead tired. Now it is decision time. What say you, Sergeant Ordway?"

Ordway looked Captain Lewis in the eye and said, "Sir, I agree with your thoughts and I feel that we should retrace our steps to last night's resting place and put the decision to a vote of the corps. The alternatives are not promising, but if one makes a mistake it must be recognized as such."

Captain Clark asked, "Sergeant, do you feel that your thinking represents that of a majority of the corps?"

Captain Lewis interrupted and said, "We should put this up to a vote of the corps, but let's go back to last night's resting place before we put it to the men of the corps."

So saying, he looked at Sergeant Ordway and Captain Clark and as they nodded in agreement, they returned to the corps and told them that the Voyage of Discovery needed to make a major choice.

Captain Lewis talked to himself as they were walking down to the river below. *Why do I always feel that we have made a bad choice? My nature tends to look at the bad side of any situation facing the corps. I hate to be pessimistic, but I can see danger in the offing. However, I will go along with Captain Clark and the vote.*

The next morning the sun came up. It was going to be a hot day and after taking breakfast the two captains assembled the group before them and Clark said, "We have a decision to make today. It is a simple one, but very important. Captain Lewis explain what decision it is."

Captain Lewis turned and faced the corps and said, "You are voting whether to retreat toward Mandan or continue on the course of the river we have been following as it has approached its source. We can tell that a mistake has been made. We should go back and retrace our steps to the juncture of the river and take the north fork, which is called Jefferson and follow in that direction. Though it is going north, it will lead us up the Rocky

Mountains and will be the way to the Northwest Passage. That is all I have to tell you."

This was what Captain Lewis had felt and it was his opinion that they should try again, but in a different direction. They would take the Jefferson fork, which would not go west, but Captain Lewis was pessimistic as to it providing the Northwest Passage Route to the Pacific.

Lewis turned to Captain Clark and said, "We will try one more time Captain Clark, but I'm willing to give it a go."

With that the corps spent the night and faced a dismal prospect ahead. It was pessimism and reflected Captain Lewis and his concerns. He knew the future was very chancy to predict and the two captains knew it.

Captain Lewis said, "William, you are the risk taker. I play it safe. You know that the sun will come up. I just hope so. You are sure a great good will come from the Voyage of Discovery. I will wait and see."

That this was a coin flip the two leaders were in accord. They were as Captain Lewis thought to himself *pessimistically optimistic*. The future is known by no one.

CHAPTER 34

Return to Reality

THE FALL EQUINOX OF 1806 found the Corps of Discovery returning to St. Louis after a brief stop in St. Charles to pick its settlements officials and a great many of leaders of the Kanza and Missouri Indian tribes. This welcome crowd included many of the tribes' braves and squaws who lived in the teepees that dotted the plains adjacent to the Missouri River.

Chief Thunder Cloud and other leading members of the tribe wanted to board the keelboat and travel across the Mississippi to the larger settlement of a thousand residents. Captains Lewis and Clark were dressed in their uniforms and the rest of the corps were wearing the coonskin caps that they had received at the start of the great journey. The captains gave the members of the corps leave to spend the night to celebrate their return to civilization and told the well-wishing crowd that President Jefferson had sent a message by special messenger to greet them in St. Louis on the morrow.

The following morning the dawn sky saw the moon sink below the rolling hills in the west. The sun rose in the east and the mighty Mississippi, the major water route to the Caribbean, was shining brightly bathing the landscape with its golden rays.

To the two captains it was a beautiful day in September 1806. It seemed to them that God was sending them a message—*well done my children*. The band was playing Yankee Doodle as the corps hustled to re-board the keelboat and head down river to their sister city a few miles away.

The dirty wagon tracks were used as path by the settlers who numbered less than two thousand if you counted all the dogs and cats and pioneers in the area. This tiny settlement servicing the central Midwestern part of the United States of America had been named in honor of the French Saint Louis before the territory became part of the United States. The territory itself was named after the Missouri Indian tribe that lived in the area.

It was a busy scene that greeted Captains Lewis and Clark as the keelboat returned to civilization with the corps of discovery. The streets of St. Louis were crowded with the residents of this river town. It was a holiday declared by the Governor General of the Missouri territory. The Corps of Discovery had returned from a three year exploration of the Northwestern territory bought from France. The President of the United States had announced a national holiday celebrating the triumphant return of the two Army Captains Meriwether Lewis and William Clark.

These leaders of the Corps of Discovery were being received at the docks of St. Louis with the Navy greeting them and five thousand people involved in the celebration. Captain Lewis had spent twenty-nine months finding the Pacific Coast, claiming the Northwest Territory for the United States of America, and notifying all the residents, Indians and fur trappers that they were now American citizens.

The celebration was set up by President Thomas Jefferson who could not be in attendance, but sent his Secretary of War to meet with Meriwether Lewis and escort him back to Washington, D.C. The band had struck up the National Anthem and the Governor of the Northwest Territory was in attendance as well as the Indian chief who represented the Missouri Tribe. The weather was perfect and the area adjacent to the dock was packed with canoes and other river craft assembled for the event.

Meriwether Lewis looked around and could not believe his eyes. He felt that his return from the voyage into the Northwestern Territory had been a tremendous success. His co-leader, Captain William Clark had left the expedition at the final stage to go back to Fort Plotin in the Ohio Territory, his former command post. The Secretary of State had been sent by President Thomas Jefferson to talk with Meriwether Lewis and accompany him back to Washington, D.C. to meet with President Jefferson and give a report to the Congress of the United States. This visit would be a report on the Squaring of the Triangle mission entered into on May 14, 1804. It was now a fait accompli and Captain Lewis accepted the accolade of the crowd and the fact that there would be a three day celebration of his return held in front of the nation's capital.

At the end of this time the two captains and a military guard would go back up the Ohio River to Fort Pitt in Pennsylvania and from there travel to Washington, D.C. and meet with President Jefferson in the White House. His former job with the office of the president had been to be the private secretary. The president had notified him that he had another job in mind and it would involve the Louisiana Territory, specifically the State of Louisiana, which was in the process of being formed.

As such he would be stationed in New Orleans and would be involved with the president through the Department of State, which had a secretary and would be receiving information from Captain Clark, Captain Lewis, and the other part of the Union. This appealed to Captain Lewis primarily because he had developed a sense of independence.

Captain Meriwether Lewis attended a number of state functions during this organization period of the state government and he was especially busy visiting various parts of the state of New Orleans to see local governments and explain what the new status of Louisiana and its territories.

In the meantime Meriwether Lewis started making the rounds of evening clubs and in one of the clubs of Orleans he met Francoise Diderot. After exchanging niceties they departed and arranged to meet again the following Saturday for lunch in the French Quarter at the Bastille Restaurant after which they'd visit an art gallery in the French Quarter.

New Orleans in the springtime was magnificent with its geraniums in pots hanging from the light standards in the streets, the cool breeze coming off the Delta, and no fog or rain in sight. It was the kind of a day meant for an afternoon of perfection. Neither of the two, Francoise or Meriwether Lewis, was aware of the time and the afternoon passed quickly. After lunch and the walk through the art gallery in old town both Francoise Diderot and Meriwether Lewis were impressed. They made arrangements to meet again the following Sunday and Monday.

CHAPTER 35

Betcha Can, Betcha Can't

THE TWO CAPTAINS HAD BEEN on the trail for almost two years The same men were getting a little tired of each other's jokes, stories, and fantasies. As a result the two leaders discussed the problem with each other. They decided that homesickness was at its roots and it was time to head for home.

After talking it over with Sergeants Ordway, Pryor, and Gass and taking a vote, the co-captains found that all of the corps wanted to return home as soon as weather conditions in the Rocky Mountains would allow. The corps did not want to spend another tough winter away from their loved ones.

According to messages from the Indian tribes who lived in the Bitterroot Mountain, the ice had not quite melted on the rivers and the Columbia was turbulent and dangerous, too rough for canoes as it flowed to the Pacific. Every day the captains met after breakfast to make the decision. They looked eastward. The two would discuss the wind, the cloud cover, the ice and snow, and the possibility of the melting snow pack allowing them to leave for home sometime in early 1806.

Their focus was to the east. When the fog lifted the two saw Mount Jefferson, over two miles high, capped with snow. The resulting decision was the same; get the gear prepared, work on their diaries, and let the others of the corps explore the surrounding areas.

The daily excursions were tediously the same. The brown bears were wandering about waking up after their long winter and hungry after their five months of hibernating in caves. The holly berries were framed by the shiny green leaves. The salmon had started up the Columbia River seeking the spawning pools found on the Columbia. Nothing could stop them but the environment being so unfavorable. Once Astoria Bay was free of ice and the rough water had calmed down the corps was homeward bound.

On the return to civilization the Corps of Discovery had been divided into two groups, Platoon A and Platoon B, each to be headed by a captain. The two captains would keep the platoons together until they had to cross the Rocky Mountains. The plan was to have the Great Race to see which captain would be the first to reach the finish line which was the junction of the Missouri and Yellowstone rivers.

When the Great Race was over the corps would leave and return to St. Louis in the Missouri Territory. The first one there would win the gold ring and a thousand dollars prize which President Jefferson had offered.

The Great Race was to start in June 1806. This date was set by mutual agreement even though some of the ice was still coming down the Columbia. The men were picked—alternately one by Lewis and one by Clark. The men were told of the gamble and that it would be the first group there despite what difficulties Platoon A or B encountered.

The day of departure was April 7th, a gorgeous spring day and also the birthday of John Newman, the last man to join the voyage. It was Lewis' selection to take Platoon B and go up the Marias Branch to contact the Blackfoot tribe which controlled the territory after which his fellow corps members were to continue descending the Missouri to its juncture with the Yellowstone.

There would be about six Indian tribes inducted and told that the Great White Father in the east was their leader.

If Platoon B arrived at the juncture of the Missouri and Yellowstone it would win. Each corps member of Platoon B would receive a bonus of twelve months pay, a prize worth winning.

Captain Clark and Platoon A would explore the Yellowstone area in the Wyoming Indian territory and confirm Captain Lewis' exploration of 1805 the previous summer. After doing this Clark would follow the Yellowstone

River and notify all the tribes in that area of the change in authority and their allegiance to the president, the Great White Father's desires.

President Jefferson had approved the grand award that whichever platoon reached the juncture of the Yellowstone and Missouri Rivers would have naming rights for the exploration. Thus if Clark won the name of the exploration would be THE CLARK AND LEWIS EXPEDITION and if Lewis won it would be THE LEWIS AND CLARK EXPEDITION.

Captain Lewis and Captain Clark had decided to use the Three Rivers Junction in Idaho Territory as the starting point for the race. It was planned for Captain Lewis' platoon to go up the Marias Branch to find the route to the joining of the Missouri and Yellowstone Rivers.

Captain Clark felt secure in the decision that he made to pick his men. The men were alternately picked from the thirty-three members of the Corps of Discovery. Clark picked first and wanted to have Sergeant Pryor. Captain Lewis then picked his Sergeant Ordway who had been his right arm from the very first. After these choices the rest followed. Alternately, Captain Clark, then Captain Lewis, then Captain Clark, then Captain Lewis until all thirty-three members had been selected. The remaining non-members of the corps such as York, Sacagawea, and the rest of the retinue were left to choose which of the captains they would follow. It was to bed that night and an early start on April 8, 1806.

On the following morning Captain Clark raised his pistol and shot in the air. Then quickly holstering his pistol he faced his followers and again raised his right arm high with his palm facing away. It was as if Clark was pushing the future away. Then Clark closed his fingers into a fist. He looked at Captain Lewis and as he did so he opened the index finger of his right hand, pointed it down the in the direction of the Yellowstone River and said, "I plan to go from the Yellowstone River and see the unusual features of the surrounding area from the Teton peaks to the bears feeding and mating nearby. Captain Lewis described these wonders so my visit will be to see for myself."

With that statement and exchange of military salutes, they started the Great Race.

CHAPTER 36

Going Back to Traveler's Rest

THE GULLS WERE CIRCLING OVERHEAD chasing and eating minnows driven up to the top of the river by the salmon that were heading to spawn. The corps was tired from the portage around the falls. It was a conflict between the privates and Captain Lewis' desires to get home. The men were arguing among themselves. Did the sergeants request a meeting and a vote about the delays getting home as fast as they could?

Captain Lewis was not concerned that his men did not care that he had recorded the corps daily locations. Lewis did this religiously. Captain Clark was unhappy with the dissatisfaction. The corpsmen wanted to get over the Rockies—now—and told the sergeants so.

This crisis came to a head when the three sergeants called for a meeting of the entire group. It was a rest stop for the purpose of building a number of canoes to be used to transport crew and supplies down the Missouri to St Louis. The corps was stopped at the Clearwater River where it merged with the Snake. Sergeant Gass was the one chosen to present the position of the corps.

Captain Clark said, "Now that the corps is assembled let the record show that President Jefferson and Congress provided that everyone on this expedition is entitled to vote on important matters and this matter was brought up by the corps. Is that true Sergeant Gass?"

Sergeant Gass answered, "Aye, Aye, Sir."

Captain Lewis interjected, "Let the record show I will enter all that happens today. Gass, present the complaint."

Gass, being a man of few words said, "Captains, all of us on this expedition want to get back home quick and dirty if need be. The Indian squaws have given sex at times but no love or affection. As all of us know that men have used each other if given an opportunity. Take us back to St Loooee . . . now!"

Sergeant Ordway volunteered, "Us sergeants vote. Get home. You can tell us any cockamamee scheme, but we don't want no excuses."

At Clearwater the corps rested and made plans to go up the Clearwater River portaging over the Continental Divide at the fastest pace they could. The paddling of canoes against the current was tiring and it was exhausting the corps.

Captain Lewis saw the male fish fertilizing the eggs. He saw the fish turn belly-up after doing so. He turned to Captain Clark and said, "William, the salmon eggs will hatch several months from now. After growing to be six inches long these fingerlings will head downstream to the Pacific. As far as we are concerned we will be halfway home if your planning works out."

Captain Clark commented, "Meriwether, this nippy weather is good news for us. It is late March as shown by the yellow daffodils in full bloom. Remember it was last week we watched the Scappoose tribe going up the Columbia to net the spring run of salmon. The Indians are experts at fishing. Once caught the fish are gutted, cleaned, and smoked over a smudgy fire and should provide their tribe salmon for the rest of 1806."

The two captains marveled at the way the tribe of Indians had made an impassable hazard in the river a thing of value to them. The Scappoose could fish this difficult obstruction whereas the other travelers going up the Columbia would find the fishing impossible and consider the hiking around the falls an unnecessary hindrance.

Commenting on the conflicting alternatives facing the corps Captain Clark said, "Meriwether, I intend to use Sacagawea and Drouillard to communicate with Chief Fastwater of the tribe as soon as we can meet them."

Captain Lewis replied with a smile, "Let's face it... it is early in the morning on the Fourth of July and here we are paddling the pirogues up the

Columbia with westerly wind at our back. We are all physically pooped out. Let's portage around the falls tomorrow"

Captain Clark answered, "You make the call."

The captains took the brief pause for lunch with Lewis talking to Clark saying, "William, the Celilo Falls is something we did not see on the way to the Pacific Ocean. This is an awesome sight. Look at the swarms of the silver salmon circling around the pool of water below the Celilo Falls. Is there any way we can get the Scappoose tribe to help us?"

Not waiting for an answer Captain Clark called out to Drouillard, "Tell Chief Fastwater to throw a couple of the silvers our way. About five or six will do!"

He asked himself, *perhaps Lewis knows why the fish are going up stream during such high water.* Without waiting to find the answer Clark ordered the corps to take lunch as it was noon. This conversation had taken place while the Crops of Discovery were resting before starting to portage their canoes around the Continental Divide. It was an interruption on the return to St Louis, 1200 miles away.

George Drouillard, the interpreter who knew Indian sign language, gave the chief the message. The chief answered, "Ugh. Fish time to spawn. We eat 'em now. Eat 'em all summer long."

Captain Lewis asked Chief Fastwater, "The summer is very hot. We are hungry. We need food. Can we rest here for a day or so? We are going back where the sun rises. We have spent the winter on the ocean. I have important message from the Great White Father to tell you, the chief, about our going around the cliffs here and resting tonight above Celilo Falls."

George Drouillard said to the chief, "After sun goes down, I will tell you story about big, big fish we found near where Clatsop Indian tribe lives."

It was the story of the beached whale and how the corps spent the first week returning home. It was lucky the two captains had decided to make sea salt and trade it to the tribes such as the Scappoose. The salt-making was a stroke of luck. They traded salt for everything the captains needed.

The farther east the corps traveled the more the value of sea salt increased. Captain Clark asked his fellow Captain Lewis, "Meriwether how come you're so damnably smart? How did you know that the salt we are carrying back with us can be traded for everything from horses to young

Indian maidens? I wish I wasn't such a prude." Clark made the last comment in jest.

During the week after the Fourth of July the two captains watched the way these Indians from hue Oregon tribe fished from the crude scaffold by using a net to catch the salmon jumping over the river rocks as their rush to get to the spawning grounds. While a slip during the netting action might meant death to the fishermen, it was certain death for the salmon as they would die from spawning a new generation of salmon or by crashing against a deadly rock.

The Corps of Discovery ascended the falls by portaging around the falls. It was a tricky portage on the part of the Captains Lewis and Clark. Once the ten canoes and their crews had overcome the Celilo the corps once again hiked for their needs.

The daily routine for the second week of July was fish, cook them, and use a fire built to warm themselves in the evening. The fresh salmon roasted on the campfire put the entire corps to sleep as happy campers!

The days of resting found the two captains wanting to keep charging onward toward home. In the morning, Captain Clark said, "We have dallied around long enough. It is the first weeks of summer and in the fall bad weather may haunt us."

Both leaders knew there was no time to dally. Sacagawea and Otter Moon were anxious to get to the Clearwater River where they could exchange the canoes for horses and mules to go over the Great Divide, the Continental Divide. There were two mountain passes that could be used to get past the Rocky Mountains. The first was Lemhi Pass. It was Captain Lewis' choice. He felt it was the easiest. Captain Clark was not sure and talked to several of the Shoshone braves to find out if the Lemhi Pass was the best. They told Clark Camp Fortunate is the place for the corps to choose between the two paths over the Rocky Mountains. The two captains agreed. Two and a half days later the corps arrived at Camp Fortunate.

It was decision time. Captain Lewis faced Clark and reminded him, "We are about ready to wrap it up. You want to use the southeast route going through Yellowstone country, Red Bluff, passing Beaverhead, Pompeii's Pillar, and the gates of the mountains. Right?"

Captain Clark answered, "I have not been that route. I want to take it exploring the wonders of Yellowstone—seeing its water spouts, its bears and other wildlife, meeting with the Teton Indians, and the snowcapped mountains, and mapping it all. I have a big job, a lot at one time, but I will do it well."

Captain Lewis then said, "As for me. I will take my group and head north going up the Marias River, see where it reaches the 54th parallel our northern border. I will visit the Blackfeet tribe its chief and elders of the tribe. I will go down the Missouri Rover listing all the other Indian tribes I find along the way. As President Jefferson wanted, I will make a list of the tribes and who the chief is as I go down the river. As part of this procedure, I will present the American Flag, a copy of the Presidential Friendship Medal, and ask them to send a tribal elder to come with us to visit our leader in Washington, D. C. This meeting will make them all citizens."

Captain Clark bargained, "We will pay you in salt if you will assist our group of thirty-four over the passes and down the other side."

Charbonneau was acting as interpreter and translating the Shoshone into French and then into broken English for the two captains. It turned out that Sacagawea's brother had been sick and was failing. He needed Captain Lewis to provide Dr. Benjamin Rush's Elixir of Life. This and several days' rest would benefit the chief and the corps on its trek home.

At the end of three days, Kamawaiht, the half-brother of Sacagawea and chief of the Shoshone since his parents had been killed recovered and was able to provide fresh horses to the Corps of Discovery in return for salt and strings of beads. The powwow that followed his recovery was ended by the Shoshone Tribe celebrating the return of Sacagawea. It was the case of the Indians wanting Captain Lewis to break out the rum for and pouring a gill for each man.

Drinking rum was coupled with the braves selecting a squaw. It seemed to Captain Clark that the frivolity of the powwow was coupled with the braves feeling no pain. By eleven o'clock in the evening, the fire had burned to ashes and the Shoshones returned to their teepees, no questions asked.

In Shoshone country summertime has a beautiful night with the smoke from the campfire curling up through the teepee peak and floating lazily up to the mountain. It was the kind of night Captain Lewis remembered from home when he went out to the barn and fed the cows alfalfa and put them down for the night. *The farm life,* thought Captain Lewis, *is a twenty-five hour a day job and when I grow up I will never look at another cow in my life. Today I have trouble remembering what it's like to have to not get up with the chickens crow and proceed with a day that never seems to end. I wonder if Captain Clark has had the same experience. I'll talk it over with him to see.*

The morning sky was blue and there were a few white puffy clouds starting to float in from the west. It seemed that nature was always beautiful and unless it was your job on the farm it could be very inspiring.

Now on the Voyage of Discovery had just turned back and were going up over the Lemhi Pass. He was supposed to meet Captain Clark at Three Rivers Junction. That is where the Maria Rivers met. It was close to the Shoshone Reservation and Captain Lewis remembered that Sacagawea and Otter Moon, two sisters, came from the Idaho reservation and its neighboring Teton Mountains.

Indian braves standing straight and tall were waiting for Captain Clark to finish his greetings. The brother-sister relationship flourished in 1806, the chief of the Shoshone tribe and most of all, Sacagawea's brother. It was to be a powwow that night to celebrate the re-joining of brother and sister and never-seen-before baby Pompeii, the first child of Charbonneau and Sacagawea, his common-law wife.

Captain Clark had gone on a special ride with his corps and said to the guide as he left to tell Captain Lewis that he would return in in several days and that he would appreciate Captain Lewis reserving the morning breakfast for them to discuss future plans. This was set up so that the balance of the return trip could be discussed.

Captain Clark realized that three years was a long time for the Corps of Discovery to keep charged up and raring to go. Now the way to race to the finish was to race to the finish

The only thing the two captains had agreed upon was the fact that St. Louis, Missouri would be the end point and should be accomplished by October 1st so that they could be greeted by a representative from Captain Lewis' part. It was to be the race of a century. It would be exciting and profitable to the winner. While there was no monetary prize, the prize was the name of the trip. Would it be called Lewis and Clark or Clark and Lewis? The winner of the race would be the deciding factor.

The two captains said goodbye. Captain Lewis wanted to follow the Missouri River after reaching the Maria's Pass. Captain Clark's contingent would go south following the Yellowstone River until they reached Red Lodge and from that point at they would go through the most unusual park that Captain Lewis had seen two years before.

It was the Yellowstone Lake region overlooking the Tetons to the south and the Lemhi Pass to the northeast. It was to be the race of the century and it was to start on the Fourth of July, 1806. The winner would be the captain and his platoon who reached the junction of the Yellowstone River meeting the turbulent and muddy Missouri that ran down the northern part of Montana. Once it passed Fort Mandan, the race would be over. The two captains left with a handshake and a good luck. Whether by luck or skill, this would be the highlight of the Voyage of Discovery. Who would it be, Captain Clark or Captain Lewis?

It would make the captain famous forever. From the captains to the privates each had something to gain. The coming six months in 1806 would be the climax of the voyage and determine naming rights.

CHAPTER 37

Heading For Home

ECSTASY WAS IN THE HEARTS and minds of all thirty-four members of the Corps of Discovery. Sometimes it was physical, sometimes it was imaginary, sometimes it was emotional, but always it was a difference of opinion about deciding which way would get the corps home in the fastest time.

This difference of opinion reached the ears of Captains Lewis and Clark just before the return trip up the Columbia River. Captain Lewis though not as well versed in the operation of the Voyage of Discovery as Captain Clark sensed that the shortest route to take was going through the Bitterroot Mountains. This was over the Lolo Pass and downstream on the Missouri River. Lewis' reasoning was that to ride down the Missouri in canoes with the current and wind at their back though a longer distance could be shorter in elapsed time. This route included riding by horseback over Lolo Pass in the Bitterroot Mountains, reaching the Great Falls of the Missouri, recovering the canoes that they had stored on their way to the Pacific Ocean, and going down the Missouri by canoe to the St. Charles meeting place.

On the other hand, Captain Clark felt that going down the Yellowstone River to the juncture with the Missouri then going down the Missouri would take the least amount of elapsed time. This way was longer to travel but could be shorter time wise.

Now that Captains Lewis and Clark had found the Northwest Passage they agreed to disagree. So they put it to a vote of the Corps of Discovery. Every member voted and it was so close that the captains divided the party and each said, "We will win the bet. See ya in St. Louie"

Both Captain Lewis and Captain Clark wanted to choose which way to go home but could not agree on which route to take to the St. Louis settlement. As established by the President Jefferson's rules of the Voyage of Discovery the captains took a vote and it was Lewis 14, Clark 11. The one favored by Captain Lewis was chosen as the way to go.

Captain Clark was disappointed and asked Captain Lewis, "I have another idea, try it on for size. You go your way and I'll go mine. Take half of the supplies and horses. The first one of us to reach the place on the Missouri River where the Yellowstone River joins it wins. We'll go down river to St.Charles – St Louis together and have President Jefferson send us the money deducted from the wages we got during the three years we have spent together."

Captain Lewis said, "It is a friendly bet, you're on!"

Both captains were yearning to get back to their loved ones. So were twenty five privates who were spending their spare time in writing letters home saying, "I will show up at home; I am very lonely but soon we will be back together again."

It was so awesome to know that going back to their loved ones caused a niche in the armor of the captains which was supposed to be all sweetness and light. The difference in routes favored Clark and made Lewis decide that the place to meet was where the Yellowstone met the Missouri. This would determine the winner.

There they could send a messenger on a fresh horse. Every day difference meant twenty dollars to the captains and and a dollar to each corps member. These bets would be payable in St. Louis after the men got the paychecks from the federal government. It would be sent to the corps member's home or last known address.

The details of their bet that the two captains made included the starting place. It was to be the Travelers Rest near the Lolo Pass area and each would head in an easterly direction. Captain Lewis elected to take the northern route through the Bitterroot Mountains. Captain Clark would take the southern route and go down the Yellowstone River which traveled east. and joined the Missouri River.

This juncture was a logical choice. It was near the border where the Montana and Dakota Indian territories joined. It was in the Black Hills which were made of granite and had been discovered by Captain Lewis during the previous spring of 1805. These hills had withstood the ages and the Dakota tribe treated the as the place of the Great Spirit in the sky.

Thousands of furs from beaver, bear, deer, antelope, and big horn sheep were sent to market. Even buffalo and bison were killed and their hides tanned and used by Europeans to grace their floors as rugs that and were shipped to Europe.

The two captains of the corps, Captain Lewis and Captain Clark, looked at each other in the eye and said jointly, "What a wonderful day it is. We have conquered the conflict of jealousy that has sprung up between us by great joint effort. The smell of success that had not been evident in the recent past; now we will compete for being chosen by the future as the best explorer in the Corps of Discovery."

Captain Clark in his blustery voice said., "Let the race begin."

Captain Lewis commented as he shouldered his gun, "I am sure that my route will lead me to success. I remember the saying of the past, 'he travels fastest who travels alone.' I am on my way. See y'all down the river." He saluted the flag that was being carried by Sergeant Pryor, mounted his horse and trailing three extra horses behind him headed north toward the the Bitterroot Mountains and the Lolo Pass.

Captain Clark, who was now in full charge of the Corps of Discovery, looked over the roster; he and many others would go to Yellowstone River to see its wonders. It was one of the most beautiful lakes in the Northwest Territory. They would visit the Teton Indian tribe's domain including the Teton Mountains whose tops had snow and glaciers year round. He had read the summary of Captain Lewis' survey of the area from the previous year on the way to the Pacific Ocean. Now it was Clark's trurn to take the corps to see this national treasure.

Sergeant Ordway had been there in 1805 with Captain Lewis. He told the corps it was a must see before they continued toward St. Louis.

It was from a different viewpoint that Captain Clark, the optimist, and Captain Lewis, the pessimist, viewed the same picture. The joy each felt sprang from a different well of confidence in human beings ability to overcome many life altering difficulties utilizing their God given abilities used to achieve the end one sought.

At this juncture Sergeant Patrick Gass got up and said, " I know that I speak for the entire Corps of Discovery each of the thirty-four brave men and one woman on this expedition have 'axes to grind.' We now feel that success is ours. Our corps has fulfilled commitment to the President of the United States that we would find the Northwest Passage through the Rocky Mountains to the Mississippi/Missouri Rivers.

'The Louisiana Purchase' is ours to manage it as we see fit. We members of the corps have left the safety of the St Louis settlement and proceeded northwest by keelboat and other means of transportation suffering many hardships and keeping our eyes on the goal of linking the two oceans of the United States of America. Again I say we have won the battle. Hip Hip Hooray!" So saying, Sergeant Patrick Gass sat down amid the applause of all.

Being a man of letters and a Democrat/Republican President Thomas Jefferson thought that his party wanted a central United States located in Washington, D.C. Captain Lewis agreed. The conflicting party was the Federalists. They felt that self government was best, but for the United States of America each state would be its own master. This was the ruling party for John Adams who was the second president.

Small wonder that the Corps of Discovery and its followers were promoted by President Jefferson whose expansion of the country was called "Squaring of The Triangle.' It applies to government in the time of Lewis and Clark and the Louisiana Purchase. How farsighted he was to sponsor his dream: a land route across the continent, shorter, more efficient and safer despite the Indian tribes trying to protect the land purchased from the French at a bargain price.

CHAPTER 38

Making Salt Saves the Bacon

SUMMER WEATHER WAS A PLEASANT 65 degrees Fahrenheit and the corpsmen wore their dungarees, went barefoot, and huddled around the fire primarily to keep the mosquitoes away. That evening as he tended the fire was Francoise Diderot, an interpreter, hired during the trip from St. Louis coming up the Mississippi/Missouri River. He had the capabilities of being able to speak French, his native language. He hailed from Canada and knew the Canadian version of English. He understood Indian sign language, which allowed the different Indian tribes to talk with each other even though they could not do it verbally.

The other two at the fire were bilingual: Corporal Richard Warfington reporting to Clark, and Francis Labiche who was a naturalist and helped Lewis collect specimens and provide names of flowers, rodents, and other potpourri for the corps' return in 1806.

These three had been selected by Captain William Clark for duty that night and the balance of the week, which meant that they would come at sundown, relieve the daytime watch, and keep boiling sea water to make plain old table salt. This was a necessity of life and vital for the world's population.

The Native Americans who lived away from the Pacific needed to get a valuable condiment desired by everyone, but not available in the interior of the northwestern part of the Ohio Territory, an area of the United States that was east of the Rocky Mountains.

Captain Clark, having served in the Frontier Country knew the value of salt to not only feed troops, the Frontier Forces of the United States Army, but also all the settlers that were west of the Appalachians and east of the Rockies. These people had no salt and relied on the Indian tribes that traveled from the Pacific Coast in search of antelope, buffalo, deer, and other mammals inhabiting the Rockies and the Plains.

The Plains Indians wanted salt and the captains planned to use the salt making process to provide it to them. It would be The Voyage of Discovery coin of the realm for the return trip home.

Captain William Clark, who was in charge of discipline, assignment of duties, and all the organization and matters of the Corps of Discovery had decided to inspect the salt-making trio that had been assigned for the week of the Fourth of July. He reasoned that if the men were going to shirk their duty they would do it on a holiday.

The trio of Warfington, Diderot, and Labiche anticipated a celebration would be held at Fort Clatsop and where the balance of the Corps of Discovery had been quartered during the winter prior to returning to their home base of St. Louis, Missouri.

The start of the Voyage of Discovery was nearly two years before. The men were lonesome and wanted to do anything to assuage their doing nothing but throwing wood on the fire and adding salt water as the salt crystallized and settled to the bottom of the large pot that had been placed above the fire. The boiling water sizzled as the hot pot was emptied. Cold metal scoops removed the salt and new seawater was poured in to replace that lost by the steam evaporating from the boiling pot.

Captain Clark and Captain Lewis had tried to think of how they were going to get horses to return up the Columbia River over the Rocky Mountains and down the Missouri River to their starting point. At that point of time they would be able to let the world know that the United States of America had confirmed the Louisiana Purchase and doubled its size. Furthermore the Voyage of Discovery had established a settlement there to support its claims on the Louisiana Purchase.

In true army style Captain Clark took a three-plus mile horseback ride during the early evening. He reached the salt making from seawater operation at Seaside. He saw the salt making operation was proceeding as planned. This operation had been going on since the arrival in October of 1805 and the building of Fort Clatsop by the Corps of Discovery had been erected.

A joint decision of Captains Lewis and Clark had decided that they would stay at Fort Clatsop until April 1st, at which time the Corps of Discovery would start their journey back to civilization. The salt for needs trade plan seemed ideal because it was a non-cash way of paying for the Corps of Discovery's return to civilization and their homes.

Reflecting back on the travel to Fort Clatsop the corps had met with a number of Indian tribes and after each meeting, the Indian chief, their medicine men, and the tribal group were told that the tribe was part of a new country. They were told that because of the Great White Father in Washington, D.C. they had become citizens of the new country.

Just as he came to Seaside Salt Site to see if everything was A-O.K., he noticed that they had the fire burning low. Captain Clark approached the fire and could not see the two men who were producing salt, tending the fire, and supposedly observing the night to prevent any interruption in the seaside salt operation.

At the edge of the beach area forest, the Captain heard rustling in the bushes and crept up to see what was occurring and if it involved the trio of Warfington, Diderot, George Julliard and their activity in the salt making. He came upon two of the men naked engaging in sex oblivious to their duties.

Captain Clark yelled, "Get up. What are you men doing away from your duty station? Stand at attention. Julliard, give me your explanation."

The two men, one a private and the other an interpreter, stood at attention. Naked and not knowing what to do they grabbed their dungarees that were hung on a bush nearby and quickly put them on.

They said, "Sir, we don't know what got into us. We were so lonely and it seemed that we would…" This weak response fell on deaf ears.

Captain Clark said, "Attention, no explanation. We will court-martial you tomorrow in front of your fellow corpsmen. Sleeping on duty is a crime punishable by death, but you are entitled to a court-martial trial of your corps."

The two men kept standing at attention and Captain Clark ended his tirade with, "I will send relief to take your places immediately. Stay here until they return with Sergeant Gass to usher you back for the court-martial tomorrow at eleven a.m." He turned and rode back to Fort Clatsop.

The two awoke to reality. They quickly put on their dungarees and tended the pot of salt water. Warfington said, "My God, we will be court-martialed in front of the troops—our friends and the rest of the corps—and either whipped or sentenced to death by a firing squad."

Julliard said, "I don't know that you will have any problem as you are an interpreter and not a member of the military organization of the corps. You will be punished but not sentenced to death. I mean that Captain Clark is a strict disciplinarian and authoritarian. He believes that obeying all the rules and regulations established at the beginning of our Voyage of Discovery. Everybody, including you, took an oath to fulfill the duties and obey the rules and regulations and other commands of the officers in charge."

Both Julliard and Francoise Diderot were shivering. They gathered more firewood and went back to tending the boiling pot. They figured they may as well stay busy until the next day at which time the replacements would come and they would be taken back to Fort Clatsop where the court-martial would take place.

Francoise Diderot had served duty as a common private after which he was employed by the captains when they were wintering at Mandan. He had served his duty since that time and his being a homosexual had not been known to the two officers in charge.

The next day the replacements came and the two prisoners, their hands tied, were led by Sergeant Gass. It took about an hour to walk back to Fort Clatsop. The gate to the fort was opened and the two men were taken inside and places in a confined area to await their court-martial. Captain Clark and Captain Lewis had reasoned that they should appoint a court panel of three members and assemble the twenty-five remaining corpsman to observe the hearing.

The court-martial was held inside the stockade with the two captains seated and the corps assembled in front of the two captains. Sergeant Ordway, who was in charge of this trial, made his appearance and the other member was Private Windsor, who had been appointed by the captains.

Captain Lewis said, "As senior officer I hereby call the trial be held to court-martial Francoise Diderot and Private George Julliard for unmilitary actions. These charges are sexual misconduct while on duty and leaving their posts to do so. They are being tried for such activity. It occurred last evening and we are taking this action at 11 a.m. today."

He then turned to Captain Clark and said, "Captain Clark, do you have any other particulars to add to the dereliction of duty these two members of the Corps of Discovery are involved in, one a corps member, a private, the other a hired member, an independent?"

He turned to Clark waiting for an answer. Hearing none he heard Sergeant Ordway say, "Captain Clark, Sir I wish to hear an explanation from the men themselves as to any other particulars or any explanations of the activities, which were contrary to our regulations and punishable by death in the case of George Julliard and discharge in the case of Francoise Diderot."

The two men said, "No Sir, we have no explanation. We admit to the charges and ask for leniency by the court."

Francoise Diderot added, "I am not a sworn member of the Corps of Discovery. I have been hired by you as an independent contractor working for wages and assisting the corps for other activities. You have the right to discharge me and I will abide by your decision. However, I wish to say that George Julliard was not instrumental in making this arrangement. I approached him and in actuality seduced him into the homosexual act we were engaged in that you discovered. I respect your decision will await it."

The two captains went back into their private room in Fort Clatsop and discussed the matter. Captain Clark said, "Well, as far as I'm concerned I think we should abandon Francoise Diderot after discharging him here on the coast and leave him to fend for himself when we make our return to St. Louis. He will stay here with the Indian tribes and continue his life as he sees fit. What do you say Captain Lewis?"

Captain Lewis turned and said, "I am not nearly as surprised as you are and realize that we must have discipline and enforce infraction of the rules and regulations, but since we have no authority over Francoise we should take this in consideration. Our only course of action that we can take in his case would be as you indicated. Abandon him after discharge, confiscate his things as part of his punishment, and let him return to his former activity but not be with our Corps of Discovery."

Captain Clark interrupted, "This does not appeal to me. I realize that we should treat Francoise Diderot differently than Julliard; however, the punishment to Julliard will be much more difficult to enforce and choose between the alternative by firing squad or being lashed. The punishment to Julliard is much more restricting and Francoise Diderot being an independent contractor can only be discharged and we can abandon him here, leaving him at the mercy of the elements and the Indian tribes. They may scalp him or provide any other physical or mental punishment. I personally, as a co-equal captain, do not support the death penalty but would subject Julliard to one hundred lashes by bull whip on the morrow. These lashings would be done by Sergeant Ordway for four consecutive days, twenty-five lashings per day."

Captain Lewis said, "I think we should discharge Francoise Diderot immediately, confiscate his back payment, and cancel the contract immediately leaving him to return to civilization on his own. The corps would divorce themselves completely, terminate any activities with him, and the corps as far as he's concerned no longer exists. This is extremely harsh, but I so move."

Captain Clark said, "I heartily agree with your suggestions and motion. I so approve. The punishment will take place tomorrow at eleven o'clock in the morning. Assemble the troops for four successive days in a row at eleven each morning. Sergeant Ordway will administer the punishment of twenty-five lashes. I, as co-leader of the corps, will submit this recommendation and ask that on an ex post facto basis President Jefferson and Congress confirm our decision. With that I ask the men appearing before this court-martial if they have anything to say."

Francoise Diderot stepped forward and said, "I am not a sworn member of the corps and you hired me under contract. Does this mean my contract is canceled and all my monies forfeited?"

The two captains nodded their heads affirming and said, "Yes."

Diderot backed up a step or two and waited for George Julliard, a private to speak. George Julliard said, "I, I, I have nothing to say except I admit to the violations of rules and regulations and deserve any punishment I receive, Sirs." He saluted and stepped back.

Captain Clark said, "This court finds that the punishment for Francoise Julliard will be that his contract has been canceled and funds or other remunerations he would be able to collect from the government is forfeited and he will be abandoned here at Fort Clatsop to fend for himself. We no longer need or want his services.

As far as Private George Julliard is concerned, he will pay a fine, namely his remuneration will be confiscated, both past and future. He will be allowed to stay with the Corps of Discovery and finish the return voyage to civilization, but he will be subject to twenty-five lashings each day for the next four days by his sergeant. This will take place tomorrow morning at eleven o'clock in front of the corps and they should be aware that this happens to any member of the corps who violates the book of regulations we have adopted. The court is hereby adjourned."

Captain Clark motioned to Sergeant Gass and said, "Will Sergeant Gass please take the prisoner, George Julliard, and confine him to quarters and have Sergeant Ordway deliver one hundred lashes, twenty-five lashes each day at eleven a.m. starting tomorrow?"

With this, Captain Clark got up and said, "All our Corps of Discovery dismissed."

The corps got together afterwards and talked over what had happened. Was it for the better of the corps? Would it improve the possibility of a successful finish of the trip into the unknown? They had reached two of the goals by President Jefferson. The third goal was to return safely with all the information that they had collected and report to his office in Washington, D.C. after returning down the Missouri River.

The two captains went back to their quarters and spent the next hour discussing what effect this disobedience, court-martial, and punishment would do to the enthusiasm of the corps and their dedication to complete the president's dream to link the Atlantic Coast to the Pacific Coast using the Northwest Passage. This discussion showed that despite an incident of erotic performance by George Julliard and Francoise Diderot, the interpreter, that the Voyage of Discovery was continuing until concluded

The next day the lashing of George Julliard was administered by Sergeant Ordway and in three subsequent days, the total of one hundred lashes was completed. The effect on the Corps of Discovery was pronounced. They saw and had an example of what it meant to not follow orders, to desert their post or duty, and the punishment after conviction. The court-martial was quick, sure and painful.

The services of Captain Meriwether Lewis in administering first aid learned three years before came into play. Julliard had been confined to quarters and was lying on his stomach recovering from the wounds on his back. The salt that had been rubbed into the lashings was done as an antiseptic, but it was also very painful and resulted in Julliard passing out each day.

The other members of the corps wondered why the two had gotten into a personal love affair and saw what happened if they violated the rules. It had been known that other erotic activities had occurred during the trip up the Missouri. Captains Lewis and Clark condoned these dalliances. Thus, sex reared its ugly head during the Voyage of Discovery. It was condoned but not encouraged by the two leaders, Captains Lewis and Clark.

However, Captain Clark as a Presbyterian, a religious man, believed that sex should be confined to his spouse and was for the purpose of raising a family. As far as Captain Lewis was concerned, he had never been married. He was in his twenties and had noticed that he was attracted to some of the men he had met during his officer training in the Frontier Forces as a young twenty-year-old lieutenant.

CHAPTER 39

Up the Marias Fork without a Paddle

CAPTAIN LEWIS LOOKED AROUND AT the corpsman on his team. He was pleased to see Sergeant Ordway. Ordway had the fortitude to overcome the conflicting dangers facing Platoon B. The privates Ordway had selected to face the unknown had asked to enter the Great Race on Lewis' team. They were volunteers. Lewis had been happy with those who had chosen to be with him

Meanwhile Clark had chosen to travel down the Yellowstone area of the Wyoming Indian reservation. It was a gorgeous square area of land which was covered with many unusual features considering it was just 1,600 square miles of God's country only the American Indian tribes had seen. They called it Yellowstone and adopted it as their habitat. It was the Red Bluff Indian reservation where he was greeted with open arms.

Neither of the two captains knew where the other leader was, but both sent out scouts to cross the Bitterroot Mountain Range noting the land features and animals as they went along.

Captain Lewis went up the Marias River and noted that the mountain goats were cropping grass on the hillsides and barely looked up as the platoon climbed up the riverbed. It was a strenuous path and it was an overnight with the coyotes barking waking the men several times.

Lewis rolled over and commented, "Corporal Warfington note this problem."

Warfington murmured, "Yes sir."

The dawn interrupted the platoon's night's sleep.

As Captain Clark visited the Red Bluff Indian reservation, he had a full view of the panorama laid out by the Great Chief in the heavens above. It was the 270-degree vista extending from the north entrance of the park to the land area of the Yellowstone River Basin sweeping from the north and to the east.

Clark's platoon A was lined up. Twelve men in a half-circle behind the leaders included York, Clark's slave, Charbonneau, Sacagawea, and her sister. It included a climb up the bluff, a welcome powwow, drums, a ceremonial feast, and for the corpsmen their choice of a bed companion for the evening. It had energized the group of explorers as never before.

CHAPTER 40

The Return on the Columbia River

CAPTAINS CLARK AND LEWIS BEGAN the discussion heatedly. When to leave Fort Clatsop was the matter at hand. Captain Lewis wanted to wait for the ice on the Missouri to break up. Clark wanted to leave in March as he thought two months would be enough time and the rivers would be okay. The leaders had had conflicting plans during the past two years but had been able to work them out. Not so this time.

Captain Clark was anxious to get started as he had a young lady waiting for his attentions. He wanted to get married. Captain Lewis wanted to get back to being President Jefferson's private secretary.

Captain Lewis was first to talk about it. He said, "I feel that the three plus months we have spent at Fort Clatsop has been very productive and from my point of view, we could spend another week or two before we head back to civilization."

Clark smiled and said, "Meriwether, I knew you would find some way to change my plans. We always seem to have conflicting ideas as to what should come next. I favor an immediate start as we do not know what problems we may have along the way."

At that Clark and Lewis left the quarters they had at the fort and had Sergeants Ordway and Pryor assemble the corps. Captain Clark was the first to speak when the corps had been gathered in front of the stockade. They had left their duties and assignments. They wanted to hear the details so that they were as ready as they could be.

Regarding the details of the corps next move Captain Clark said in his military voice, "Sergeants, call the men to attention and have them take parade rest."

Both captains were standing at attention as the sergeants gave these orders to their platoons. The captains, after seeing their orders had been followed said, "Stand at ease men. We will explain what will happen now that it is springtime. There is no snow on the ground and the rains have stopped. We thought we would go up the river to our destination at the three rivers junction on the east side of the Rocky Mountains. We anticipate this will be in March so we'll buy ponies from the Indians along the way."

He added, "Fortunately, we had the salt making process going for the last three months. This natural stuff is the same as gold is to a miser. We have something that is not available on the other side of the Continental Divide. The Indians will trade for salt and we can get food from them. We will need at least twenty horses as each of us will ride and tow a pack horse behind. We will be going from dawn 'til dusk. Going up the Columbia with its bad spots is not a practical way for us to go upriver. Our canoes are fragile. The river contains the Celilo Falls and even the sockeye salmon have to be jumping up to pass them. We will travel up river for nearly two hundred miles to get by them and other problems. Are there any questions?"

Sergeant Pryor said, "I have one. My men have told me that they wished to get back as rapidly as possible. Could you tell the corps your best guess as to when in 1806 we will be back in St. Louis, our start point nearly two years ago?"

Captains Clark said, "We feel that we should be back no later than the first of November as we know the lay of the land and will go from dawn 'til it is so dark that we can see the trail. Obviously, this is subject to the weather, not having any Indian conflicts, and taking the baby Charbonneau along with Sacagawea. Since there are no questions. I propose we leave tomorrow, March 27th. Have you anything further to add Captain Lewis?"

Captain Lewis said, "I think this idea stinks, but you know how I feel Captain Clark. Say no more! Please dismiss the men."

The next morning, bright and early, the Indians were eager to see what was left behind in the Fort Clatsop stockade by the corps that they would be able to use. Their Chief Long Braid liked the idea of occupying the stockade and keeping the sleeping quarters for their meeting area. It was a wonderful gift for the chief who could live where the two officers had lived.

Captain Lewis and Clark had watched as the pack mules were loaded and the pony for Sacagawea and Pomp was prepared. Each said almost as one, "The west is won for our union. Now is the easy part of our Voyage of Discovery—the quick route home."

The Corps of Discovery had successfully found its goal, the Pacific, and had staked claim to the area for the United States of America in spite of the two officers not agreeing about many things such as leaving the American Flag flying in the Pacific breeze.

It was a very tearful goodbye on the part of Sacagawea as she felt that going back with her papoose and her husband Charbonneau and leaving the new friends she had made would be a telling experience.

Going up the Columbia River, they found that the Deschutes' Indian tribe lived on a river of the same name. It had a reservation called Portland since it was an island. It was at the base of a snow capped volcano, which had been dead for a millennium.

The corps saw that the Columbia River was fed by small streams, one of which was called Bridal Veil Falls, which spurted from the cliffs towering above the riverbed. The spring winds whistled through the yellow pine trees extending to the river's edge. Red headed black birds and woodpeckers attacked the trees. This forest hid the Indian red beaked totem pole and a lodge, which guarded the Columbia at the base of Mount Hood.

The Shoshone Indian tribe was the tribe from which both Sacagawea and her sister Otter Moon had been kidnapped some six years before. This reservation had a log lodge where its Chief White Arrow had the teepees scattered near the river.

Captain Lewis noticed that the Indian features were different than the other tribes that they had visited. Even so Lewis made them citizens of the United States of America. It was at this reunion of the Shoshone the two Indian maidens Sacagawea and Otter Moon were surprised to learn that the Indian chief of the Shoshones was their half-brother. She remembered his name was Chief Kamahwait and he welcomed them back.

The Indians at the Red Lodge lived off of the seafood fish that was found such as salmon that migrated up the Columbia. The "land locked mountain trout," which was found in the Deschutes River itself were the main source of sustenance.

The captains met with another Indian Chief, White Arrow, and the whole Shoshone tribe were sworn into the United States as citizens and asked what information they could provide to aid the corps to return to civilization as they knew it in St. Louis.

Captain Clark was reminded that the rivers at this time of year were at flood stage because the snow in the mountains had been melting. The trip up the Columbia was marred by a huge thunder storm that had gathered over Mount Hood and it proceeded to hail, thunder, and lightning. The north wind stopped The Corps of Discovery from going up the rivers. Canoes were forced to the banks to wait for the spring storms to be over.

Captain Lewis turned to Captain Clark and said, "This is a fine kettle of fish we are in. Weather should improve in a few minutes. In the meanwhile there may be bear in the area because this is salmon country and they often fish by the banks. On the way down the Columbia we saw the bear catching the fish that had spawned, but now it is the fish going up river that will draw the black bear to the Columbia."

Just as Captain Clark predicted, the spring thunderstorm was over. The expedition continued up the Columbia by canoe and they reached the Indians who were catching trout on rickety scaffolds made of quaking aspen branches lashed together and hung over the river banks.

These were the Celilo Falls and the water was falling and the salmon were jumping against the falling water. It was a conflict of man and his arch rival Mother Nature and her silver sided competitors in their struggle to go up the icy river and to procreate.

This battle was was as old as time. It was the battle of men and his salmon stalwarts in the age old struggle to bring the new generation of life aboard. It was to lay eggs in the silver sand to be fertilized by the ardent male willing to die for his young. The Corps of Discovery watched in wonder before the contined their travel into the future.

CHAPTER 41

The Third Year Unfoldeth

FOG ROLLED IN ON the Oregon shore and blanketed Fort Clatsop where the Corps of Discovery had settled in after reaching the coast less than a week before. It was a joyous time and the subliminal warfare between the captains had subsided.

Captains Clark and Lewis had welcomed the New Year with a little grog and a lot of satisfaction having accomplished President Jefferson's goal to find a land route to the Pacific. However, the Northwest Passage as it was called was not found. This thwarted Jefferson's primary purpose of the Voyage of Discovery, which was to find a land route across the North American continent.

The corps had remained together while crossing the Continental Divide. It had taken a great deal of effort on the part of Captain Clark, Sacagawea, and the Corps of Discovery. They had suffered from the cold and the fact that their moccasins had worn out. They were above the timberline. The nights were cold and the days were warm.

Captain Clark finally said, "We will descend to the Clearwater River just ahead and take the time to build canoes that can take us down the Columbia River. Our scouts have found Indian tribes who have told us that we are within two hundred miles to the coast of the Pacific and that if we cross to the Oregon coast, we'll be ahead of the game."

Captain Lewis chimed in, "We're getting into the land of the Oregon tribe. By doing so it would prevent Britain's claim below the 54th Parallel."

Lewis took the pirogues built to travel down the Columbia. He had Sacagawea and Charbonneau guide them west. He wrote in his journal, *The efforts of going down the Columbia River by canoe was accomplished using three men pirogues, taking our meager belongings aboard going down the river on the northern side of the Columbia, and indoctrinating all the Indian tribes as we went along.*

Lewis said, "According to Old Toby before the end of the year we'll be on the Pacific Coast and safely in a fort, which we will build."

Captain Lewis told Clark, "I am planning to collect many specimens and record all the features of man, women, and children within the coastal area including the fish and flowers we see and the other elements of the environment. As we pass I will spend my time doing this with the help of my platoon members and Sergeants Ordway and Pryor. It will be a busy time but fascinating."

The sight of the Pacific Ocean north of the Columbia was recorded by Clark and after staying overnight on the northern coast from the Columbia River's mouth, the voyagers found that the weather conditions were not conducive to staying north of the Columbia.

A vote was taken by the corps and Captain Clark marveled that the thirty-four members of the Corps of Discovery voted to spend their time south of the Columbia in a camp in a fort to be made during the last two months of the year, 1805. The construction of Fort Clatsop would be in the charge of Sergeant Gass. It must be done by January 1806.

The conflicts of the corps as to where they should spend the winter was between Captain Clark and Captain Lewis. Captain Lewis wanted to build quickly and for the shelter to be made relatively warm because of the many trees that quickly could be used in the great fire place.

This was unacceptable to Captain Clark who said, "I think we should put this to a vote. We have had our scouts look south of the river and also look north of the Columbia along the shore. It is suggested that a vote as to which place to winter is necessary and called for by our charter."

The vote was taken the following day. All but three of the corps wanted to go across the river in the more sheltered area where the three or four months could be put to useful purpose getting ready for the return trip home.

Captain Clark was upset that his suggestion was not accepted and he indicated his displeasure with his abrupt, "I'm finished with this meeting! I hereby call the meeting closed."

The next day Captain Clark had cooled down. He said, "Now I want to cross to the south side of the river and find a much more sheltered area, still close to the ocean and also close to the river."

The meeting was dissolved and the event showed that there was now a rift growing between captains that been smoothed over but could erupt at any time. The camaraderie they had displayed during the first fifteen months of the Voyage of Discovery had all but disappeared. Both captains had tried to avoid rubbing his opposition by not voicing any criticism. They had some but this was kept under cover.

The next day sixteen pirogues loaded their equipment and personal items and proceeded to cross the Columbia, which was thrashing by the wind blowing from the northwest. They came upon a small fur trading village called Astoria. Clark's advanced scouting found out that John Jacob Astor from New York Commonwealth had established a trading post there. It was where the Indian braves traded the furs pelts and raccoon tails in exchange for buttons, bows, and glass beads. It was busy and went on till darkness came.

The next day the two captains surveyed the area on the south bank a mile up from the Columbia. There was a small stream of fresh water and plenty of forest wood that could be cut and used for fire. There were also disadvantages to this location, but that was true of any location within five or six miles on the land.

The Indian tribe called the Tillamooks were trying to trade cheese for beads, bangles, and bows, but Captain Clark told Sacagawea,"Not for today lady."

The corpsmen were eyeing the squaws for a tangle at an angle and were hard to keep under control.

Captain Clark was saintly as he said, "Thanks but no thanks." On the other hand, Meriwether Lewis disappeared into woods.

Upon Captain Lewis's return, he heard Clark's sharp voice, "Meriwether, I am disappointed with my selection of permanent camp on the north side of the Columbia. I realize that the wind blows more than there, but it also has a tendency to keep the mosquitoes away since it blows out to sea and the mosquitoes do not like the salt water. However, since the die is cast, you won, I lost, we'll move tomorrow."

Captain Lewis said with venom in his voice, "I will let the men know and you inform your platoon as well so that we do not have visible split between our two platoons as to who is in command."

The Corps of Discovery had set up its headquarters in the area near the Pacific and deployed there. The following week Captain Lewis told Captain Clark that he wished to take Sergeant Patrick Gass, the best hunter of the company, to shoot fresh game for the Christmas celebration.

All the food and drink had been assembled and at sundown two fiddlers started doing the "Virginia Reel" and "Turkey in the Straw," two songs that they had known while they were back in the states. They noticed the local Indian tribes started to dance around the fire and before they knew it the party was on!

They had been given very little alcohol, but were enjoying the rum that Captain Clark had provided. It was a party to believe. Sacagawea had left baby Pomp in the hands of one of the Indian squaws while she found Charbonneau, her husband, and proceeded to dance with him. Charbonneau, quite a ladies' man, as his wont proceeded to find the Indian squaws who were dancing around the fire to find one that met his fancy.

The next day was Christmas Day and Captain Clark, having gone to church in his youth, gathered the members of not only of the Corps of Discovery but also the Indian braves and squaws of the coastal tribes to hear about the birth of Christ. It was a way to celebrate the religious holiday but also have the two races intermingle. Thus, the various confrontations were temporarily put aside.

Two individuals, Lewis and Clark, found out that despite having different backgrounds together they could achieve great advancement for their nation. Division of duty and aims of the corps were placed ahead of their personal gain.

CHAPTER 42

The Captain's Challenge

"RAIN, RAIN, GO AWAY, COME again another day." It was the case of 'nonsense chasing practicality'! This couplet kept racing around in Captain Lewis' head! He was a dreamer and idea man. This was true as Lewis met the challenge of keeping the spirits of the 33 officers and men of the Corps of Discovery ready to face the rigors of returning to their homes almost 4000 miles away.

It was January 1st of 1806. It was the New Year but the fog and rain enveloped the stockade at Fort Clatsop. This weather occurred daily and made collecting the information about the Oregon Indian tribes difficult. The entire corps was restive. It had been almost two years away from home

Chief Bold Eagle told Sacagawea that the bay had been formed by the Columbia River pouring its fresh water into the ocean. The Oregon Indian tribe seldom had foreign sailing ships enter their bay. When the vessels did the visiting sailors landed and there would be a powwow and celebration for several days. There was an excitement of the new and different cultures meeting. These visitors spoke a foreign tongue and traded rum for sex with the Indian maidens.

Sacagawea asked, "Captain Lewis, what questions do you want me to ask the foreigners?"

Captain Lewis thought a minute and replied, "Where are they from, where are they going, and did they have any tobacco to trade for food or souvenirs?"

The answer they heard was, "No, but they had been on the water coming from the Hawaiian Islands. We are lonely and the diddling of a girl would suit us just fine."

The next few days saw partying that would have made history the world round.

The two Captains, Lewis and Clark, used this time of rest and relaxation to prepare for the return journey to civilization.

The two Captains had a difference of attitude about the trip home, but they agreed on one thing certain—it was senseless for them to go up the Columbia in the dead of winter. Coastal rains meant snow in the Rockies.

Every night following, Captain Clark took his flint and steel and used it to light his briar pipe. The tobacco smoke curled in the air as he puffed on his pipe and said, "The corps is running low on smoking tobacco and the men can't wait till they get back to where it's grown. This is the last of the tobacco. We should accommodate the corps desires and start now so that we can finish our return trip in early fall of 1806. I want get back to present to the world the result of our voyage to the Pacific. I feel sure that the president wants to hear about our success immediately."

Captain Lewis had listened to Captain Clark patiently, and then said, "William, I want to get back to Washington, D.C. as much as you do BUT, as the old saying in my family goes, 'a half a loaf of bread is better than no bread at all.'"

Captain Lewis said, "For your information, I have caught up organizing my data and information of the two years on the road. I think the time is not ripe. Let's wait for good weather, especially in crossing the Rocky Mountain passes as we go back home."

Captain Lewis knew that Captain Clark had kept the Voyage of Discovery on its course and moving ahead at all times, except when the weather was bad. He located his position and all other features of the trip. These included all changes of direction of the corps as they had continued their travel to the Pacific. These daily diaries included longitude and latitude. It was a tremendous job as it was 3000 miles of travel with many topographic land features of the unexplored 800,000 square miles of territory.

The two leaders and thirty men had proved that there was no Northwest Passage, but reaching the Pacific Ocean overland was possible but not practical. There was no Northwest Passage. This information was needed by President Jefferson and the federal government. These results were fruitful and the nation's funding of the Voyage of Discovery would show the American people that the United States of America was growing all the time.

The next morning Captain Lewis turned and watched the misty rain roll in from the Pacific just a few miles west. However, Fort Clatsop had been a good wintering spot. It had seen lots of fog, some rain, but no frosty days. Snow and ice was only on the eastern side of the Bitterroot Mountains.

Captain Lewis said to himself, *I am pleased with my efforts. I have much data for the president and many specimens for the National Museum. Co-Captain Clark has been a great pathfinder and we have had only one man, Sergeant Charles Floyd, die on the road despite my limited training as man of medicine."*

That night after the evening meal, Captain Clark said to Lewis, "My major regret about our trip is that incident at Seaside where the privates were lollygagging around playing with each other rather than making salt. I should have used the lash, but my not listening to your warnings is not the first time we didn't agree. But we'll see who wins what you have dubbed The Great Race. I want to be the winner of our private bet as I have phrased it. The prize for me winning is fame and fortune. I would kill in order to be the first successful exploration of the Louisiana Purchase."

Clark added, "Meriwether, you should put your money where your mouth is. I feel it in my bones and I will bet you half of my share of the money that I can finish all the duties left to do for the president and get back to our meeting point before you do. I am going to win The Great Race!"

Captain Lewis replied, "I want to beat you out of it William. Let's sleep on the idea. We will discuss what the rules are, including which routes to take to win the grand prize. Fame and fortune ring true the world round."

Captain Lewis shrugged his shoulders as he waited for the next day. He turned to retire as he changed the subject, "What do you think the president will say to us? We only accomplished half of what he asked me to do. I suppose a half a loaf is better than none. I can report that there is a way from the Atlantic to the Pacific, but the Rocky Mountains stand in the way. Do you think that you can find a route that is closer to St. Louis than our going over the Lolo Pass? This was the first mountain range we encountered on our western trek." Lewis added, without waiting for an answer, "It was the one that we traveled through to get here. I almost froze to death. Sacagawea pulled porcupine needles from your feet and Charbonneau tipped out of the boat. We were lucky to save our diaries."

Captain Clark interrupted, "And baby Pompeii cried and cried, but thanks to Old Toby we found the Shoshone tribe and her half-brother Chief Kamawaiht before we all died on the trail."

Captain Clark stated, "I hope so but winter weather on the coast doesn't mean a thing according to the Chinooks. This is the month of January 1806 and we agree to leave the route to get home undecided until the ice on the Columbia River breaks up. This should be in late March or the first of April."

The weather was so blustering and icy cold that the only exercise the corps had was to go on hiking trips. Sergeant Gass took the corps on skiing trips using homemade skis made from quaking aspen saplings. The leaves fell off the trees from cold, but below freezing temperature had killed the young trees, which were not old enough to live through the winter. Sergeant Gass had lived in the northeast, and showed the men how snow skis were made.

The two plus years of constant togetherness was not healthy for the corps and its leaders. Everyone including Seaman Lewis' dog was on edge.

Realizing this situation was threatening, Lewis decided that opportunity could be a saving grace! Therefore, when the two captains got together in early February 1805 Captain Lewis told Clark that he had an idea for Clark to consider. The two captains went to their quarters and proceeded with the discussion as to what to do to make the return trip an adventure.

Captain Lewis started the meeting with, "William, I chose you as a co-captain with equal rank but with special duties and responsibilities. I told you from day one that you would handle the operations, and I would be involved with collecting the information and making a written report that President Jefferson needed. Now our Voyage of Discovery is on its way home, but..."

Captain Clark interrupted Captain Lewis with a wink and a smile. "The men are all tired and want to get back to civilization in the shortest time possible. I am sure that the corps members are anxious to see their girlfriends and socialize. I wouldn't mind a little fond company myself. We need to get their spirits up and give them cash and land as an incentive to be on the way home. The old saying cash is king holds true."

Clark added, "Even for us, Meriwether, believing that there is something in it for each and every man in the corps including us is true! I believe here is what the government can do for the corps. It can give something to each man including us. Pay the corps a grant of the land we are exploring. Such a payment would be earned for each and every one of us all in the Voyage Discovery. It should be paid from the treasury coffers upon our return to St. Louis. It is for risking our lives in hostile Indian territory. It will make all of us energetically cautious."

With this goal in mind, Captains Lewis and Clark worked together to make the trip home a race to the finish. They agreed that the corps would be split into two sections, with one headed by Captain Clark and the other by Captain Lewis. Each Captain would choose one man at a time—Lewis first then Clark, then Lewis then Clark. Each would be choosing his team alternately. In order to jazz the men's spirits this effort by the Corps of Discovery would be labeled the Great Race.

The winner of the Great Race would be which of the two sections Clark or Lewis reached the point on the route home where the Missouri and the Yellowstone Rivers met. The prize was both tangible and intangible— money and fame.

Each and every person who was on the Voyage of Discovery was governed by this set of the rules for the Great Race. The two captains told the men and woman that rules for such a contest are bound to be complicated and they should agree before they started.

"We leave from Camp Fortunate near the Clear Water River and the Columbia River to return to the starting point where we left almost two years ago, April 7th, which is two months from today. We will keep the corps together until we have reached the Bitterroot Mountains and the pass over the Rocky Mountains."

The Travelers Rest where the Clearwater River turns south and the Bitterroot River continues, some distance from the Columbia, was a good starting point for the contest to begin. The two groups would meet at the finish line where the Yellowstone River and the Missouri River join. The race would be about six hundred miles in length.

The winner would get to name the exploration and the prize would be a thousand dollars to the captain who won and each man in the winning team would receive $120. The men in the losing platoon shall would receive $60 for the extra effort each man expended in trying reach the junction of the Yellowstone and Missouri Rivers first.

"Is that correct Captain Lewis?"

Captain Lewis answered, "Yes, Captain Clark, but I have some other conditions that have to be met. I want to explore the Marias River and develop the information the president has asked us for about the territory that we move through. There are at least seven or eight tribes that are to be found on the Missouri near the Bitterroot Mountains. So for my part, I will induct the chief of each tribe I visit into the United States of America as a citizen and include all the members of his tribe. They will be governed by the laws of the United States and will be completely independent other than obeying their new country's laws.

"On the other hand, Captain Clark, you will go southeast to the Yellowstone River's point of origin. While there, you are to visit the area I have called Yellowstone Parkland where you will see the eight wonders of the world. You will make mention of this in your report to President Jefferson. It will be your own report as to what you find in this magical wonderland. As you may have heard it has never been explored except by fur traders and few have lived to tell the tale."

Captain Clark said, "By gum Meriwether, even I am looking forward to this race to the finish line. I will win and explain what it means to all members of my team if we win the prize."

Captain Lewis said, "Well, I always think of you in your buckskins with the foxtail fur leading the Frontier Forces onward to success, but you must be first to be the winner of this the Great Race. Good luck and God Speed!"

Captain Clark always the optimist said, "Meriwether I always thought you were a winner in all you do, but this time you will be last. My platoon will be waiting for you at the finish Goodbye!"

CHAPTER 43

The Voyage of Discovery Part 1

THE VOYAGE OF DISCOVERY HAD accomplished one of the two goals that President Thomas Jefferson had in mind. Unfortunately, it was not the one two Captains hoped for. The stay at Fort Clatsop was boring. It was around the mouth of the Colombia River. It had proved to be a disappointment. The two Captains had been traveling for more than two years and had found the Pacific coast and that it was occupied by the Tillamook Indians. This tribe was one of the most peaceful the voyage visited on the journey.

Captain Lewis was specializing in what Clark called "La Dee Da." One instant Lewis looked up at the blue skies dotted with white cumulus clouds as white as the driven snow. It was a conundrum that had made Captain Lewis seem unable to concentrate on the task ahead. Stability was not one of Captain Lewis's strong features. Now came the new idea, the Great Race. The Great Race progressed with Sergeant Gass and Ordway directing activities with Platoon B. Each day Captain Lewis pushed his twelve privates to greater effort. The raid by the Nez Pierce Tribe was to steal the pack and horses that Captain Lewis was using to get to the Canadian Border and place the American flag claim. Lewis planned to head back and win the Great Race.

The winner of the Great Race would decide who got the naming rights of the race. Would it be "Captain Clark and Lewis" or perhaps named after the order the expedition was conceived by President Jefferson? Each of the three had a major job to do. Jefferson was the author. Captain Lewis was the organizer and choose the four non-commissioned sergeants and the 25 privates who did the President's grunt work.

If the truth be known the two Captains were fast friends at the beginning of the "Voyage of Discovery" a multiyear trip to the west coast of the North American continent. The two accomplishments desired by the "Voyage of Discovery" were to go west and claim the land rights purchased by the Congress and claimed by the United States of America, 800,000 square miles of land mass extending from the Mississippi River west to the Pacific Ocean and from the northern border claimed by France and Britain. This was approximately the 54th parallel in the North to the southern border tip of Florida. These are chain islets in the ocean.

The fact that Napoleon Bonaparte the emperor of France would accept $15,000,000 for the Northwest is one of the President Thomas Jefferson's greatest land purchases of the 19th Century. The Voyage of Discovery claimed the unknown lands when the treasury transferred gold bullion in 1803. This land purchase was completed when France and its emperor accepted that was paid.

CHAPTER 44

Fishing at Fort Clatsop

THE WEATHER IN JANUARY 1806 WAS not much different than the fall weather of 1805. The Corps of Discovery was suffering from the dampness in the air and despair of the men living inside the fort. The weather conditions were caused by a misty fog brought inland by the shore breezes. The humid air clung to the ground like mustard plaster sticks to your chest. The leaves were rotting and still hanging on the trees.

Captain Clark, the commanding officer of Fort Clatsop, could sleep all night and still take a nap in the afternoon. The privates of the corps could not and instead would play *Territory*, a game made up by the next in command, Captain Lewis.

To start the game a player would drive a small stake in the ground, cut a five-foot piece of rope, tie the rope to the stake, and use it to scribe a ten-foot circle on the ground. Two or three men would play against each other at one time. The game began by dividing the circle on the ground into pie shaped pieces. Each player bought a piece of the pie. The object of the game was to end up owning the most of the property of the pie.

To add property a player would stand in his property and not invade his opponents. He would take his hunting knife by the blade while standing with his two feet completely inside his own territory. He would throw his hunting knife at his opponent's territory so it would stick in the ground.

If the knife stuck in the ground the player who threw the knife would add the pie shaped piece of territory to what territory he owned. The winner was the player who won all the territory in the circle. A player lost when he could not stand with both feet in his own territory.

The winner would then start the next game against two new opponents. The winner would be the one with most territory. The privates from the Kentucky Territory were the most skilled. The winner would collect a chaw of tobacco from each of the losing players.

Captain Clark had Sergeant Pryor learned the game of *Territory*. He was the best among the players and this was the only fraternizing between officers and the men of the corps.

CHAPTER 45

Captain Lewis Races toward Three Forks

"IT'S THAT TIME. LET'S GET a move on." Captain Lewis saw that Platoon B was ready to go. Lewis had tried to imitate Captain Clark as he barked his orders to Sergeant Ordway his noncom. His platoon was mounted on the horses that they had received for the ocean salt they had made while waiting the winter out.

Captain Lewis knew that the Great Race had started. With this thought in mind he summoned Sergeant Ordway by shouting, "The time to leave is now."

It was an electrified group of men who came on the double led by Sergeant Ordway. The end of March had seen the weather to change for the better, and Captain Lewis wanted to meet the requirement to get to the Canadian border. Captain Lewis had not realized how precious salt was with the interior tribes, but now he knew. For every handful of salt it was one pony. To make travel easier he wanted to have packhorses too.

Platoon B was an interesting group of explorers that headed down the Missouri River to the three rivers area of the Blackfoot. It was from this point that Captain Lewis wanted to go up the Santa Maria Branch and meet the chiefs of the Black Feet to inform them that their new White Father, President Thomas Jefferson, would welcome them when they visit his reservation many moons away.

All of Lewis' platoon were mounted on Indian ponies. The five scouts were fanned in front of Platoon B. The corpsmen followed and Sergeant Ordway guarded the rear. Even though Captain Lewis had never visited the area where the Blackfoot reservation was established, the Blackfoot tribe's territory was reported to be one of the most dangerous through which to travel. Captain Lewis thought the reason for such antipathy was the conflicting cultures of two races: the Indians and the Americans. The interior tribes were nomadic and resisted efforts of white men exploring and settling down in what was their territory. This attitude of the natives had never been resolved. There were fur trappers killing the buffalo or Elk to mount their heads to hang upon their office walls and red fox boas to adorn their wives.

As they hurried along the Missouri River's bank Captain Lewis saw a family of brown bears in the shallows of the Marias River. They were using their front paws to fish for trout.

Lewis called, "Halt," while he studied the bears. He realized that it was the time of year that the twin cubs born in mid-winter would be protected by the papa and mama bears. He raised his musket and shot the papa bear in his right shoulder. This stopped the bears in their tracks and Lewis was spared having to kill them.

Captain Lewis knew that he should continue at a pace where they could reach the Marias River in a few days. He signaled to the platoon to gather around him. He said, "I'm glad that's over. The wounded bear will recover and we are safe. We must continue to march north exploring this river until we reach the Canadian border. I estimate this trip would establish the northern border of the Northwest Territory. Sergeant Ordway, assemble the platoon in fifteen minutes."

Sergeant Ordway gave the order, "Take a fifteen minute break. Then we will move on."

The privates were glad for the rest. They were upbeat at the prospect of getting back home and were pleased that Lewis' attitude was one of being careful and protecting their rear. Private Richard Windsor pulled out a plug of tobacco and said to Ordway, "Sarge, that was almost a ball buster, but we got away with it. Here have a chaw, and if not now maybe tonight after chow."

They reassembled and Captain Lewis said, "We are just below the timberline. We will continue north and make camp at night fall. Sergeant Ordway let's go."

As they continued to move ahead Captain Lewis made some notes for his report of activities. As he looked around himself he listed the wild flowers and saw two rams butting heads on the rocky slopes ahead. He noted that it was rutting season and they were fighting over which of them would service the ewes.

Lewis noted, "It is the law of the wild; survival of the fittest."

Just as the action was getting to the final effort all three sheep bounded away, sure-footed, up the slope. The privates laughed as the saw the drama of the wild. One yelled out, "Just like my girlfriend."

That evening as they made camp they saw evidence that the clearing had been used by the Indians. Seeing this Captain Lewis summoned the sergeant and pointed out the blaze marking the path that the Indians had made. The two men talked over what protective moves the corps was following. They had the corps get near the fire so they could go over the next day's schedule. It would be sun up before the corps could go over what went on during the night.

The guards said, "The night is quiet. The horses though hobbled still moved closer together and Seaman, the dog, growled several times after the campfire burned into embers."

Six days had been needed to reach the meadow on the Missouri where the Marias River bordered. Stately pines encircled it. As one of the smallest tributaries of the Missouri the forest came to the river's edge. Red squirrels romped in the trees and looked for nuts on the ground—the pine nuts that had fallen the year before.

That night half of the corps slept in a meadow with the horses in hobbles centered in the middle of it. It should be noted that the Marias River was located in the shadow of the Bitterroot Mountains.

Lewis said to Sergeant Ordway, "The men are tired so let's stay here another night. Tomorrow I will take Private Williard with me as well as Interpreter Drouillard. These two men are two of the best-prepared explorers the United States has produced. We will scout the area before we continue on to the border of Canada. Lower Canada is the boundary of our newly purchased territory. I bet that President Jefferson will be very pleased that we did this."

The next night the corps planned to get a good rest for the race to the Missouri river three forks. It was early to bed, but Lewis had a fitful night's sleep and shortly after midnight he heard Seaman growling. Lewis raised up from the pillow and looked over at the horses, He saw several Blackfoot Indians trying to steal the horses. Then Lewis reached under his pillow of pine tips. He had pulled his loaded pistol up, cocked it, and the bang of his gun woke the rest of Platoon B. They heard the shot of Lewis' gun and the pounding of hoofs as the Blackfoot braves mounted their ponies and sped away. The raiding party had jumped off the Indian ponies. They loaded both the wounded brave and took the mortally wounded brave with them. He was tied to his pony's back. He seemed to be dead. The other Indians had taken the dead man with them. He was draped over his pony, head on one side, feet on the other.

It was chaos for the rest of the overnight stay. Lewis surmised that an Indian war party was probably being assembled to take revenge. Captain Lewis surveyed the situation. He felt that the Blackfoot tribe would be on horseback. Therefore it was vital to return to Platoon A, the one headed by Clark.

Captain Lewis could not wait to get started, but it took Platoon B till daybreak to get their party together and to get underway.

The path as to what action to take was vital. Lewis thought of his family at home in Virginia waiting for him to return from the outback. Would the world think of Captain Meriwether Lewis as Chicken Little who thought the sky was falling? Or would it be better to fall back to a safer site and finish the nation's assignment as the corps did so?

After a sleepless night filled with bad scenarios, Captain Lewis made up his mind to put his solution to a vote of the corps. He decided and confided in his Sergeant Ordway to assemble the platoon at daybreak.

At dawn the next morning the sky was clear and cold. Lewis remembered his father's ditty, "Red clouds in the morning, explorers warning. Red skies at night, explorers delight." How true it was. No sight of the Blackfoot revenge seekers. The weather was better and the privates' attitudes had improved. There was a sense of putting a successful alternative to the test.

The Co-Captain of the Voyage of Discovery, while still not out of the woods, was delighted by a unanimous vote by Platoon B to withdraw down the Marias tributary of the Missouri River watershed and meet Platoon A headed by Captain Clark. The question lingering in the minds of the corpsmen from captain to private remarked, "I make my vote saying, 'Discretion is the better part of valor.'"

CHAPTER 46

Travelers Rest Becomes the Start

THE FIFTEEN HORSES WHINNIED JUST before the sun came up. The morning cold was causing them to want to move to keep warm. Captain Clark had ordered them to be hobbled to keep them from moving around during the night, but their uneasiness could be the result of Indian scouts of the Nez Pierce tribe. These devils might be nosing around looking for stragglers, man or beast to capture.

The captains had used a different strategy to come back from Fort Clatsop. It was having one of the two leaders, usually Captain Clark, heading the parade with the scouts following him. Then came the rest of the corps and lastly Captain Lewis protecting the rear. This was a necessity because the corps was in Nez Pierce country. This tribe was rumored to steal the packhorses, even those for which they had just traded to the captains and received sea salt in exchange. This was known as Indian trading.

The Nez Pierce tribe said, "What's mine is mine and what's yours is mine." This included the deal made for the sea salt from the Pacific Ocean.

The canoes the men had made from the directions of Sergeant Gass, had been nested and dragged behind the platoons so that the return trip could be on the water where river conditions allowed. Captain Clark had wanted such boats when the corps started down the Missouri.

Traveler Rest was just that. A week of resting up for the exertions to follow.

After the two captains had decided to have a Great Race, they went to their quarters and created the rules that both would follow.

The two captains had picked their men and proceeded to start their separate journey to the junction of the Missouri and white water Yellowstone River. The race included Captain Lewis's trip to go up the Marias River toward the Canadian border.

Once reaching the border called the 54th Parallel they should turn and go back toward the junction of the Missouri River and the Yellowstone River. There were approximately six tribes that had been described by their Indian guide, and Lewis was to stop at each tribal reservation and let the tribal chief know that the territories they now occupied would remain the same but be under the control of the Great White Father in Washington, D.C.

The junction of the Yellowstone River and the Missouri River would be the terminus, the end of the race.

Captain Clark decided that he would leave immediately. He had the southern route going first to the Yellowstone area where Captain Lewis had been once before, but they wanted to verify by having Captain Clark include his inspection of the area and his description of the wonders of the beauty and unusual features found in this portion of the Wyoming Territory.

Captain Clark left after provisioning his group for a six-week venture into the unknown as far as he was concerned. He first proceeded down the Missouri River and the route they had taken adjacent to the Bitterroot Mountains and the fact that the Columbia River flowed north after being east-west for the first two-hundred and fifty miles from Fort Clatsop.

It had been a great trip up the Columbia. They had traversed the Celilo Falls and had traveled up the Columbia to where the Clearwater River ran into it.

The Bridal Veil Falls they saw going up the Columbia were gorgeous. They extended one-hundred feet up into the green loveliness and the gray cliffs that provided a lip over which a stream of water, twenty feet wide, gushed and developed a sound that was like a murmur and then a thunder and then a murmur and then a thunder as it tumbled down the cliff to the pool below.

The cliff itself was gray granite and evidently had been cracked by a recent earthquake some hundred million years before and the rain and snow every year had eroded the cliff so that the waterfall, twenty feet wide, became turbulent as it fell down the hundred foot trough looked like a white ribbon against a gray box during Christmas time.

The other features they saw going up the Columbia on their return trip were magnificent and Lewis and Clark, the two captains, and their crew had enjoyed the return up the Columbia and reviewing the efforts of the Indian tribes pulling their canoes through the rapids, traveling one hundred-twenty odd miles to the point at which the Columbia heads due north and to Fort Mandan about four hundred miles away.

The men were joyous in the two platoons. They were on their way home and that evening they surrounded the fire and sang songs, drank a gill of whiskey, and made merry celebrating their return.

Captain Lewis told Captain Clark, "The return trip should not take as long as it had for us to come up the river. I anticipate that it will be a much easier journey since we know the way and the hardships we are about to overcome."

Captain Clark replied, "That's true, and I think we should find a shorter way back to civilization if we can. I know you have sent President Jefferson the report of our first stay at Fort Mandan and have taken with us the notes and diaries that both you and I have kept getting from Fort Mandan to the Pacific Ocean. It was so unexpected that we did not realize the impact of our explorations. Now we wish to have a race to the point of our departure two years ago. During that time, we should complete my study of the environment, notes of the Indian tribes we have met, and the rest of my diary and you have kept your own diary and should be up to date as I have."

Captain Clark said, "You know I'll do that. My army training and having to report to my commander when I was in the Frontier Forces has trained me well. I will also keep map making so that the hundreds of thousands of dollars we have spent will be worthwhile and both President Jefferson and Congress will be glad of our claims to the Northwestern Territory for additional land for the United States expansion."

Captain Lewis said, "We'll have a number of days to discuss this matter, but now I want to talk to you about the Great Race and which part of our group, either yours or mine, will win the prize. I've been thinking about the prize we should ask for upon our return as we wish to get back to the St. Louis start point as soon as possible."

Captain Clark said, "Well, I have had forced marches with my platoon when I was in the Frontier Forces and know how to get to a point of destination in the most rapid way."

Captain Lewis interrupted, "Well, that's the purpose of the Great Race. To do our job, split the Voyage of Discovery into two platoons, Platoon A and Platoon B. Choose our members for the Great Race alternately so that you choose a man, I choose a man, and so on. That way it will enlist the efforts and the energy that each of our corps has and will get them vitally interested. Let's go back for a few minutes and discuss what the Great Race will involve and what you envision. I envision starting tomorrow. Choose the members of our corps alternately so that half the corps will be going with you and half the men in the corps will be going with me."

Captain Clark said, "That is what I feel is your end of the exploration, but I heartily agree to take half of the Corps of Discovery and investigate and report on the lands surrounding the Missouri and Columbia Rivers and supply a report of this.

I will be responsible for doing the mapping that is required to present a visual account of our experience and you will see that it is presented to Congress and the result will be worth the monies we have spent. I also feel that we as the leaders are entitled to benefit from organizing and commanding the Corps of Discovery going from St. Louis and returning there also."

With that, the two captains retired for the night and proceeded to make detailed plans as to where they'd gone and what they saw. This enabled each to know where they were during the estimated two months it would take to get back to the starting point, but they were allowing the trip to continue past the October 1st if necessary.

The two captains bid each other goodnight and proceeded to get Sergeant Ordway and Sergeant Gass to awaken them in the morning. The next day Captain Clark arose and after Reveille and breakfast assembled his men. "Sergeant Gass, get your men ready with all their belongings and to the canoes. We are off and running."

CHAPTER 47

Conflicting Siblings

T HE FIELD BROTHERS JOINED THE Corps of Discovery in December of 1803. They joined at Camp Woods where Captain Clark was stationed. Clark was a Lieutenant in charge of a platoon of U.S. Army Frontier Forces. The conflict between brothers occurred on duty while guarding the stockade located at Camp DuBois. The two had gone to the local pub and had one Jamaican rum too many. While returning to Camp Dubois the brothers tried to sober each other up by slapping each other in the face and realized that Captain Clark would be extremely upset by their unsoldierly action. This event occurred as they were returning from the local bar.

It was a case of two enlisted men who that happened to be brothers. The oldest brother, Reuben Fields, told the bartender that they were supposed to have returned to Camp Dubois. He added that his younger brother also wanted to return to the camp, but he wanted to sneak past the sentry that Captain Clark had appointed for the evening.

If the sentry was elsewhere the two of them could return to the camp, sneak in, and go to bed. When they awakened in the morning they would be as fresh as the morning dew having slept off the rum hangover.

The two men staggered back to the gate of Camp Dubois and waited until the sentry on duty stopped and called out, "Twelve o'clock and all is well."

Hearing this, Reuben Fields proceeded to climb up the eleven-foot spiked stockade wall using his brother's shoulders as a way up to the top. He proceeded carefully and did not fall.

Reuben whispered, "Watch what you're doing. I don't want to fall on the sharp poles of the stockade."

The other brother, Joseph, looked up as he held his brother and said, "Got the message, Reuben."

Once over the wall, Reuben went down into the stockade area and found a rope that had been left in the ready room. He took it and went back to the stockade and tied it to the top, throwing it down to Joseph who proceeded to climb up the rope, hand over hand, but slipped back and had to start again. Luckily, he did not sprain his ankle. On his second attempt he whispered "You dumb bumpkin, give me a hand."

Reuben tried helping him over the twelve-foot wall, being careful not to make too much noise in the process. Just as they were finishing this operation, the sentry came and said, "Who goes there?"

Reuben whispered, "It's us, the Fields brothers, returning from special duty. Please assist us to our beds."

The sentry said, "I must take you to the Captain's quarters and turn you in. It's my duty and if I don't I will be punished for aiding you to come back into the compound. I was not told about this. Without permission or a pass, whatever you want to call it, I can't let you by."

So the three of them walked from the sentry tower to Captain's office. The three men stood at attention and saluted Captain Clark.

Captain Clark addressed the men, "Stand at ease. Now what are you men doing here with the sentry?"

The sentry replied, "Sir, they were climbing over the stockade wall and had reached the walkway to my post trying to get back to quarters. After I caught them they mumbled something about being on the way back to their sack. They tried to get past me, declared themselves, and we immediately came to you, Sir. That's what happened."

Captain Clark asked, "Field brothers, what do have to say?"

Reuben, being the oldest spoke. "Sir, we went to the local store and bought some liquor, which we drank as we came back to Camp Dubois. We were gone for just thirty minutes and to our surprise were stopped by the sentry since he knew we belonged here as part of the corps. That's our story Sir, and it's the truth."

Captain Clark turned to Joseph Field and asked, "Is that what you have to say too?"

Joseph Field snapped to attention. "Yes Sir, we beg your forgiveness and would like to return to our beds."

Captain Clark replied, "You may do so as I will talk this over with Captain Lewis in the morning and decide what punishment is deserved."

The next morning the corps got up at Reveille and were asked to stand at ease. Captain Clark spoke, "Would Private Joseph Fields and Reuben Fields please step one pace forward?"

They each said, "Yes, Sir."

The Captain ordered, "All but Private Reuben and Joseph Fields are dismissed. You may return to your quarters now."

Captain Clark turned to the Fields brothers. "Follow me to my office. Captain Lewis is there and since you belong to his platoon he will hear your case with me and then as the co-captains we will decide what punishment you will receive."

In the captain's office the two privates were asked to tell their stories. After a garbled account of their conduct was heard Captain Lewis looked at them and said, "I cannot tell you how much this bothers me since you are the first privates to be disciplined, and I wish that it had been Captain Clark's platoon."

The Field brothers saluted and in unison said, "We are sorry, Sir."

Captain Lewis said, "We have to render punishment but feel that this first offense should be punished by extra guard duty and five lashes to be given by Sergeant Ordway tomorrow morning at ten o'clock." Captain Lewis turned to Captain Clark. "Have you anything else to add?"

Captain Clark said, "You tell Ordway to administer the five lashes to each man. Since this is the first incident of breach of security this punishment will serve as a warning to the Fields and all others in the Corps of Discovery any further actions of this kind will receive much harsher punishment."

This was the outcome of the first breach of duty in the new territory and the two men saluted and returned to their quarters.

The next day, the other members of the Platoons A and B were policing the area of the camp of anything that was littering the place. When the corps were sent back to their quarters to relax after a full day of training, they sat down and talked.

"Shall we desert the corps? Shall we go over the wall and go back home or shall the corps tough it out?" The four sergeants two from each platoon led the meeting. There were several who wanted to call it quits—to split and go over the wall tonight and be AWOL (Absent Without Leave) and go down the Missouri River even though it was the middle of winter and disappear into the great nothingness of the Missouri Territory.

Giving it serious thought the men decided that the Field brothers ought to take the punishment and never do anything as foolish as that again. The next morning at ten o'clock the two sergeants, Ordway and Floyd, arranged to have the punishment in the center of the stockade. They had a pole from which the men could be suspended by their wrists to expose their backs to the touch of Ordway's whip.

The group of thirty-four were assembled and the Captain Lewis said, "At ease men. We are hereby rendering punishment to Reuben Field and Joseph Field, both privates of the Corps of Discovery and who are guilty of being away from the stockade without permission. They also were stopped as being drunk. As a result, they will receive five lashes each administered by Sergeant Ordway."

Both the Fields brothers had their shirts removed and their bare backs exposed and each was attached to the pole with hands and wrists bound. John Ordway, the sergeant, took a bull whip and alternately gave each man five lashes. The men groaned and as salt was rubbed into their wounds as a disinfectant they screamed in pain.

After John Ordway was finished he turned to Captain Lewis, "Sir, punishment administered. May the men be dismissed?"

Captain Lewis replied, "So ordered."

The two Field brothers were cut down and taken to their bunks and laid on their stomachs so they would not bleed on their bed covers and were left to recuperate.

After coming to, Reuben Field said to Joseph, "That is a punishment I will never forget. You should not forget it either. We will notify Captain Lewis through Sergeant Ordway that we beg forgiveness and that we will be good soldiers the rest of the way and models for the other privates to emulate." The two went back to their tortured dreams.

Captain Lewis and Captain Clark observed the conflict between officers and men. They felt that such conflicts should be avoided wherever possible and once a transgression occurred the conflict between the whipped and the one who whips was a conflict that the corps wanted to minimize. The corps numbers was small and the duty asked of the men was great. The two officers should be firm but just. They should gain the confidence of all.

CHAPTER 48

Winter's End—The Last Leg of the Triangle

THE TWO CAPTAINS FACED EACH other at Traveler's Rest in early March of 1806. Captain Lewis would celebrate his thirty-second birthday by giving his word that the Voyage of Discovery would be over before the snow fell. Meriwether made this solemn pledge to Clark even though it was voluntarily given. Lewis wanted to assure his co-captain that he was dedicating the rest of his life to prove his being alive and well was a gift from his Lord and Redeemer. This conflict was within himself. He was feeling both confident and unworthy at the same time.

The past six years working for his president had been stressful. His position had been a new one known but to President Thomas Jefferson. He was selected by the leader of his country to save the third residency of his country from disgrace.

After authoring the expansion project called the Voyage of Discovery it was up to President Thomas Jefferson to confirm the mammoth acquisition to the rest of the world, but especially to all American citizens.

As the sponsor of the Louisiana Purchase Jefferson had handpicked the leader, but he had been unsure of the future. He felt the Voyage of Discovery would end the speculation that Jefferson was heading a do-nothing administration.

As to the other side of this equation, Captain Clark, a known friend of Lewis was a practical optimist. He had led the group of explorers and was ready to lead them back to St. Louis. He had mapped the route of the first half of the three-thousand-mile journey precisely. It had taken the corps less than two years. The two men, Captains Lewis and Clark, had done what they had been ordered to do. Clark was the operational leader. He arose each day positive that that day would be more productive than the day before.

Captain Clark, slightly older than Lewis, was looking forward to celebrating his thirty-sixth birthday and felt that he was the old codger who had successfully led the troops to the Promised Land, the Pacific Ocean. They now were returning up the Columbia River retracing their second leg of the Voyage of Discovery in 1805—this time traveling east toward the sun and home.

The countryside of the Columbia River would be examined as the corps rowed up Columbia river toward Celilo Falls where the Walla Walla Indian braves fished for salmon, and the point where the Columbia River turned due north and flowed through unexplored countryside.

Having completed two-thirds of the trip the two captains thought that the way back up the Columbia would be far easier. Captain Clark knew how to shorten the trip by eliminating former course errors. They would have already visited and explored the virgin forest along sixty miles of the Pacific shoreline. Going up the Columbia Gorge, where many species of birds, fish, and animals were to be found Captain Clark kept accurate records of twists and turns in the river portaging around Celilo Falls. Captain Lewis was concerned with the topography and unique geographic features, which showed how fishing had become the principal source of food and basis of living close to the river and its having a different living pattern.

The braves fished the year round as it seldom snowed in the winter and the Indians stood on a framework of poles lashed together netting salmon as the fish jumped up to reach the spawning grounds of the upper Columbia River. Creating the next generation of salmon fingerlings would be the last act of the salmon's existence as the fish died after laying their eggs. Once fertilized by the male both the female and the male floated belly up down river dead. The salmon's spawning was the final act of a seven-year drama.

The 14,000-foot high snow topped mountain was named Mount Hood by the captains after it was sketched by Captain Lewis. This was just one of nature's miracles.

The other natural features were drawn and recorded by the men who were risking their lives. It was to be a happy trip as they had made sea salt from seawater during the winter from talking with the Indian braves on the way west to the Pacific. They had learned that there was a commodity (sea salt) that was more valuable than gold. It was a substance the Rocky Mountain Indians would eagerly trade horses to get. The two captains had learned from Sacagawea that it was so treasured that her Shoshone brethren would ride five hundred miles to get salt from the Utah Indians and the Great Salt Lake.

Captain Clark told Lewis, "Meriwether, we will need canoes and horses. We can get them by swapping our sea salt for them, but we will give them as little salt as we can. I can make a better swap than you can."

Lewis said sharply, "We shall see . . . we shall see."

The canoes that were needed to transport the explorers were bargained for by Captain Clark. Captain Lewis had made salt from seawater and he brought it along as a trading substance and it was to be used to trade for horses before going back over the Rockies.

The inland Indians told Captain Lewis they could trade a powder horn full of salt for each horse the Voyage of Discovery needed. Since there were thirty-one people on the return journey, the corps needed nearly 40 three man canoes to travel up river and many ponies to travel back from the Snake Clearwater junction until they reached Travelers Rest in Idaho Territory.

Captain Lewis was interested in going across the Snake River and meeting with the Indian tribal elders who had instructed Chief Raindrop to attend to tribal needs, tribal rules, and the best of living circumstances that could be provided.

At that time the Boise Indians and the Walla Wallas were at war with each other. This would complicate the Corps of Discovery's crossing the Rocky Mountains to return to the Missouri River. These two Indian tribes had raided each other seeking marriage partners and taking such kidnapped captives to trade with Indians from other regions and interior forests.

The two tribes had powwows to appeal to the Great Spirit in the sky that the winter weather be mild. After the weather improved and the rivers were not frozen over the Clearwater tribe would travel over the Rockies to the Southeast. This would be aided because both the Missouri and Yellowstone were not frozen over. Travel by horseback over the trails was not hampered by snow in 1806. It made getting from the Indian tribes in the interior such as the Shoshone, Sacagawea's Tribe, to the American explorers and settlements much easier.

The first visit of the Americans consisted of both Captains Lewis and Clark, the Sergeants Ordway and Shannon, and a few of the other corps members crossing the frozen Missouri to see how the Indians lived.

It was a wonderful day but cold even though it was the first week in March 1806. They notified Chief Yellowknife that the spring equinox in the third week in March would be fine for the powwow. Having it on the Missouri side of the Rockies would be a wonderful gesture on the part of the tribe.

The day of March came and the twenty-four members of the Corps of Discovery from Fort Mandan prepared to cross the snow topped mountains and walk to the Shoshone Reservation. The Indian tribes lived in different types of homes made of mud and bricks. Covered with tanned skins, each of these structures had an opening facing toward the center of the family living quarters, which allowed the Indians to visit each other; vital in taking care of the old, the young, and the women squaws that were part of the Mandan Tribe.

The chief introduced the captains to the medicine man and the tribal elders. It was a meeting of two cultures and both the captains were impressed with the Shoshone tribal development.

Sergeant Ordway tried to collect the Indian brave's shirts, leggings, and head bands. In the ceremony he pointed to a girl and to himself and took her inside. It was not that unusual an event as to raise any alarm.

The Indian Chief Yellowknife was wearing another headdress decorated by polished opals, sapphires, and other semi-precious stones. Glass beads were used to provide decoration and each had a leather pouch in which personal items could be kept. They had a comb, money belt, and a broken mirror for looking at themselves after they were dressed.

At this stage of the event a hunting party had horse harnesses draped around their waists when they were leaving camp to hunt with their horses. They had western style saddles with the saddle horn sticking up to hold lariats.

That evening two groups formed to entertain. The Lewis and Clark group went first and the Indian tribe followed with a ceremony of a dance in which Indian braves formed a large circle around the campfire used for cooking and a feast and tom-toms pounding a staccato tune and the Indians shouted and sang the tribal songs. These songs celebrated the establishment of the tribe and the wonders of the rivers and forests in the Shoshone Territories.

The two captains soon tired of the powwow and began conversing. The talk centered on how soon the ice would break up. The medicine man drew a sign on the ground that showed ten days.

The dancing, rowdy celebration, and feast lasted through the evening hours. Knowing the territory, the Indian chief suggested at the end of the meeting that a group of braves escort the Corps of Discovery back to its stockade and living area.

Clark told the Indian chief that the celebration and aftermath of dancing and singing had been pleasant and they should meet again before the Missouri became a flowing river again. The Indian chief raised his hand in the salute of friendship and said to disassemble and prepare to return to Fort Mandan and Lewis, who had been talking to the Indian braves asking them questions through the interpreter, George Juilliard, had been able to conduct a conversation to send back to Washington, D.C. The ceremonies being over they exchanged the peace sign and the Indian braves took the corps back to the river's edge and bade them farewell.

Captain Clark turned to Captain Lewis and said, "I will dismiss the men unless you have any further work for them to do."

Captain Lewis paused for a minute and said, "No, I do not have further work that won't wait until the morrow. Goodnight gentlemen and we will return to quarters and prepare for next day's activities."

The two captains retired to their quarters and discussed the day's activities. Captain Clark said, "I think we pulled it off Meriwether. I think we have friends and they will make our spring trip back to civilization much more pleasant and give us some information about fishing in the frozen river and how they catch the trout and catfish that are found there. I have seen them ice fishing along the southern bank of the Missouri and have noticed they have pulled up trout there."

Captain Lewis said, "I will prepare information concerning fishing in the territories of Montana and South Dakota. Not only can we learn fishing techniques, we can call on the Lord to prepare for other activities such as a celebration for the spring equinox."

CHAPTER 49

Off, Off and Away

"**H**OORAY! HOORAY! 'WE ARE OFF, off and away', going home again" chortled Reuben Field to his younger brother Joseph. The two men in their early 20's were more like identical twins than just plain brothers. *The Brothers,* as they were often called, had discovered that they did not have as much in common as each of them thought.

When they joined up Joseph asked Captain Meriwether Lewis, "Are there two spots in your crew? I am a carpenter and my half-brother is a master tinsmith."

Guessing that he grew tobacco Captain Lewis queried, "Your plantation you must be big enough to need both trades. Tell me why your brother is not with you applying for work. Why isn't he with you now?"

Joseph Field looking uncomfortable answered, "Now he and I don't get along so well. He is willing to play house with the Indian squaws and I am loyal to my sweetheart Betsy. He is not loyal to his wife to be. I don't feel that even if he tells me that a lot of his friends play house makes it okay. However, even though Reuben tells me that with him and his wife to be togetherness is not his being totally hers. He has told her so and by doing so it makes it right. I promise working for you, if it be hard and long, we put out the work. We will do the job, honest!"

The eagerness of Field was apparent. Lewis sensed that the two brothers would fill the bill and the corps would benefit if the two had jobs and worked hard filling them.

Captain Lewis thought for a minute and then said to Clark, "Now we, argue now we don't. This won't cut the mustard."

Turning to Field he said, "Bring your brother down for me to talk to and when my partner meets you and we four are together both must tell me 'I want to be on your team Captain Lewis.'"

When Captain Clark was consulted, being the authoritarian he was, he said, "Meriwether, I better not make such a commitment. If I do and others ask to work with us despite their not being compatible it makes for chaos and almost impossible to say 'No' to any such request."

Captain Lewis thought for a moment and said, "William, you might be right, but let's give it a try. Have the two come in for an interview. We have told the two it was okay. How can we as officers and gentlemen now say, 'no way' to the Field brothers?"

Captain Lewis thought a moment and said, "William, if I were in your shoes I would also say, 'No,' but I'll take Joseph at his word."

The Captains knew that the Field brothers might become the best scouts of the expedition. The two men were disappointments, but they were allowed to work one for Lewis' platoon and the other in Clark's platoon. This would satisfy their need for separation and adventure for each of them but also being at the forefront of the corps as scouts.

Alas, this did not turn out to be the case. The two requested that they should become scouts at the head of those sent to explore the wilderness. This request was denied unless it was approved by a vote of the entire group of the twenty-five men. The vote was twenty-three yes with the Fields not voting.

During the six months of 1806 with the brothers as scouts the corps had traveled 1200 miles by pirogue, canoe, keelboat, and walking and the two brothers had been assigned many a scouting duty. The Fields had performed their assignments well. Captain Clark, the expedition leader, wanted flexibility and did want the Fields assigned scouting as permanent duty.

The winter weather had caused them to interrupt the journey. The Field brothers proved to be expert woodsmen during the building of Fort

Mandan and Fort Clatsop in 1804 and 1805. It was a time for reflection. Would the brothers withstand the conflicts caused by the loneliness and being away from home? In truth, the two missed the home fires, their sweethearts, and Kentuckian camaraderie.

CHAPTER 50

Rise and Shine

THE TRAINING PROCESS WAS SET up by Captain Clark for the Corps of Discovery.

The Voyage of Discovery, the President's baby, was his effort to blunt the bad publicity that former President John Adams had raised of his being defeated. The general public wanted to have a strong judiciary independent and chosen by the new president in the 1800 election. John Adams had become the former leader of the country and was a Federalist rather than a Democrat–Republican, as was Jefferson.

The $500,000 was a huge amount of money that President Jefferson had asked Congress for to prove there was a Northwest Passage to connect the two oceans by land. Such an endeavor was expected to require several years to complete. The first year of this expedition was half over and the winter weather was mellowing. The first leg of the Voyage had seen the Missouri river freeze over and several feet of snowfall.

It was April and they were waiting for the Voyage of Discovery to start up the Missouri River again. Several new people had joined the corps replacing those who had died, deserted, or disappeared. The interplay of individuals and/or sergeants would be heard by the two captains sitting as a court for disobeying the captains' orders. There would be punishment by lashing using a bullwhip. Captains' disputes would be voted on by everybody on the craft.

Lewis told Clark, "Let's not wash our dirty linen before the crew."

The results of trying to have discussions by Captain Clark and Lewis was that each felt the other would tell him to go to hell in a hand basket before asking for a vote.

Both were army officers true and true. Both expected complete subservience from his men and would tolerate no breech of duties as he saw them. It would be a conflict of the greatest importance in one life and mean nothing to the other.

Seeing the ominous black clouds ahead, Corporeal Warfington thought to himself, *What more can I expect but trouble? I must steel myself to the fact that when we reach Fort Mandan we will have our first opportunity to meet with the Hidatsu and Mandan tribes.*

He talked this over with the men. He said, "We are making contact with the natives. They look at our coming as an invasion. The captains should be low key. Do not be belligerent. I have been selected to lead the men that have not met the standards of the Corps of Discovery. It is with great sorrow that I was hired on from Fort Wood to be the leader of those men in the corps who were not expected or did not deserve to be with the permanent party as we continue our search for the Northwest Passage."

Warfington turned back to look at the Missouri River as it was passing in front of the Mandan Indian Tribe Reservation. This was in the southern Dakota Sioux area and the Mandan tribe was peaceful and primarily lived on the Missouri and smoked fish for use in the winter months. They had almost exhausted their supply of dried fish and the Mandan braves would be out fishing as well as planting wheat for use in making bread.

The Mandan tribe had learned from the pioneers and fur traders that went up the river that the Northwest Passage did not exist except in the mind of President Jefferson. The president himself felt there was no such thing, but he wanted to continue with the permanent party of privates that would be traveling with the corps. He realized that this conflict of interest meant much to him, but Captain Clark was a military man, the operations man of the Corps of Discovery. He had taken his duties seriously. He had trained all of the men in increments and had made an army platoon for himself as well as for Captain Lewis, his counterpart, taking care of relations with the Indians and the scientific portion wanted by President Jefferson.

He had many observations and every day with Captain Clark had made the sightings of the sun using the astronomical instruments he had practiced in his preparation for this trip. Warfington felt that with his experience he could help Captain Clark and Sergeant Pryor along with Sergeant Gass as to the necessary discipline, which would be a vital cog in this machine put together for this mission.

Pryor, Clark, and Lewis met and after deciding that now was the time to have the men return downriver to St. Louis from whence they came, they would be paid for their time on the river and for each month of duty would receive five dollars.

Thus, the die was cast and Corporal Warfington asked Captain Clark, "When do I take over this party of ten plus the boatman in going back down the river in the keelboat?"

Captain Clark said, "We officers have decided that you are to spend the next three days getting the keelboat ready and the men prepared to make the eight hundred mile trip to the fort we plan to build there. We will have enough men to construct a fort and live on the other side of the river. The river will provide us safety on our flank and the fort will provide us additional safety."

Corporal Warfington said, "I understand that, but I want to know how you want us to proceed down the river. Will I be in complete command?

Captain Clark relied, "Absolutely. You are to see to it that the men man the keelboat and return to the Kansa Tribal Reservation on the way back to St. Louis." He turned to Captain Lewis. "Can you please give further instructions?"

Pryor said, "Sir, may I ask a question?"

"Certainly," said Captain Lewis.

Corporal Warfington then said, "Sir, what are we to take with us of your scientific information and who do I give it to?"

"Details I have collected are to be returned to St. Louis and from there sent to the National Museum in Washington, D.C." Captain Lewis looked Warfington in the eye and told him, "The information that you are taking back represents what we have found out during the past nine months as we have come up the Missouri at a leisurely pace, met the Indian tribes that are found along the Missouri, and told them they are now citizens of the United States. In addition, the scientific information that I have collected will be vital to the country and should be sent immediately from St. Louis to to be delivered to the National Museum. The delivery will end your duties and the men should be paid for the time they have spent on getting as far as Fort Mandan and your return trip, however long it takes. The contract we have met and made is five dollars per month and you are entitled to be paid for your training period when you were trained by Captain Lewis as to the military bearing. You should learn and return the specimens discovered. Here is a packet for your information regarding the route to take and the tribes to contact on your way back to St. Lewis. Any questions?"

Corporal Warfington said, "No sir. If I have I will report them to you."

Captain Clark said that he should review them prior to their leaving. "That is my understanding Sir." Corporal Warfington saluted and turned to the men he was taking with him.

CHAPTER 51

Celebrating of Clark Winning the Great Race

C APTAIN LEWIS REGRETTED THAT CLARK left the Voyage of Discovery at the location of the two rivers merging into the Missouri River. Lewis wanted to have the reminding river called the Missouri, since it was now going down to meet the Mississippi River some 1,200 miles away.

The crowd had reassembled at 12 o'clock, the mayor of St. Louis yelled out "We are here to celebrate the "Voyage of Discovery" in honor of Lewis, Clark, 34 men, and especially Sergeant Floyd who died of unknown causes during the trip. His body lies overlooking the Mississippi River. It is located on top of a mount about 100 miles toward the Canadian border. It has a wonderful view of the prairie surrounding the Missouri River and the path of the expedition."

The mayor continued, "We have 34 of the privates making up the corps with the exception of one Sergeant Floyd. President Jefferson could not make the voyage. The British have been making noises concerning a potential difference facing the two nations. The ceremonies included a speech by Captain Lewis. Lewis turned to face the corps who had assembled by the riverside and had pulled their canoes up on the bank and were standing at attention. Captain Lewis looked around at the crowd, and said, "Here are the 33 privates ready to receive your congratulation and eager to head home. Each of these men are to receive a payment of $30 per month. The corps was

on the road for 2 years 8 months including their training time before they
started in May 1804. In addition, to the $30 the corps was to receive 320
acres of farmland in any of the areas controlled by the United States of
America."

With that the mayor turned to Captain Lewis and said, "I hereby declare
the week of October 1806 a holiday and we will ask the President to get
Congress to approve the national week. The band which was in front of the
crowd where the mayor was speaking started playing the Star Spangled
Banner. The words of this song "O say can you see, in the dawns early light
will forever grace our country." These words were expressed and the band
repeated playing the song as the mayor signaled for the crowd assembled to
sing along. At the end of the bands rendition of the song the mayor said that
this would end the ceremony and the celebration will continue for dinner at
the town square with dancing and revelry to continue until 9 p.m. "Good
afternoon, and see you at the celebration tonight"

The assembled crowd included the Missouri Indian tribe who were
dressed in feathered head dress and deer skin leggings and a beaded head
band with the red, white and blue feathers. The new affair resumed in the
town square at 6 p.m. with the Missouri tribe assembled in their loin cloth,
deer skin leggings with the chief sitting cross legged on the dais and the
medicine man smoking the peace pipe of Virginia grown tobacco. Captain
Lewis had returned to his living courters at the Mayor's home to prepare for
the next weeks celebration.

The Mayor and the three council people met Monday morning at his
home. Lewis ate breakfast having enjoyed a good night's sleep in a bed for
the first time in three years. He did not realize what comfort was until the
down quilt and window blinds made the room dark. Captain Lewis got up
and went for a walk on the dirt streets of St. Louis. The area he surveyed
were truck farms growing vegetables and larger parcels of land growing
wheat, tobacco, and corn all of which had appeared out of the fertile soil and
the plentiful water nearby. Lewis wondered what his co-partner was doing
since Clark had headed to Fargo, North Dakota. Captain Lewis spoke to the
mayor and asked about the farming was being done by the settlers that came
in from the east. He noticed that log cabins were being made in the outskirts
of town. The incoming settlers that came down the Ohio River to occupy the

territory that had been joined to the United States and almost tripled the size of the country.

Captain Lewis thought to himself that Clark should have joined him in this celebration ceremony. But Clark wanted to be discharged from the United States Department of Indian Affairs that was being acquired through settlement from east of the Adirondacks Mountains. The next week Captain Lewis visited the ten most prosperous men in the St. Louis settlement and indicated that he had a concept he had received from Washington D.C. the previous day. He had discussed this correspondence and read it to those people in St. Louis most likely to help in this endeavor.

Lewis had considered the affect that the Voyage of Discovery would have in growing the US into a nation dedicated to expanding the 13 colonies into a coast to coast country that would merit the world interest as to what was happening to the North American continent. This growth from a rinky-dink nation to a potential world power, even President Jefferson had trouble imagining. All this was done by the US purchasing 800,000 square miles of virgin land. The mountain ranges stretched from coast to coast.

CHAPTER 52

The Question before the House

" 'WHERE IS THAT MAN?' THIS was the question being heard loud and clear. It was coming from inside the president's office at the United States Capitol building. The voice was authoritative and demanding. It was the voice of the President of the United States.

Thomas Jefferson was summoning his newly appointed personal secretary. The president needed to hear about progress of Captains Lewis and Clark.

It had been over two years since he had had any information from the Corps of Discovery. As it was, President Jefferson felt his pet project of both his first and second terms in office was being neglected.

Captain Meriwether Lewis' exploratory trip to the Northwest Territories was funded by the United States at the president's bidding. This was a major request, a five-hundred thousand dollar expenditure. It came out of the 1804 federal budget. It was spent and no progress had been reported by Captain Lewis. A progress report would tell the American people.

President Jefferson had but a few weeks left in his first term as president to report to the nation and account for the money provided by Congress to pay Napoleon Bonaparte for the Louisiana Purchase. The treaty had been signed by France, Spain, and England. The money had been paid to France. The U.S. Congress had reluctantly provided the money, but had not received the report of the progress of the expedition. Jefferson wanted to show the world, but especially the American people, that the $15,000,000 had been spent wisely by the fourth Congress of the infant nation. Was President Jefferson a wise man or a fool for funding such a project as the Corps of Discovery?

President Jefferson had sponsored the Louisiana Purchase and President Thomas Jefferson had to show his nation it was a wise purchase. Ex-President John Adams who was beaten by Jefferson was telling the nation, "I told you so. It is Jefferson's Folly."

The Voyage of Discovery was to be undertaken on President Thomas Jefferson's watch. After nearly two years of effort on the part of the president on May 14, 1804, thirty-four Americans calling themselves the Corps of Discovery left St. Charles settlement on the Missouri River to try to reach the Pacific Coast and this Voyage of Discovery would find a land route. It would connect the fur trappers of the Northwestern Territory to the customers of furs in Europe.

President Jefferson's dream would be the life blood of the Midwestern North American settlers who could come from Europe and the orient and become citizens of a new country that was expanding. It was a triangle of three men: the president and two military officers who would squarely face a project that was to become the envy of every nation of the 19th Century.

The Mississippi River to the Pacific Ocean overland looked like a pipe dream. The promised report had been written by Meriwether Lewis and then given to President Jefferson for presentation to Congress.

The election of James Madison as president in November 1808 made Thomas Jefferson happy. Jefferson felt that the Louisiana Purchase made during his presidency was vindicated. Now, the new President Madison would reap the benefits of the three to four years of expansion to the Northwest.

The two captains, Lewis and Clark, knew that centuries thereafter their names would be attached to the journey and of the mystery of the Northwest Territory. The conflict the Corps of Discovery had with the environment and the Indian tribes were to be found in great numbers on both on Missouri River Drainage Basin and from the Bitterroot Mountains.

Captain Lewis said to the newsmen, "It would have been easy for us in the corps to not be involved in three years of searching. We wanted a

Northwest Passage. We could have given up the ghost and given up our hope of finding the direct route the Pacific."

The head reporter said, "I speak for all of us news hounds. You two captains will have satisfied President Jefferson's greatest dream to have a land route from the East Coast of North America to the West Coast if the exploration is successful. Most of us reporters are very skeptical."

President Jefferson had given specific instructions to the two captains to keep the spirits of the men at a fever pitch from start to finish on the way home to St. Louis. If not, any second term would be a failure.

Clark said, "I will tell my men that this race will be the greatest thing since men invented sex. It will stimulate the imagination and the hope of the Corps of Discovery to win the race."

His counterpart Lewis replied, "Having two equal sized groups leave from Camp Fortunate and pass on a different side of the Bitterroot Mountains will show which captain is the better one."

The first of the two to reach the place where the Missouri and the Yellowstone rivers join would be declared the winner. It was an idea that appealed to both Captain Lewis and Captain Clark. They decided that starting from Camp Fortunate they would proceed with one group run by Clark to go through what they called Yellowstone and investigate and report to the president its wonders.

Captain Lewis on the other hand had a different target in mind. He wanted to go north up the Marias River Gorge and reach the Canadian border at the 54th Parallel. His platoon was to secure general information regarding the Blackfeet Indians in that area and join the Boise tribe. Doing this would allow the captain to influence both to join the United States of America.

CHAPTER 53

Returning to the Virgin Territory

CAPTAIN LEWIS JUMPED OUT OF bed the next morning. Lewis had received direction from Jefferson summoning him to make a report to the Congress, the peoples of the United States of America, and those native Indians that occupy the land purchased from France. Lewis had the feeling the President wanted to be involved with making the Louisiana Purchase worth all the time, effort, and money he had provided the two Captains. President Jefferson had received word from Clark that he wished to be discharged from the armed forces of the United States of America and proceed to form the American Fur Trading Company.

Captain Lewis was very excited when he received the notice that the American Philosophical Society had invited him to become a member of the organization of 100 citizens of United States. Their primary interest was to see how and when to continue growing this infant nation. They advised the President and Congress to induct the Captain into the Society.

This notice from the American Philosophical Society caused Lewis to direct his activities to making the purchase of the land north of the Mississippi River, from St. Louis to the Canadian border and from the Mississippi River west to the Pacific Ocean. As a condition of making a valid claim of territory the territory so purchased must be occupied and settled by the country making the purchase and a treaty of the major nation involved in the transaction. The purchase of the area called the Louisiana Purchase was acquired by the payment of 15 million dollars offered in gold bullion by the US. However, the treaty must be drawn up by the major powers in Europe, namely Germany, Italy, France and Great Britain. This treaty was signed by those nations during 1802 but by the time the purchase price was paid and became signatory of the document.

It was at this point that President Jefferson conceived the idea of the Voyage of Discovery and the confirmation of the Northwest Territory. The seller was the empire of France and Napoleon Bonaparte.

France and its Emperor Napoleon had no claim to any territory from the Pacific to Atlantic Ocean. The Northwest Territory represented France's interests in the North American continent.

President Jefferson summoned Lewis and upon reaching the capital all the requirements of the treaty had been met except the development of the territory thru its occupation. Jefferson greeted Lewis at the White House indicating his joy with Lewis having acquired the Northwest Territory. The President wanted to have Congress including the speakers of both institutions meet the new President of the American Fur Trading Company that Jefferson was planning to sponsor. President Jefferson proclaimed a national holiday to be set aside for this new expansion. Jefferson was pleased that Congress confirmed his plan and that the date of confirmation should be July 1, 1803. This was the preliminary of the Voyage of Discovery and the acquisition of the Northwest Territories. The Pony Express carried the news to Philadelphia, St. Louis Missouri Territory, and Indian tribes located in the area purchased. The news was delayed and the date altered to be the 4th of July 1803. Church bells rang throughout the land and though the people did not know how mammoth the purchase was the President did. The US would be one of the most important nations.

Captain Lewis was asked to become the President of the American Fur Trading Company. It would be established as a private enterprise. During this period the President asked Lewis to notify the tribes along the Missouri River that all fur trading in the Northwest would be thru an agency private but under the international law and said purchases and delivery would be thru a firm to be established by the end of 1804.

Hearing this Lewis started his journey up the Missouri and went as far east as the city of Fargo, North Dakota Territory where his ex-co-captain was living. Lewis, President of the American Fur Trading Co., went to Fargo to meet with two gentlemen, one of which was Mr. Clark. Clark and Mr. Wells had formed a new organization, which was to supervise all fur trading activities in the Northwest Territory. This accomplishment by Clark "fait accompli." There was one factor that was over looked and all three members of the American Fur Trading operation were shocked to find that the Indian tribes that were trapping beaver, deer, and bear to make items to be sold throughout the world was not to be. The American Indian tribal chiefs extending from St. Louis down the Missouri up the Colombia said "No way." The United States of America while controlling the territory was not to be approved by the American Indian tribes. The Indians wanted to deal with the individual trappers and not have the federal government interfere with the trade.

CHAPTER 54

Going Down the River

G OVERNOR LEWIS REFLECTED ABOUT HIS life and what was going to happen to the balance of it. The point of return had been reached. It was now or never. The past three years had gone from bad to worse--from his last week in September of 1806 to the first quarter of 1807. The day the United States sought its expedition to find the Northwest Passage come to prove that there was a route from Washington, D.C. to the Pacific with the last barrier being the Rocky Mountains that must be crossed on route to the Pacific.

President Jefferson was told how Captain Clark had been lucky in looking to the heavens and then to the ocean as he shouted, "Oh, the joy!"

Captain Lewis was awakened by the sound of horses hooves and he looked up and saw the Blackfeet Indian raiding party start to unhobble the horses and were about to steal them back.

With great care, Captain Lewis aimed his gun at the shadowy figure silhouetted by the fire and a shot ran out. The startled horses were still hobbled and whined. The Indian that had been stealing them slumped to the ground and one of his party jumped off his pony, picked up the dead Indian, threw him over the horse, and started the group racing back from whence they came.

Captain Lewis raised the other members of corps, gathered them around him, and said, "Now we've done it. We've killed a Blackfoot and they will bring a raiding party back to scalp all of us. Get your horses and let's head back down the Marias River to the Missouri and run for home."

Sergeant Hardway said, "That's a great plan and I'm all for it. The Indians will be back. Let's get going."

The group headed down the Marias going much faster than they should because of the twisting and turning of the path and the many rocks that were on it. From then on it was, *get going and God speed.* They went down to the Marias in less than a day and a half and camped there while they made plans to continue.

Sergeant Pryor came to Captain Lewis and said, "We should stop at all the Indian tribes that are on the Missouri and follow President Jefferson's orders to make them citizens of the United States."

Captain Lewis replied, "I'm aware that we have this job to do on our way to the junction, but we should do it in an orderly fashion rather than starting helter-skelter and follow the president's command."

They started down the Missouri stopping at the first Indian tribe, the Oto tribe, and met with Chief Yellow Finger and proceeded to make the president's demand a reality.

Chief Yellow Finger was sworn in with the statement, "You are now members of a great country, the United States of America, and are expected to follow the orders of the Great White Father."

Having done this, Captain Lewis said, "Let's go men!" and proceeded to follow the Missouri. At each tribal reservation along the Missouri the same routine was followed by Captain Lewis and his corps.

The rest of the journey was relatively simple and it was at the Great Falls Junction that Captain Lewis dismounted and said to the men, "We have to portage by foot around the Great Falls. It will take us at least a day and a half to do this. Be careful, if your horse falls down and breaks his leg we will have to shoot him and you will be on foot the rest of the way until the junction point."

Captain Lewis turned around and heard a shot and saw a smoking gun as he felt a searing pain on his rear. He felt around his back and brought back a bloody hand and realized he'd been shot by one of his men that turned out to have been Private Shannon, who had mistaken him for a bear and thought he was protecting the captain.

The corps gathered around Captain Lewis and Lewis recovered from falling to the ground. "I'm bleeding but that is what I need to do, to get any of the germs out of my system."

Sergeant Pryor proceeded to load Captain Lewis on his horse laying across the saddle and expecting Captain Lewis to recover his senses as they continued down the Missouri toward the junction.

Captain Lewis recovered his senses the following morning and said, "It looks like I will be incapacitated for the balance of our trip down to St. Louis. Sergeant Pryor, you will be in charge. Sergeant Ordway, you will follow up the rear and see that we are not ambushed as we travel."

Captain Lewis had a miserable time going down the Missouri until they reached the Yellowstone Junction and he met with Captain Clark and said to Captain Clark, "I've done it to the corps. Why don't you leave me here and I will catch up as best I can."

Captain Clark said, "Don't be silly. You would be bear meat in less than an hour. Let us keep going down the river. I won the Great Race and when we stop again I will tell you what my plans are to get back to St. Louis."

That evening the corps gathered around the campfire and heard Captain Clark say, "You men should follow Captain Lewis' and the two sergeants' instructions to the letter. You should continue down the river, and I will head back to the North and meet with the Sioux and become their agent for their negotiations with the Corps of Discovery and the United States Government. I intend to ask the president to make me Indian Agent for the new Northwest Territory as I am interested in this duty."

That ended Captain Clark being a member of the Corps of Discovery and its co-captain. Captain Lewis brought Sergeant Ordway to him as he was resting on the ground for the night. He said, "Sergeant Ordway, I feel that you should be the leader while I am recovering. I should be treated as the privates are being treated, no better, no worse, and this is an order."

This was the way the day went every day for the next three weeks going down the Missouri. At each stop along the way the settlers would gather around and hear Captain Lewis tell them of the adventure of the century and that they were now American citizens that the Federal Government would be sending parties up the Missouri to settle as they had settled and get to the Pacific Ocean if they wanted as it was now part of the United States.

CHAPTER 55

Lewis, Governor Louisiana Territory , January 1, 1807– end of 1807

"**H**APPY NEW YEAR AND GREAT work Governor Lewis! You have set a new standard of performance under fire."

Captain Lewis, now governor of the Louisiana Territory, was still bothered by the shot in his ass he received from his own man by mistake. He could sit down tenderly and realized it would still be a while before he was back to normal. He was in front of the government headquarters in St. Lewis and the crowd that stood around as he made his New Year's speech was enthusiastic and very interested in hearing what the governor had to say.

Governor Lewis said, "This event in my life climaxes what thirty years took to create, a man with a mission. I am a servant of the United States Government and its people and will govern the Louisiana Territory to the best of my ability, I hereby accept this honor and privilege."

Governor Lewis turned to face the President of the Senate and the leader of the House of Representatives. He said, "I will be able to get my cabinet together and we will beware of the English and the French, both of which are getting ready to fight for their interest in the North American Continent and we oppose them directly."

It was a case of a new government expanding its opportunities in an area that he controlled. Captain Clark had not yet received his appointment as a colonel and as the head of the organization of the Indian tribes west of the Mississippi. He would be stationed in Sioux City and would make various trips up the Missouri to visit the tribes, telling them that the President of the United States had appointed him as Indian Agent to represent a conduit from the Indian chiefs and their tribes to the President of the United States, the Great White Father in Washington, D.C.

After so accepting this he got in touch with Governor Lewis and told him of his new career as an Indian Agent for the entire United States and specifically of the new Northwest Territory who would deal with the Federal Government in Washington, D.C., representing the Indians of the country and their Indian tribes and chiefs. This appointment was received gratefully by the new Indian Agent, Colonel Clark, and had been acknowledged by the House of Representatives and the United States Senate as well as the president.

The Governor of the Louisiana Territory left Washington, D.C. and headed for the Louisiana Territory and St. Louis, its capital, and proceeded to set up his government. As he saw it, he realized he would be traveling to the far reaches of the territory and looked forward to that. He realized that at thirty-three he was going to have his hands full in getting the government of the Louisiana Territory set up and running. He also planned to go up the Missouri River retracing at least the first leg of his trip to the Mandan Reservation and the fort that had been built. He felt that this three-step process of getting set up in St. Louis and getting their settlement of the territory involved as Clark's Indian Agent philosophy would be wonderful and helpful, not only to the Federal Government and President Jefferson, but also to the Indian tribes that would be involved.

Each one of these spots along the Missouri River could have a fort built and have a contingent of American troops represent the Federal Government as best they could and keep the peace.

This was pretty much his goal during 1807. He proceeded to travel up the Missouri and contact various Indian tribes as well as the settlers and promoted his idea of governance while the territories became states when they became large enough to support such a government. It would be the pinnacle of his career if he did this because he wanted to establish a fur trading organization which would take all the furs that were trapped in the Missouri Territory and get them assembled at a meeting point in the territory. They would be sent down the Columbia River to Pastoria, a shipping point to both receive the goods and services from the Orient and also provide the Orient with the vital product that could be processed by them to fur pelts of the deer and the otter and the beaver. This was his dream and represented his major desire during his tenure as the Governor of the Louisiana Territory.

Governor Lewis proceeded with his plan and attempted to organize the settlements, but found that the reason the settlers had moved was to get away from such government interference and establish their own homesteads on the Missouri River so that they would not have anything but their own homestead and perhaps a fort that would be built under their control and not that of the Federal Government.

This was a wild-eyed idea, but it proved to be a stopper of the fur trading organization that Governor Meriwether Lewis wanted to establish and have a fur trading empire located in the United States where the supply was available and where the fur traders could get their product to market as well as purchase product from the trappers. A wild-eyed dream and the beginning of a worldwide operation centered in the United States of America and its territories.

Disappointed, Governor Lewis was willing to give it one more year as long as Jefferson was president and he had contacts in Washington, D.C. that could be so powerful that it would be unstoppable. Thus, the division of organization would be available but on a local basis rather than on the North American wide basis that President Jefferson wanted to have established during his term in office.

Governor Lewis said to himself, *I will give it one more year and will do my best to contact the various elements of this worldwide organization including the suppliers as well as those who needed the fur hides. The hides would be shipped from the mouth of the Columbia River to the Orient and from the Orient back to the United States and its headquarters wherever it might be established either on the West Coast or in St. Louis, which would be centralized as far as the North American Continent was involved.*

It was a case of who controlled the operation as well as where it would be controlled from and it would be conflict between the suppliers and the users and between the Federal Government and the settlers along the Missouri Columbia Corridor.

CHAPTER 56

Mandan, a Home Away from Home

IT WAS THE SECOND YEAR of the exploration. The year 1805 started with the boom of the cannon of the Voyager. The two captains had decided to celebrate the week from December 25th to January 1st by giving the corps a break. This effort would pit the winter snows against Captain Clark's skills of protecting his men in the wilderness.

The two captains celebrated by having a roast deer dinner shot by Jean Batiste Le Page, a private who had been apprenticed to a gunsmith while in his native state of Virginia. It was a joyous time and rum was distributed as a special Christmas treat. It was hot and buttered and tickled the palates of the twenty-five privates who were incarcerated by the winter weather. The prison being Fort Mandan, which had taken two months to build and had sleeping quarters for Captain Lewis and Captain Clark to meet and plan the future operations, especially for the next day.

Captain Lewis said, "Happy New Year, Meriwether."

Captain Clark said, "Same to you Lewis."

The problem that Captain Lewis saw was getting on with the trip to the Pacific Ocean—if there was a passage up the Missouri. The mission was clear. The first leg up the Missouri River from St. Louis had been reached by the 1st of November. The ensuing two months had resulted in the meadow in which the Corps of Discovery was living and had the forest gave up its logs so that a stockade could be built to protect the corps from the weather and specifically the Indian tribes, which were found from St. Louis to Mandan customs and culture in force and most of which had never seen a white man in the tribal area.

Meriwether Lewis had pledged as his New Year's resolution to do a wonderful job as co-captain. He was in charge of interfacing with Indian tribes and recording their activities. He also needed to gather specific information about weather conditions, the land they traversed along the Missouri, mineral specimens, and other environmental characteristics.

The locations were shot using the Adelaide—the air temperature, and the readings taken by both he and Captain Clark to whom the instruments shooting the sun and interviewing any of the Indian chiefs or braves that were available on the date involved. January 1st was celebrated by a dance and dinner with the Mandan Indians across the Missouri.

The two captains, Lewis and Clark, had made as their New Year's resolution the goal of reaching the Pacific Ocean or determining there was no such Northwest Passage and to take such information back to Washington, D.C. It was still an exploration that had completed the indoctrination and notification of the Indian tribes found along the Missouri, meeting their chiefs and notifying them that they were now citizens as of the United States of America.

Lewis was clever enough to realize that the social structure of the tribe was composed of a chief, his medicine man, advisor, the use of men of adult age, the squaws of adult age, and the children from fourteen down to papooses on the backs of the squaws. The tribal structure was so different than that of the corps that Captain Lewis spent a great deal of time interfacing with Chief Littlefoot of the Crow tribe which was located twenty miles above the Platt River from the south banks of the Missouri.

The Mandan tribe was three miles south of the Missouri and was within walking distance, but the tribe had snowshoes available and Captain Clark wanted to have those available for use by the Corps of Discovery. The snows of late December impeded any outside activity of the men with the exception of taking a walk to relieve themselves. The pit that had been dug at the beginning of the construction of Fort Mandan had taken two months to build and had taken the efforts of all the five privates that the corps contained.

Captain Clark had two sergeants, Patrick Gass and George Juilliard, who was also an interpreter. Captain Clark had later found out that Julliard's last name was Shannon and had been wrongly entered into the corps' personnel directory of privates.

The other members of the corps were under the control of Captain Meriwether Lewis. They consisted of twelve men, Sergeant John Ordway, and his co-equal Nathaniel Pryor. The men assisted Captain Lewis in getting the technical information regarding the territory and collecting specimens to return to the National Museum in Washington, D.C. at the end of the trip.

January 1, 1805, was celebrated by the Mandan Indian tribe who lived across the Missouri and were peaceful but very interested in seeing what the Corps of Discovery was doing at the fort. The twenty-five members of the Mandan tribe came across the frozen Missouri on horseback, tied up, entered the compound of the fort, and met with Captain Clark and Captain Lewis in a powwow celebration.

This meeting of the two groups was an event that Captain Lewis recorded in his memoirs. He wrote: *The Mandan Indians were peaceful, knowledgeable in the way of living in the Northwestern Territory near the Missouri River. Their homes are made of mud and straw contrary to the normal Indian teepee. The bricks of dried mud and straw were piled upon one another by the Indian braves to a height of five feet and then covered by leather deerskins. These skins were tanned and formed a tent like opening cover for the living quarters for the tribal families. The braves were warriors from young to old.* Lewis estimated the size of the tribe as being several hundred.

CHAPTER 57

After The Ball Was Over

T HE EXCITEMENT OF THE RETURN of the Corps of Discovery to Kansas and Missouri was palpable. The Missouri River had never looked as good to two captains, Clark and Lewis. They had spent the past month going down the Missouri from Holloway and Boise, Idaho over the Bitterroot Range. The Great Race, which Captain Clark had won but had given up his prize in naming the Corps of Discovery. The Voyage of Discovery was now Captain Lewis' treasure.

The celebration in St. Louis lasted some ten days from the end of September past the first week in October. It was a whirl of parties meeting dignitaries. They were there to explain the meaning of the Lewis and Clark Expedition to President Jefferson and to the United States.

Jefferson was overjoyed when he heard the news that the expedition that had left in May of 1804 had found a route to the Pacific but had not found a way that it could be done at sea level as the Rocky Mountain Range stood in its way.

However, Captain Lewis and Captain Clark realized that half a loaf was better than none and after waiting for the ice and snow to subside in the Bitterroot Mountain Range they had decided to stimulate the interest by having the Great Race of the Corps of Discovery. Platoon A, which was Clark's platoon, left from Camp Fortunate going south and east through Yellowstone National Park and the pillar which Clark named Pompeii and the wonders of the park itself leading to the juncture of the Yellowstone River and the Missouri Rivers.

Captain Lewis on the other hand, took the eastern route down the Missouri up Marias Branch, struggled over the riverbed that went up to 9,000 feet and came out in northern Oregon territory, and crossed over the Canada border. It was there that Captain Lewis had killed two of the Blackfoot braves and caused him to head for the meeting where the race would be over and Captain Clark or Captain Lewis would be declared the winner.

It was an exciting time. The Blackfoot tribe had sent a raiding party after the horses and pack train that Captain Lewis had created to go to the 54th Parallel, the border of Canada and the United States. Captain Lewis had awakened and shot two of the Indian braves having a raiding party to return to its base in eastern Washington State and Northern Idaho along the Missouri. This caused a change in plans and Captain Lewis went down the Missouri River into the State of Montana. He was able to see the wonders of the Missouri and meet with the Indian tribes, their chiefs, and locations. This was vital essentially. It was to enlist the new Indian tribes, their chiefs, and their warriors into the United States of America now proving the Northwest Territory.

Captain Lewis had agreed that the terms of the Great Race, which represented a challenge between the two captains. Each selected men and hastened to return to St. Louis, Missouri as quickly as they could.

Captain Lewis, having killed two of the Indian warriors of the Blackfoot tribe, hastened his descent of the northern fork of the Missouri through the Bitterroot Mountains and he made a presentation of the President's Medal of Discovery that President Jefferson had given to the corps and its two captains to present to the tribes found along the Missouri River.

The juncture of this Great Race was where the Yellowstone River and Captain Clark's contingent would meet. Captain Lewis had the Missouri Juncture some five hundred miles to the east. It was a noble challenge and Captain Lewis realized that he wanted to have his name attached to the Corps of Discovery's voyage to the Pacific Ocean and return.

As the expedition went ahead Captain Clark had gone through the Yellowstone and its lakes, waterfalls, animals, and Indian tribes that inhabited the area.

The Teton Mountains towering to twelve thousand five hundred feet were part of the area in the Yellowstone River. On the other hand, the Indian tribes around the Missouri River were important to say the least and required Captain Lewis' utmost skill in the negotiations to get each of the chiefs as shown on the map.

These tribes were wild and woolly. Braves and squaws were always afraid of being attacked by competing tribes and then kidnapped for sale into the slave market. All Indian tribes were involved in trapping furs and existing nomadically in the territories of Montana, Wyoming, and Idaho.

Captain Lewis and Sergeant Pryor were well aware of the fur trading opportunities this tribe had that distributing such furs to be processed in the Orient after going down the Columbia River Basin would be very valuable and make the Indian tribe more important than they ever were before.

The Blackfoot tribe with its Chief Thundercloud was not one of Captain Lewis' favorites as they proceeded down the Missouri River. It was during this juncture that Captain Lewis was shot by one of the men. They never found out who shot him by mistake and he was incapacitated during the continuing race down the Missouri.

CHAPTER 58

Meriwether Lewis has just come up the Missouri into the Northwest Territory

DOWN THE RIVER TO NEW ORLEANS was the intent of Meriwether Lewis, the new Governor of the Northwest Territories secured by the Louisiana Purchase. It was a welcome crowd that met Governor Lewis in New Orleans and the first person to greet him was Francoise Diderot, fur trader and acquaintance of Governor Lewis. He was greeted with a big smile, a wave of the hand, and the words "Hello Stranger. I hardly recognized you. You're dressed in finery that belies your position as the Governor appointee of President Jefferson."

It was the intent of Governor Lewis to visit the pearl of the Louisiana Territory, New Orleans, and its Basin Street—the quarter of shops and restaurants surrounding the center of the settlement, which had housed the French settlers since the territory purchased by the United States was a French Colony and had the same amenities as Paris, France, some three thousand miles away.

Governor Lewis smiled and said, "Francoise, I hardly recognized you in your finery too. You have the look of the Paris French dandies and it will be of great interest to me after I find lodgings to have dinner with you at Antoine's Restaurant on Basin Street and see the nightlife that you let me know about in correspondence we had a year ago. I have come a long way since our conversations and meetings before I returned to St. Louis and the Governor's home. I am looking forward to organizing the fur trading company and will see you this evening for dinner so that we can exchange information about what we expect to do next."

It was with a little surprise that Meriwether Lewis, Governor, was quite interested in meeting with Diderot again. He had several meetings with him up the Missouri during the last year and expected to have good conversation of joint interests that evening.

Promptly at nine p.m. Governor Lewis went to Antoine's by carriage and was greeted at the door by the owner of the restaurant along with his manager, chef, and other retinue who were assembled at the door. Francoise Diderot helped Governor Lewis get out of the carriage and the two walked over to the owner of Antoine's where he was introduced by Francoise Diderot to Governor Lewis.

After having a seven course dinner the likes of which Governor Lewis had never experienced before with service and food presented in the main dining room in a special area reserved for famous people that frequented this well-known restaurant in the Louisiana Territory.

The seven course meal took several hours to present and eat as allowed. The talk was about the past year and a half. Francoise Diderot led the conversation. The interest of the governor was to see what the crown jewel city of the territory he was governing was like and to make a needed contact with the city government and former French location.

The candles burnt low by midnight and Francoise Diderot said, "Let us see Governor Meriwether what the nightlife is like on Basin Street. The many restaurants and cabarets do not close until sun up. We should have a great time together, meet some interesting people, and get you familiar with the French ways of entertaining."

Meriwether Lewis answered, "I'm with you Francoise. Let us depart."

He thanked the manager of Antoine's who said as they left, "It's been a pleasure, Governor. There is no tab for dinner. Come back and visit us again when you return to New Orleans."

The two men, Diderot and Meriwether, walked to the center of Basin Street. They stopped at every cabaret along the way for champagne and cognac. By the time they reached a burlesque show in the center of town the two men were having a tremendous evening.

The girls came over and were introduced by the owner to Lewis and Diderot. "This is my friend and I wish you to show us your gambling casino in the rear and your entertainers upstairs."

Governor Lewis said, "Bonsoir," the only French he knew and then followed Diderot and the owner upstairs where there were roulette tables with the usual hostesses by their side. The men were introduced to those who frequented the premises—girls of ill repute and various gays, who they called fairies. It was a wild time and Governor Lewis was approached by several of the entertainers with a wink and a smile.

He returned to Francoise Diderot and said, "What am I supposed to do? In my capacity as Governor of Louisiana I must be careful of contacts that I make because word could leak out and my reputation as a philanderer other than a government official will become known throughout New Orleans and hence throughout the territory."

Francoise Diderot winked and said, "We will make it discreet. I will take you to a private room where entertainers will join you."

And so it went. They retired to a private room, which was lavishly decorated and had a bed fit for a king at the center and a small dance area where the entertainers could perform. The manager of the dance hall excused himself and the owner of the establishment and Francoise Diderot also left saying, "We have business to take care of. Enjoy yourself Meriwether with Robert and Nancee."

As they left Nancee kicked Diderot and the owner retired. Meriwether Lewis was nonplused. He had had various sexual experiences while on the Voyage of Discovery up the Mississippi/Missouri halfway to the Pacific at the various Indian Reservations during the year and a half he had been gone, but he was uncomfortable with this new situation that had developed. He did not realize that Francoise Diderot was gay and had formed an alliance with the owner of the cabaret. Robert and Nancee proceeded to dance together and the music from downstairs could be heard. The room was filled with candles and their flickering. It started to become mesmerizing to Governor Lewis.

CHAPTER 59

Governor's Last Visit with President Thomas Jefferson

G RINDER'S INN WAS A REST stop for travelers in New Orleans who came from various cities on the Natchez Trace, a path that extended from New Orleans to the capitol of the United States where the central government of the young country operated. Governor Lewis addressed the host of the Inn, "I am Governor Lewis and am on my way to Washington, D.C. to meet with the president. Do you have a resting place for me and my horses?"

Mrs. Grinder said, "I am the wife of the owner of this establishment. Our rooms are available to somebody of your eminence. I am Nancee and will have our slave prepare for your visit here. How many days will you be here Governor Lewis?"

Meriwether Lewis said, "Since I am traveling alone I will be here one day and proceed on my way as I have been summoned by the president for an important meeting."

He signed the register and went into the dining area of the inn, which was an L shaped log cabin with two wings perpendicular to each other. One housed the host and hostess of the inn, the kitchen, and the dining area, which also served as a place where the travelers could smoke tobacco and talk with each other.

There were three other guests at Grinders Inn and they were introduced before dinner at cocktail hour where each of the guests told of their purpose for staying there and what news and travels they had while staying there. One of them, a young man dressed in the travel clothes of the day, said that he was on his way to New Orleans to meet his prospective bride and that they were to be introduced by a mutual friend. It would be his first meeting with the young lady who was several years his junior and if they got along they would be married immediately so that he could return to the tobacco plantation owned by his family where he would be working the rest of his life.

The second guest said that he was on vacation from New Orleans and that since it was autumn in the year of 1809 he wanted to see the turning of the leaves of the maple trees, which was supposed to be exquisite during the fall. He had heard from other travelers that the beauty of the eastern Adirondacks was apparent. Maple trees, box elder trees, and sycamore trees were to be seen along the way and that he would continue on to Washington, D.C. on personal business with the United States Government. He was a salesman for a clothing firm.

Governor Lewis interrupted, "I am going outside to feed my dog, Seaman. I can't be with you anymore at this time as after he is fed I will bed down at the inn since Mrs. Grinder was so gracious to give me a room for myself and my dog. I bid each gentleman goodnight and will see you tomorrow morning before I leave for Washington, D.C."

The two guests and Mrs. Grinder said, "Goodnight Governor Lewis. Have a pleasant sleep. If you wish, we will take care of your dog in the main building."

Governor Lewis said, "That won't be necessary. You have been very kind to me and I would like to pay my bill tonight so that I can leave anytime in the morning."

With that Governor Lewis paid the bill presented to him and took Seaman and proceeded to the cabin next door. There he had a bed, a fire that was burning, and all the amenities of such a traveler's rest. For the rest of the evening Governor Lewis planned what he would say to the president when he met with him the following week. Governor Lewis felt that his friend, neighbor, and the president would chastise him for not following through on the trip he had made exploring the Missouri River Basin and the connection to the Pacific. He had made notes of what he would say and of course, had taken his diaries with him having recorded what events took place each day of the almost three years.

He had been dilatory in making such use on his part including specimens he had collected, his diary in which all the activities, both of his and those reported by Captain William Clark, his co-leader, and what he felt the benefits were to the United States of America. This outline had been prepared mentally for the past two years though Governor Lewis had not gotten around to preparing the specimens and cleaning up the draft of the three year exploration.

He noted the most important efforts were that they had survived two winters on the trip, met with over thirty Indian tribes, and inducted the tribe members as citizens of the United States.

The preparation for his potential meeting with President Jefferson was time consuming and it was well over twelve o'clock before he finished making copious notes. He got up and started pacing his room and speaking aloud as if he were talking to the president from the notes he had made. He had taken and made use of the bathroom facility outside the area, stopped by and awakened Mrs. Grinder, and said that he was going to bed and that he would be talking about a meeting with the president and practicing aloud what he would say to imaginary questions asked by Thomas Jefferson. He had to have a bottle of cognac and wanted to see if she had any tobacco available so he could have a cheroot before he went to bed.

Mrs. Grinder proceeded to get what Governor Lewis wanted, writing it down in the register. "Do you want to pay me for this now or upon leaving early tomorrow morning?"

Governor Lewis said, "I'll pay for it now so that I can leave as early as I want provided the stable is open so I can have your man get my horses ready for travel."

Mrs. Grinder said goodnight to the Governor, "I'll do that right away," and accepted his money.

Then Governor Lewis returned to his room, locked the door, and prepared for bed. He started pacing the room, presenting his case to the imagined President of the United States. His voice cracked from the excitement he expected upon his arrival in Washington, D.C. He realized that he should do this several times at the end of each day so that he would be prepared to for any questions he was sure that President Jefferson would ask. He wanted to be ready for any contingency.

Thus, the evening of October 10, 1809, was coming to an end. The locked door provided the security that Governor Lewis expected. He wanted to continue his practice. As his candle burned low he went to his bed to get several of hours sleep before continuing by horseback up the Natchez Trace and toward Washington, D.C.

Around three-thirty in the morning, Mrs. Grinder heard a loud discussion in Governor Lewis's quarters and knocked on the door. "Governor Lewis, you're disturbing our guests and you must be quiet. It is very late and everyone wants to leave early."

Hearing a mumble and finding the loud discussion discontinued, Mrs. Grinder went back to the café quarters where she lived with her husband. Quiet resumed and such was the case until six o'clock in the morning.

Governor Lewis had not yet arisen, and Mrs. Grinder knocked on the door. "Governor, it is six o'clock. You said you wanted to have an early departure. I have made you breakfast; it is warm and waiting for you."

She heard no response and knocked on the door again and feeling that the Governor would awaken and that she had done her bidding, went back to her quarters in the café sleeping area. At ten o'clock in the morning, she looked in the stable and saw that Governor Lewis' two horses were saddled and still in the stable.

The stable boy said that he had saddled the horses as Governor Lewis had told him and that he would be leaving at dawn. Mrs. Grinder noticed that the door to Governor Lewis' room was still locked and had the stable boy climb in through a window.

The messenger came from President Jefferson who was about to be turned out of office through the inauguration of James Madison. It was sent from Washington, D.C. to St. Louis in the Missouri Territory, not yet a state, to Governor Meriwether Lewis from Thomas Jefferson himself. The message that was given was,

My Dear Meriwether Lewis, Governor of the Louisiana Purchase Territory as well as the Northwest Territory,

The information I have received from you Meriwether has been very little and too late. As you know, I am being displaced by the Inauguration of

James Madison and he will be taking office on March 4, 1809. You have been a faithful servant to me and have performed an expedition along with Captain William Clark. This exploration confirmed that a path to the Pacific Ocean from anywhere in the United States was possible overland but not at sea level and would require a traversing of the Lolo Pass in the Idaho Reservation Territory.

You have been exemplary in maintaining the records of the trip and with Captain, now Indian Agent, William Clark, secured our Northwest Territory and connected an eastern and western portions of the North American Continent. Congratulations, and may you enjoy your retirement from service. I have nothing left to do during my term in office. As president, I will not be past president, Thomas Jefferson, the third President of the United States.

President Thomas Jefferson
United States President of America

This message upset Meriwether Lewis who was now ex-governor of the new territory. He expected to go to Washington, D.C. to meet with the president to receive the highest award of the land. He had to be there before March of the previous year, but was unable to make that commitment because of his attempt to set up a fur trading firm. The firm would encompass the entire United States and provide pelts directly to China for processing and then be returned to the United States and the West coast to be shipped to the users of the furs who made bear skin rugs and lady's fur coats as well as gentlemen's fur hats.

It was a major step in the growth of the United States of America because it shortened the time it took to get the trapping of pelts from the Northwest to manufacturers in the Orient and hence to the European and North American markets.

Meriwether Lewis felt that President Jefferson had committed the ultimate slur of his presidency on the efforts of Governor Lewis to make use of the information and quelling of the insurrection of the new territories purchased from France. The inference was that Captain Meriwether Lewis had not followed through and made Jefferson's dream a reality. As a result Governor Lewis ignored the president's dismissal and decided to return to Washington, D.C. as quickly as he could and become the governor of the

new states of Missouri and Louisiana when they were confirmed by the
action of the Congress of the United States and the signature of the still
president, Thomas Jefferson.

Gathering his paperwork and the treaties made with the Indians and the
relics that had been collected during the three year Voyage of Discovery,
Meriwether Lewis went down to the wharf at St. Louis and booked passage
to Washington, D.C. via the Mississippi River to the Caribbean Sea, across
and around the Florida peninsula, up the east coast to the Delaware River,
up the Delaware, and into Washington, D.C.

The passage was booked, but it was to be on a boat going down the
Missouri, stopping one day in New Orleans for passing out the mouth of the
Mississippi and on its way to Washington, D.C.

Meriwether Lewis got on the pirogue that was available and that he had
booked and started down toward the New Orleans port on the river. As he
proceeded down the river Governor Lewis waved at the settlers on the
riverbank and proceeded to enter his cabin and await the end of the two day
trip to New Orleans. Meriwether Lewis did not sleep well that night and got
up at twelve bells to talk to the captain and wait for the dawn. At a little after
nine o'clock in the morning Captain and now Governor Lewis just watched
as the pirogue stopped in New Orleans. He left the canoe to see his friend
and previous fur trader that he had met a number of times during the Voyage
of Discovery.

They had become extremely close and had had sex with each other at
their last meeting. Two men discussed their relationship as well as what
Governor Meriwether Lewis' trip to Washington, D.C. to see President
Jefferson might bring. It was a deep and thorough discussion for the purpose
of Governor Lewis' trip to Washington, D.C. and his meeting with the
president about his being inadequate in performing his function of governing
the Louisiana Purchase Territories, the Northwest Territories of the Indian
tribes to the Pacific Ocean.

This discussion took various pathways. The first that Governor Lewis
said that the relationship between the two men was finished and that he was
no longer interested in a close relationship involving sex. Such activity was
frowned on in all the other areas except New Orleans, which had a French
background and in which homosexual relationships between two loving men
was condoned and in Paris, even promoted in the Louis IV Court. The morals

of the French Quarter were condoned and even promoted by French citizens in New Orleans and Governor Lewis stayed up the night at Antoine's restaurant leaving at six in the morning to continue his voyage to Washington, D.C.

As the pirogue that Governor Lewis had engaged went to the mouth of the Mississippi River the owner of the pirogue looked off to the Caribbean and saw a British frigate, Man of War, offshore to patrol the coast of the Caribbean. He told Governor Lewis that he would not try to run the blockade to get around the Florida peninsula and go up the East coast.

He said this was not a possibility and that he would drop Governor Lewis off at the dock to make other arrangements. He suggested the Governor voyage up what is called the Natchez Trace which would take him up the Adirondack Mountains to Washington, D.C. and his meeting with President Jefferson. Lewis was exhausted and laid down to rest in a local bed and breakfast. He got up early the next morning and went to the livery stable and bought two horses and the necessary saddles.

CHAPTER 60

The Road to Oblivion

THE ROAD TO OBLIVION IS the road to death. This macabre thought crossed the minds of the men who were the Corps of Discovery. Each and every one knew that they had been risked their lives daily for the three years on this the ultimate adventure.

Usually Captain Clark had discussed this premise with his co-leader, Meriwether Lewis, after an event happened. The two would talk about how close the incident was to being life ending—who was involved and what was the outcome. Certainly, it became very important at the journey's end in September 1806.

However, Captain Clark left the corps after winning the Great Race and refusing to accept the prize saying, "You deserve the honor Meriwether, and I am pleased to have you take it instead of me."

Captain Lewis was stunned. Clark had never been warm and fuzzy and gracefully did so, mumbling, "You have been a co-leader with me. We have shared all the good and the bad for nearly three years. I will tell President Jefferson why you left. It was for personal reasons, wasn't it?"

Clark replied, "Yes, decisions about organization, discipline, and major changes in our goals we wished to accomplish especially."

Several weeks after Clark left the corps entered the settlement of St. Louis in the Missouri Territory. The band was playing and the entire corps was in canoes rowing slowly down the river. Seaman was standing on the prow of Captain Lewis' canoe. The crowd was cheering. The corps was lined up in their formation across the Mississippi River and swung as a body to the dock on the St. Louis side of the Mississippi. It was an impressive display of the Corps of Discovery in action.

Sergeant Pryor said to Captain Lewis, "Would you believe it, Captain Meriwether? The whole territory must be here to greet us; even the redskins are here lined up along the riverbank clapping and making noise with their tom-toms to let the world know the Voyage of Discovery is back from three years in the wilds of the Northwest. It is a wonderful feeling to be missed and greeted so wildly."

Captain Lewis yelled back, "You should draw a sketch of this to send to the newspapers when we get home in a few weeks. What do you plan to do Sergeant Pryor?"

The sergeant thought for a minute. "I am going to sleep for a month. I will find myself a good woman and make her my bride even if it takes me another month."

Lewis yelled back over the noise of the crowd, "I wish I could find a young lady that would take me," but the boat swung into shore and he couldn't hear the answer.

In the morning the populous of the St. Louis Territory greeted the corps and the rest of the hangers-on in front of the church that graced the settlement. The mayor of St. Louis came to Captain Lewis and said, "We will have the ceremonies begin at 12 o'clock sharp. Please reassemble your corps at that time. We have awards to present to those of you who went beyond the call of duty."

Then Captain Lewis said, "We will be here dressed in our buckskin attire. We will even have Seaman sit up and do tricks. But I must inform you that Captain Clark had to attend another function in the Illinois Territory, so I will see that he gets it. Captain Clark asked me to give these beaded moccasins to you Mayor. We have brought them all the way from the shores of the Pacific Ocean."

Lewis added, "The Indian tribes that we inducted into the United States of America have showed the world that our country is growing up. I hope we receive as great a welcome in the nation's capital as we are getting here. I know President Jefferson joins me in doing so."

The two men clasped hands, and Lewis said, "It was worth our spending several years expanding the United States of America. The corps will visit Washington, D.C. soon."

After the ceremony Captain Lewis started to plan his return to his home in Monticello, Virginia. It was a long way up the Ohio. He wanted to get home, see his mother, and prepare his papers for the president.

Captain Meriwether Lewis wasn't sure whether he wanted to resume being Jefferson's right arm in the president's office or not. Lewis had become accustomed to the power and prestige of heading this great expedition into the Northwestern part of the Continent. Now Jefferson's dream had been fulfilled for the most part. Lewis thought to himself, *I'll talk to the president and see what he has in mind.*

Lewis said to his three sergeants, "Let's have a good time here for the next few days since these American citizens have spent so much time and effort preparing the three day holiday with food, fun, and frenzy for all."

With that they turned to each other and said, "We are glad to be home." and left for further activities to be held later in the afternoon.

Captain Lewis rested for a minute thinking, *I have my records to update and will get the information ready to present to the country. It will take me some time after I get back East to organize the bulk of information we have collected. Mine has to do with the birds, bees, and all Indian affairs. Clark's has to do with mapping and getting those maps back to the National Museum.*

During the following week Captain Lewis continued talking to the settlers as they were getting ready to celebrate the return of the Voyage of Discovery. The population of St. Louis was a little over a thousand including all the natives. He said, "The tribes that are found up and down the Missouri and Columbia Rivers can be a major asset to the country. The resource of 800,000 square miles is a bounty beyond belief."

Captain Lewis woke up the next morning with a spring in his step. He realized that his being a leader of this expedition had made him a man. His working closely with Captain Clark had given Lewis a perspective he never had before. Just organizing it could take several years and would require much soul searching because of what would happen if Jefferson didn't want to continue in office.

With many public parties and meetings in store Captain Lewis along with Sergeants Ordway, Pryor, and Gass led the entire expedition on tour. Lewis looked at the growth that had taken place in St. Louis during the three years that the expedition was on the road. People were pouring over the Allegheny Mountains daily. They were flooding in from the eastern sections of the United States. They were not only coming to the territories of the Ohio tribe and the Indiana tribe, but also those as far south as Tennessee and as far west as the Mississippi River and the Louisiana areas.

Therefore, Captain Lewis believed that he could find a publisher and have him edit and prepare "The Chronicles of the Lewis and Clark Journey to the Pacific Coast." It would be for distribution throughout the thirteen states and the territories not yet having qualified for statehood. It was to be a publication from the nation's Congress and for the people for the United States of America. Lewis was positive that both he and Clark had made history.

That evening was the reception dinner put on by the entire community and featuring Captains Lewis and Clark. The settlement leader, soon to become mayor of the community, asked Captain Lewis for his autograph and he wondered why both captains were not there.

The future mayor of St. Louis opined, "You should commercialize all the information and what you saw and make them available not only to our own country, but to those nations and populations of Europe and the rest of the nations of the world."

This was said casually and Captain Lewis said, "I did not understand what you meant. Would you repeat that again?"

"I am just a farmer, a soldier who has had ideas of becoming the Indian the way Captain William Clark has done up in the Northern Territory. If, and it is a big if, I do the same for the rest of our country I would be based in St. Louis. My plan would be to follow Captain Clark's lead and follow the Indian tribes and induct their braves, squaws, and other people that are settlers in the area and have them become American Citizens. I would spread the word.

Fur traders one and all, bring your furs to St. Louis and get top prices. The Great White Father in the summer sky will take care of all his children. More dollars for you and the tribe."

Captain Lewis interested the mayor by saying, "You are so lucky to be alive and I, for my doing a service for my country, I plan to get President Jefferson to make our three year exploration the greatest thing since Christopher Columbus came to North America. I plan to use this map and make the United States the fur capital of the world." Lewis said this as he was waving the Clark maps in the air.

Captain Lewis added, "I want to get the word out that President Jefferson's Voyage of Discovery was a great success. During the past three years and with much effort on September 25, 1806, in the wilds of North America our expedition, known as the Voyage of Discovery, is safely back home and will eventually have its journey papers available for sale when properly edited and reproduced. I think that this one feature alone, along with the astronomical readings, will make history."

Sergeant Ordway said, "Here, here! From your mouth to God's ears." And then the two men proceeded to ask the women who had come to the dance to trip the light fantastic and they began to square dance and dance the Shodish. The violins made music not heard by the likes of Captains Lewis and Clark for many a moon.

The corps of thirty men had to learn dancing with new loves or rekindled romances. Square dancing was relearned by the happy men as President Jefferson had the dream of a lifetime come true. The Transcontinental journey from the Atlantic to the Pacific and return was proved possible and was accomplished with only one death.

Lewis and Clark were starting the final chapters of the adventure. Captain Clark couldn't wait to begin his private life. He told Lewis, "It's been great. I will treasure this adventure. I want to continue to use the experience we had in traveling through Indian country. We have had the opportunity to help our country, President Jefferson, the many Indian tribes, and I want to go back to help the Sioux and other tribes by being an Indian agent for the new territories. Let's keep in touch with each other Meriwether."

Thus, the benefits to the United States of making the Louisiana Purchase and the Voyage of Discovery had already begun. By seeking to become the Indian Agent for the Northwest it showed how forward looking Captain William Clark proved to be. He felt this in his bones and gave the entire Corps of Discovery the thumbs up sign as he left the expedition.

But for Captain Meriwether Lewis it proved to be a different matter. Even though he had friends in Congress and was in great demand for speaking engagements he did not relish the future. He sensed his future was going to be bleak.

One pundit even commented, "The Lewis road to the future is like a Rocky Mountain stream; it flows smoothly but is turbulent at times."

Even Lewis himself wryly commented, "My road to oblivion is a long one and has been but partially traveled. I have tasted the fruit of the vine, graduated to using opium, and succumbed to demon rum."

Captain Meriwether Lewis realized he had consorted with fairies and contracted syphilis from unguarded sex. In his final years of life Lewis teetered from the high of heroism to the depths of failure. The next couple of years would show how the two captains fared on their journeys to eternity.

Captain Meriwether Lewis died under mysterious circumstances on the road to see President Thomas Jefferson in the nation's capital.

CHAPTER 61

Docking on the Mississippi

RETURNING TO "ST. LOOEE" CAME after a brief stop in St. Charles to pick its officials and a great many of leaders of the Kanza and Missouri Indian tribes. This welcoming crowd included many of the tribe's braves and squaws who lived in the teepees on the plain adjacent to the Missouri River; Chief Gray Eagle and other leading members of the tribe wanted to travel across the Mississippi to the larger settlement of 900 that surrounded the wharf.

Captains Lewis and Clark agreed that this fact alone would be helpful. And so it was; all the corpsmen were dressed in buckskins with beavertail hanging on the back. The corps including the captain's uniforms were worn with pride. The rest were wearing their coonskin caps that they had received at the start of the river trip.

The captains gave those members of the corps leave to spend the night and to celebrate their return to civilization. The entire crowd heard President Jefferson's message sent by special messenger to greet them and honor them in St. Louis.

The next day the dawn sky saw pink sails to the east sky and Captain Lewis remembered his mother saying, "Pink clouds in the morning have given sailors warning, pink clouds at night are sailors delight." The sun rose in the east and the crew was chilled by a north wind.

It was a beautiful day in 1806. It seemed to them that God was sending a message, "Well done my children. The band was playing Yankee Doodle" as the Corps hustled to re-board the keelboat and head down river to their sister city a few miles away.

The settlement had wagon tracks that were used as a path by man and beast. The settlers numbered less than a thousand if you counted all the dogs and cats and pioneers in the area. This tiny piece of America was in the growth phase.

Captain Lewis smiled as he said, "Immigrants are pouring in from Europe and coming through the Cumberland Gap. Our settlement is servicing the central Midwestern part of the United States of America. It had been named in honor of the French Saint Louis before the territory became part of the United States. The territory itself was named after the Missouri Indian tribe which lived in the area for centuries.

Clark said, "Meriwether, I can operate where we go, when we travel, and map where we've been, BUT I don't know any of the birds and the bees and the hickory trees we're seeing.

Lewis commented, "That's why I chose you to operate the Voyage Bill!"

It was a busy scene that greeted Captains Lewis and Clark. The three man pirogues slid through the river water and returned to civilization. All in all 16 boats were in a double line each headed by Clark or Lewis. Seaman stood on the prow of Lewis' canoe and York, Clark's slave rode in his pirogue. It was a little armada with the Corps of Discovery strung out in two lines parallel to the banks. It was a delight to behold.

The streets of St. Louis were crowded with the residents of this river town. It was a holiday declared by the Governor General of the Missouri territory, the Corps of Discovery had returned from a three year exploration. The President of the United States had announced a national holiday celebrating the triumphant return of the two army Captains Meriwether Lewis and William Clark.

The celebration was set up by the President himself. He couldn't attend but sent his Secretary of War to meet with Meriwether Lewis and escort him back to Washington, D.C.

The band had struck up the National Anthem and the Governor of the Northwest Territory was in attendance as well as the Indian chief who represented the Missouri tribe. They greeted Captain Lewis.

Meriwether Lewis looked around and said to himself, "I must be dreaming. All this hoopla and for us." He felt that his return from the voyage into the Northwestern Territory had been a tremendous success. His co-leader, Captain William Clark, had left the expedition at the final stage to recover from the flu so he could rejoin Lewis. In the meantime Vice President James Madison and his curvaceous wife Dolly Madison had been sent by President Thomas Jefferson to talk with Meriwether Lewis and accompany him back to Washington, D.C and present his report to the Congress of the United States. This visit would be a report on the Squaring of the Triangle mission entered into on May 14, 1804.

CHAPTER 62

Squaring the Triangle

THE FALL OF 1806 WAS filled with excitement for President Jefferson and the two captains of the Voyage of Discovery. The greeting they received as they headed down the Missouri was phenomenal. The two captains had returned to the settlement of Saint Louis. This is where they had started in May of 1804, three long years ago.

The banks of the Missouri river were lined with settlers as the armada of almost 30 canoes and pirogues paddled down the river to the dock after spending the night across the Mississippi river at the St. Charles settlement. The two rows of canoes were headed by Captain Lewis and his dog, Seaman, barking his welcome at the shouting throngs. Captain Clark was assisted by his man-servant, York, who jumped out and assisted his captain ashore.

Many of the on-lookers were crowding around the corps. There were signs on the banks of the Missouri River as the canoes and the pirogues were spread out by the men. The signs read, "Welcome home captains."

The Kanza Indians had prepared a powwow for the homecoming and had circled their teepees around a large fire-pit for the evening event. As this setting up for the night the Captains noted that the area had grown and the number of settlers had grown with it. The coulee where the Indians had camped was Louisiana Purchase Territory and it was filled with well-wishers from all sections of the United States.

It had rained all night but the corps was restless and the Voyage of Discovery packed up so that the welcome home party was not delayed. The Governor of the Missouri Territory of the Northwest declared a holiday for all settlers with dancing in the streets and interviews by the St. Louis newspaper. It was pandemonium personified. Stores closed so that their clerks and customers could join the celebration.

At the first planning for the future meeting Captain William Clark said, "Meriwether we have had a spectacular expedition. I want to visit my family and by December of 1806 I want to be connected with the Northwest Territory that we have explored. The Indian tribes had been notified that the braves, the squaws, and the children are now Americans citizens and would be governed by the Constitution of the United States. This meant that no longer could they raid other tribes and steal their women and horses. All of us are American citizens and would be treated in the same manner.

I am no longer in the Frontier Forces as this is my letter of resignation. By the time this letter of resignation reaches you Mr. President I will be headed into North Dakota where the Santee, Sioux, and Yankton tribes roam. I hope you will find me a spot in the government where the years of service will benefit my country and me.

Several months later President Jefferson received a letter from the Northwestern Territories from Mr. William Clark. He wrote another message to President Thomas Jefferson.

This effort to reach the Pacific to claim the land below the 54th Parallel from the Mississippi took us three years and reached the Pacific. I think that your buying of the rights for our country from France will be of benefit to our country now and forevermore and will make our country grow and prosper.

As Meriwether Lewis had said time and time again, "We three, you Mr. President as the point of the triangle of power and Captain Lewis and I as the base of this triangle, have made your dream come true making our country a leading nation of the world, growing in population and territory. I want to help further in this effort and wish to be your Superintendent of Indian Affairs if given a chance,

I will be the coordinator of transactions between the government and the Indians. I will be the agent representing both sides to maximize each side's value of living in the same country.

I am on my way to the settlement of Grand Forks on the Red river. A Mr. Wells has a large 'spread" and has a ranch in the center of the Dakota Territory. He has plans to establish a stage coach operation he calls "The Pony Express. "

Both Captain Lewis and I want to say that the greetings of the people of the Missouri Territory have been beyond belief. He joins me to say if there is anything further we can do to assist you and our country in effort to meld our new territory of 800,000 square miles of virgin land and pristine mountains and boundless opportunity please let us know as we are anxious to help in our nation's growth in the Northwest.

Respectfully,
Captain Clark
Voyage of Discovery 1804-1806

After reading this Captain Lewis looked in the mirror and he saw a man of 32 graying at the temples and said to himself, "Is that me? I look older, every bit the age of Bill Clark who is 36. I am the one who is old." Meriwether Lewis went to Clark and said "Clark I must get back home to see my mother and the rest of my family. I need some rest and relaxation.

The mirror did not lie, Captain Lewis said after a second or two "Aye, aye sir."

The next day Lewis had his horse saddled and started home. It was to take him fifty days to get there but the weather was chilly. The maple trees were turning red. As he arrived just before Thanksgiving week his mother came out and greeted him with a hug and kiss saying, "It's been years since you've been here to see me. Your brother has been taking care of the farm, but enough about me. Let me hear of the trip."

Captain Lewis said, "I'm tired and need a bath. I am sure glad to be home for a month." Pointing to his saddle bags he added, "I'll be busy as you can see from my full saddle bags."

Thus he began organizing his report to President Jefferson. By the end of the year of 1806 he had outlined the trip and was able to go directly to

Washington, D.C. Since Congress was not in session until March 15th it was held in early January 1807 at Monticello.

President Jefferson greeted Captain Lewis formally seated at his desk in his study. He said, "How is our partner Captain Clark?"

Captain Lewis said, "As you instructed he is on his way to Fargo in the North Dakota area. Rumor has it that he is to negotiate treaties for each tribe on the Red River up to the Canadian border.

President Jefferson finished his thought aloud, "Actually his trip would be a fitting end to Squaring the Triangle. That's subject to the approval of the Department of Interior and the United States Department of State. Isn't it?"

Captain Lewis said "Yes, is that all Mr. President?"

President Jefferson said, "Yes, and doesn't our meeting remind you of your being my special secretary in 1801?"

Captain Lewis said, "Yes Mr. President."

Lewis turned and left Washington, D.C. to go to his house while planning his visit to all the Indian reservations going northwest. This mission was special since it was to establish fur trapping and trading posts along the Missouri River route.

CHAPTER 63

The Old Homestead

THANKSGIVING DAY HAD COME AND so did the first snow of the winter. Captain Meriwether Lewis had received a message from the President. The message said, "Do you know where Captain Clark is? He has resigned his captaincy. Therefore, Captain Lewis must give the report to Congress about the Voyage of Discovery. This should be done before March 15th, the day Congress reconvenes."

Congress was meeting on March 15th. Lewis was working on his report and had it outlined, but not written. He had worked on the report from dawn till dusk. His brother William Lewis was irritated by the fact of Meriwether Lewis' lack of attention. His mother said "The family must get along or Meriwether Lewis must leave."

Meanwhile, President Jefferson sent another message with the following demand, "By return messenger send me an outline of what happened during the Voyage of Discovery."

As a result, Captain Lewis thought long and hard. He had been organizing his study of the birds and the bees and the names of the trees. It had not been finished. Lewis' remaining work on the report was staggering. Lewis had been what he jokingly called "up to his ears in alligators." He had received a reminder from the president saying, "Need to present a report to Congress about the Voyage of Discovery. In it be sure to account for the $500,000 and what you need from Congress to follow up on your Voyage."

Captain Lewis looked at the piles of documents that Captain Clark had created by his nightly mapping. Lewis thought *I must explain to the president and Congress what Clark and I have done during the last three years. I must get this to D.C. in less than two months. I will flesh out my notes and get Clark's maps and other work. I must give it a go.*

Meriwether Lewis spent many a sleepless night reviewing the spot he was in. He had suggested Clark be the Voyage of Discovery's co-equal. Clark's choice of the "Gates of the Mountains" pass through the Bitterroot Mountains chain was no excuse for the outcome. Who knew that the mountains would prevent a land route from the Atlantic to the Pacific Oceans? It was not impossible, but it was impractical. Lewis thought and thought but he concluded that he, Captain Meriwether Lewis, was not going to overcome this disaster so easily.

The distance between the Yellowstone River and the Missouri River was almost 160 miles of the toughest terrain on the North American continent. Even in the summertime the Lemhi Pass was not an attractive choice for the expedition to use because of unfriendly Indians and the very unfavorable weather conditions over half of each year. The return was put on hold until some further factors were added to the route selection.

Captain Lewis thought to himself, *I'm just a youngster. I am approaching my thirty-second year. Feel pretty well and not burdened with a nasty wife and a bad marriage. I should 'thank my lucky stars.' My older brother Bill has all the family worries, but seems to be doing 'A-Okay.'*

Lewis looked up at the sky and said to himself *Blue sky, blue birds, blue bells, and even America the blue-tiful. Blue is a good color. I even wish my eyes were blue. I have a great boss, the president, who asks for my advice a lot and thinks that my choice of Clark as co-leader fits the bill. I think that he and I dividing the leadership duties is working. Sometimes I think he is too formal. I always look for problems that might be there but are the problems real? I guess it is the realist in him versus the 'may be ist'*

Wow! Just Two months to do all the preparation, segregation, analyzing, organizing, presenting, concluding and finally defending your conclusions. I can't shortcut the process. I will have too many disbelievers as it is. If, and it is a big if, I can get the average American to see the importance of the three years of exploring our great country's expansion

*from shore to shore and from border to border I will have performed a
wondrous deed. I just know I have.*

The next day Captain Lewis penned a letter to Washington, D.C., "I
need to come to see you as soon as you can work me into your busy schedule.
It was signed, "Hopefully, Meriwether Lewis." He sent it to President
Jefferson. It was signed as the President of the American Fur Trading
Company In Formation.

It was Meriwether Lewis devoting the rest of his life to a new entity
The American Fur Trading Company, which was dubbed by the professional
capitalist as a start-up. It would utilize the first three years of Thomas
Jefferson's dream, a country for the people, by the people and of the
people...a dream about to become true!

CHAPTER 64

Promotion, Surprise, Surprise

C APTAIN LEWIS WAS EXHAUSTED. THE three years exploring the
Northwest and the upcoming election of 1804 had been a scary one for
both Jefferson and his staff. On the other hand, Captain Lewis was thrilled
that both he and Clark had led the parade of canoes down the Missouri. They
docked overnight while they prepared to paddle to the Saint Louis side of
the Missouri.

Waiting expectantly for the explorers Captains Lewis and Clark nearly
1,000 settlers made up the crowd of well-wishers. It was the thrill of a
lifetime for every one!

The special sentry, Seaman, Lewis' dog was sniffing the muggy river
breeze as the corps was eyeing the crowd. It was like a circus, fun and frolic
for all. The dignitaries were everywhere. They were back slapping and
shaking hands as they waited for the Voyage of Discovery to come ashore.

Captain Lewis said, "William, I have never seen the likes of this, it is
mayhem. How will we get through the crowd to accept the key to the city?"

Captain Clark replied, "Don't know and don't care, I am enjoying being
heroes. I never had it so good when I was in the Frontier Forces. I am tired.
I wish the Mayor would get on with the show!"

The bugle sounded. The settlers sang their version of "Turkey in the
Straw." The youngster made a circle clapped their hands in unison. The

Voyage of Discovery debarked and got behind the two captains to await further instructions. The mayor said, "Gentlemen welcome home."

The crowd yelled in unison, "Welcome home, welcome home strangers."

The mayor held a brass door key and gave it to Captain Lewis who said to the crowd, "Three years ago in the month of May, we left for the unknown. Yes, very few of you were waving good bye. Today we are met with a cheering crowd. How do you explain this?"

Captain Clark replied to Captain Lewis, "You know Captain Lewis, it was having 25 brave men, their officers and you at the ready. We conquered the elements and lived to tell about it."

Turning and waving to the crowd he yelled, "It is great to be home!"

The crowd's response was loud and long. The men of the Voyage of Discovery went out into the milling throng grabbing any hand and shaking it, kissing all the girls in sight, pretty or not. They were working their way into the local bar to taste the Saint Louis grog. The noise was deafening and the crowd did not go to their homes for more than an hour.

Captains Lewis and Clark were overpowered by the crowd and pushed inside the inn to get a room. That evening after dining at the inn they went out into the street and bought tobacco that had not been available to them until they came back to civilization. They smoked their pipes while talking over the events of the day.

Captain Clark being more outspoken said, "Some day wasn't it? The whole settlement greeting us was beyond expectations and the weeklong holiday in our honor is unbelievable. What are you planning to do after this is over Meriwether?"

Meriwether Lewis slowly said, "My job is not finished. I have to get my report written and back to President Jefferson along with the exhibits we have collected. Three years is a long time, but I must get things organized the way I want them. I think I will go back to Virginia and see my family. How about you Bill?"

Clark said, "Meriwether your choosing me to be your co-captain was an honor that I can't believe. You and President Jefferson have bestowed fame and fortune upon me. You know I can't collect specimens or organize data the way you do. I plan to return to the Northwest Territories but in a quasi-military way. I want to see the Indians and the U.S. collaborating with each other. The Indians and me an agent for the Frontier Forces is finished. However, I do not see my job as being over. I can see coordinating Indian Affairs. I plan to suggest this to President Jefferson and see what he says. But what about you Meriwether?"

Lewis says, "I want to set up a public-private organization. It will be neither 'fish nor fowl.' What will you do Bill?"

Captain Clark replied, "I think that when the president looks at me he see me as a private citizen. He does see me as a man involved in returning up the Missouri River basin as a Superintendent of Indian Affairs. That is what I will tell him. If he asks my future plans. I will also tell him the last three years of dealing with Indian tribes we found a land route to the Pacific and tying the Atlantic and Pacific coast and claimed it as being under the American flag!"

Lewis then said, "May I add if he gets my report he will offer me another government position. I'm almost 32 this August and I want to help my country grow as it expands in size."

This was the first time Captain Lewis had voiced his concerns about his personal future having been transplanted by his mother to Georgia while he was growing up in the south. Now that she had moved back near Monticello, Meriwether Lewis was 30 years of age and had gone to tobacco auctions where he met and impressed Thomas Jefferson. There seemed to be an instant respect for each other even though they were on opposite sides during a tobacco sale.

1795 was the first time Thomas Jefferson ran for the Presidency. He came in second to John Adams and as such was elected as the Vice President in the fall of 1795. Thus he was Vice President when John Adams was President, but in 1799 the situation was reversed and Thomas Jefferson beat the sitting President John Adams. It was a political mess.

President Thomas Jefferson had picked Meriwether Lewis to be his Private Secretary since the two were tobacco farmers. This rivalry turned into friendship. President Jefferson needed a good man to keep the presidential agenda free from unwanted interruption and only the people he wanted to see. But Jefferson had a dream in which the United States spanned the continent of North America. President Jefferson was not popular in the U.S. Congress and Jefferson realized he must pull a rabbit out of the hat. This rabbit was to be the Northwest Passage expedition connecting the

Atlantic Ocean and Pacific Ocean using an overland route. Calling in his private secretary he said, "Please sit down Captain Lewis."

Captain Lewis's heart sank. He thought to himself *the president must be going to fire me.*

President Jefferson felt the most logical leader of the trip was his private secretary Captain Lewis. He knew what to do to get the Voyage of Discovery ready to go. President Jefferson asked Captain Lewis to come into the Oval Office.

Captain Lewis said, "You know me from the times I won bids when we faced each other at tobacco auctions. What do you have in mind?"

The president turned to his desk, picked up his pen, drew a triangle and said, "You and your co-leader Clark have joined me in drawing a triangle and squaring it for success. We three must think success. We three form a triangle; me at the top and you Captain Lewis may choose a fellow officer to form the base. Should I say congratulations? I want you to say 'Yes, Mr. President, let's start the ball rolling. I will think about who I could choose to be my partner.'"

Captain Lewis said with a tremor in his voice, "Thank you, Your Excellency; now what?"

President Jefferson said, "I need your report and we will present it to Congress as a team together. When will it be finished?"

Captain Lewis said, "Sometime before the 4th of July 1807."

President Jefferson said, "I have to give you a leave of absence. Congress is against me, I have a plan."

Captain Lewis said, "Yes, Mr. President, I will."

President Jefferson said, "As you know all my plans are stalled by Congress. Former President John Adams, a Federalist has turned against me. I have a plan so grand that it will blunt the opposition. It is to consolidate the United States with the Northwest Territory to make one country. Do you think you could do this?"

Lewis said, "Yes, Mr. President, I will do this for you and my country. When do I start?"

CHAPTER 65

Looking Forward to a Rosy Future

OCTOBER 1806 BECAME CAPTAIN CLARK'S chance of a lifetime. However, his resuming being one of the top officers in the Frontier Forces did not appeal to him. He knew that the Lewis and Clark Voyage of Discovery was "old hat" to the U.S. Congress. Thus he must look for other possible ways to better his career.

Clark had talked to co-leader Lewis about what they as partners, Meriwether Lewis and William Clark, could do as a team if they were private citizens living in their young country. Lewis was not a positive individual such as Clark. Clark had gone over the future mentally and said to himself, *I have some new ideas and Lewis is leaning toward becoming a politico in the Southern Territory. I will go it alone. I feel it is the best for me.*

As far as Captain Lewis was concerned he had liked working for President Jefferson and had been able to spend $500,000 to run the exploration of the Northwest Territory during the previous three years.

Later in the same year of 1806, Lewis had sent dispatches back to the president in mid-August saying, "Clark wanted to find a position where his talents in commanding others were to be used."

Clark said to himself *I must find opportunity NOT let opportunity find me. I think that future opportunities are mine for the asking! This exploration and its successful ending in the fall of 1806 is 'a fait accompli.'*

Thus, the first week of October found Clark traveling up the Red River alone. He planned to spread the word that as one of the two leaders of the Voyage of Discovery that he was "working alone."

Clark planned to visit some of the Indian tribes and tell their chiefs and braves that their tribe's membership in the nation would be a star in the American flag and the Dakota tribes were "brothers under the skin!" This was Clark's "pitch" as he preceded "up river."

He mentally explored his future. He had reached his 36th year. He was in good health. He had found leading was better than following.

Clark remembered that as the time passed the co-leadership with Lewis was not smooth. His sergeants though loyal were not following the rules and required discipline and punishment by the captains. However, Clark felt that he owed it to the country and the corps to accomplish his life's work. His trip up the Missouri to the Red River was his first step. Clark rolled this over in his mind. He had such pleasant thoughts.

However, he noted that the country side was changing and the golden wheat had been reaped. As he traveled the ducks and geese were flying south for the winter making their way to the Caribbean. The whir of their wings often disturbed his morning sleep.

Clark met settlement leaders along the way. These brave souls did not want the system changed. They like being their own boss. They were getting ready for the cold, dark, and gloomy nights. This reminded Clark of the second year of the Voyage of Discovery.

At the end of three weeks the width of the Missouri had shrunk in size since the flow of the Yellowstone River had not been added to it. Parts of the Missouri were iced up and the remaining flow could be crossed in a rowboat. Clark stopped one night when he had met a small group of the Dakota tribe. He greeted the chief. Both had raised their arm accompanied by the word "How." Clark smiled and using what small amount of sign language and verbal communication was at his command pointed to himself with his mouth chewing and swallowing.

The chief pointed to his interpreter who said "Chief said in sign language you want eat; chief said yes." The three men walked to a blanket and sat down cross legged with squaws serving the three amid smacking of lips, chewing of teeth, and eating the food.

After they finished the chief pointed to himself and the other two, pulled out a peace pipe filled with Indian tobacco. The tobacco they smoked was grown on the South Dakota plains. It tasted horribly to Clark as he was used to Virginia tobacco.

After the conversation the following sign language was given from the chief to be interpreted. The Chief asked "What you do here?"

Clark pointed to himself. "I go to 'Fargo' in Dakota lands."

Chief said, "What you do there my land?"

Clark pointed to the chief and to the others. "We all own it."

The chief, medicine man and other braves gathered together and started conversing with gestures and vocally. It was hectic. Clark stood up, pointed to himself, put his hands together horizontally and laid his head down on his hands. The interpreter pointed to a teepee nearby and grabbed Clark's hands and led him to it. He opened the flap and escorted Clark to a bearskin rug on the floor and motioned him to sit down. He then verbally told Clark, "You sleep till sunrise."

Clark as his eyes were closing thought to himself, *What do you know maybe the interpreter can go along with me when I leave.*

The next morning to Captain Clark's disappointment he saw the tribe leaving going south. He looked at his image in the spring reflection, just plain old Bill Clark doing something alone for a change.

Bill Clark said, "I'll go up north till I hit the Grand Forks settlement. This will be where I can find out about this Dakota Territory. It is massive, 400 miles east to west and 320 miles from north to south. Wells was a mammoth rancher in North Dakota Territory. The settlers tell me 'Nothing gets done here without Wells, O.K.?'"

The few settlers he had talked to who knew the Dakota Territories all said, "I am a farmer at heart, I raise sheep and cattle. I trade for furs that the Indians have killed or stole. Once a year I horseback to the Minneapolis settlement and trade for things I can't make, grow or trade, but Wells had said go ahead and do it."

After several weeks at Grand Forks North Dakota Indian Reservation, Bill Clark found out about life, love, and the pursuit of happiness. He met the girl of his wet dreams. He was about 75 miles from Fargo as it was part of the Dakota Tribe whose reservations were scattered from the Iowa Territories west to the Rocky Mountains and from the Canadian border south to Nebraska.

Clark had found that herds of buffalo roamed the land. It was where he first thought about making this his home on the range and it he found an Indian maiden who caught his eye. However, he was sensible enough to catalog her for future exploitation. He knew that 36 years of age was when "batching it" lost its charm. *What am I waiting for?*

Grand Forks was on the Red River and had a trading post, a café, and of all things a place where "squaws of the evening" plied their trade. It was called The Pink Angel. The most popular of the Indian maidens was Scarlet Feather. She was very light skinned, had long black hair, a great smile, and a way with men on a bear rug. Her teepee had a red feather on the flap. On Saturday night there was a line waiting with wampum in hand. It was here that Clark visited.

Having fortified himself with "firewater" in the café Clark made a deal with the old squaw before the fire. She checked to see he did not have V.D. and collected the wampum. When it was his turn the old squaw ushered him to the teepee entrance and Clark entered through the flap standing before the bear skin rug until his eyes became accustomed to the candlelight.

What he saw was Scarlet Feather wearing on her an Indian feathered headdress extending below her private parts. Clark was struck with the sheer beauty of Scarlet sitting there like a "feathered boodah" waiting for sex. Scarlet removed Clark's buckskins shirt and pants and proceeded to massage him offering her "titties" and lips to kiss.

It was over in a few minutes and Clark almost passed out from the force of the act. He dressed himself while Scarlet readied herself and her lair of love for her next arrival. Clark meanwhile went back to the Indian reservation. He remembered that he should decide where to live and what to do before the snow flew.

Clark back tracked south on the Red River. He wanted to look at putting down stakes at the village of Fargo, North Dakota Territory. This was the spread of Wells, a large landowner in North Dakota. Wells was a developer of small truck harness. He raised horses, cattle, and sheep. He used these staples to get settlers to move to the Red River. Wells had been promoting a stage coach company to carry passengers from the Pacific Coast to points of interest in the Northwest. It got the area expanding. Wells said, "Give me enough time. I have the money to populate the eastern half of the north Dakotas' William 'Bill' Clark is willing to bet his life on it."

CHAPTER 66

Passing by Sergeant Floyd's Mound

THE MISSISSIPPI CURRENT KEPT PUSHING Clark's canoe downstream. He was now a free man. He was free, white, and forty. He resigned from the Corps of Discovery. He did not want to return to his old unit of the Frontier Forces in service of his country. It made Ex-Captain Clark feel like a new man with new goals. He was looking forward to getting ahead.

It was 1808. It was now Mister, Mister William Clark. He was amused at the thought of his being just plain Bill Clark with esquire behind his name. That's progress, but he felt different.

After a few days of moving up the Mississippi he saw Sergeant Floyd's memorial mound on the right bank. He rowed to shore, walked up to the top, and saw that the cross was askew so Bill Clark straightened it.

Bill Clark went back down the mound to the canoe and passed by Sioux City in the Iowa reservation.

It was winter time and one of the chunks of ice on the river almost overturned his canoe so he returned to the Sioux Iowa settlement for a few days until the weather was better.

Clark recalled the big powwow the Corps of Discovery had held in 1804. Chief Thundercloud had assembled a number of the Indian tribes so that the Indian braves could understand their change of status. The tribes were not sure that becoming American citizens was a good thing for them, but they had held the meeting of the chiefs. Clark was bothered by the fact that the resistance of the Sioux' was more pronounced since the settlers were making homesteads in the prairie.

He took time to consider his future and realized Rome wasn't built in a day and that he should wait till spring days were upon the Mississippi.

CHAPTER 67

Organizing a Fur Trading Empire

T HE APPOINTMENT OF CAPTAIN LEWIS to a new position as President of the American Fur Trading Company was a pleasant surprise to the corps members who had stayed until the trip ended. This was not unexpected that Lewis would head the new organization. President Jefferson was pleased to have prompt use of the fruits of his idea. He nominated Lewis to be the President of the "American Fur Trading Company." It would be at Fort Mandan. It was to centralize the trading of pelts trapped in America for fur coats sewn in Japan and returned to the United States of America for redistribution worldwide.

Before starting to manage the new company Meriwether Lewis had two tasks he wanted to accomplish. The first was to get his diary rewritten and published. This would be done by one of the many publishers who asked for this right. The Second task he wanted was to be a featured speaker and member of the American Philosophical Society, also known as APS.

The request to speak and then join this prestigious group of educators was a great honor since Meriwether Lewis had only gone as far as the seventh grade. All of the above tasks and duties preceded his returning to the Missouri River. He was given top billing in the monthly organization meeting.

During the question and answer session the Chairman of American Philosophical Society asked Lewis, "What is Captain Clark your co-leader doing these days?"

Captain Lewis answered, "I know not except Captain Clark said that he wanted to be involved in a commercial organization and use the experience gleaned during the Voyage of Discovery. I will ask President Jefferson if you want me to!"

The publishers told Mr. Lewis that his book had such limited appeal that they wouldn't publish it. The month of June passed slowly. He only had one proof of his epic tale and rejections were one by one. Lewis visited the sights such as the Liberty Bell and Independence Hall. Finally he reached the conclusion that the book that he had in mind was not to their liking.

It was then that Captain Lewis came back to see the President. He was received royally by President Jefferson. As he waited in the anteroom the lieutenant who was Jefferson's private secretary said, "I told the President you were waiting. The President told me to tell you that you should have presented it to Congress for approval before taking it to private publishers. I'll see if I can overcome this misstep."

Captain Lewis was stunned and after serious thought decided to see if the American Philosophical Society would plead his case. It seemed that Meriwether Lewis was not getting anywhere. His adventures were turned down one by one. Going from being a hero to failure was a shock. Captain Lewis was stunned.

CHAPTER 68

President Jefferson's Summons

CAPTAIN LEWIS LOOKED UP AT the sky and said, "Today is not going to be a good day for me. I have to go down to the New Orleans dock and look in the Caribbean to see if I can get out of the Mississippi River and head around the Florida peninsula on my way to Washington, D.C." It took all day for him to make that trip. As he went up the Florida peninsula he saw British frigates about to intercept his boat so he turned around and retraced his steps. Several hours later he returned to the Gulf of Mexico and back up the Mississippi River to New Orleans.

He stopped in New Orleans for the night and went to Antoine's restaurant where he saw his old friend Francoise Diderot. So after a friendly hug they sat down to one of the most delicious dinners in the world: lobster bisque, vin blanc, and the usual French cooking.

Francoise Diderot said, "As usual, delicious."

Meriwether said, "Yes I think so too!"

They lit up a cheroot made up of the finest Virginia Tobacco and Meriwether said, "I have a major problem, Francois. I have been called to come to Washington, D.C. I think I know why it was sent by special messenger. You are a man of the world, please listen to my predicament. I have reason to believe that my last two years of my governing the Louisiana Purchase Territory has not been to the Presidents liking."

Francoise said, "Yes, go on."

Governor Lewis said, "You know I screwed up when he wanted me to run the American Fur Trading Company in 1807. After this federal government sponsored effort failed he had Congress approve my being appointed as the Governor of the Mississippi River Basin Territory. I think I know why he is calling me to come to his office. He will ask me resign as Governor of the Louisiana Purchase territory and I will have to find a new occupation. I have returned from the Caribbean and am on my way up the Mississippi to the Tennessee River to get to Washington, D.C. through the Natchez Trace."

Francoise answered, "Oh you poor man, you are about to suffer one of the worst experiences of your life. You should think about this visit, carefully. The effect makes your future dim. Jefferson is a difficult master and as President of United States he has the power to do anything he wants."

Lewis took out his handkerchief and dabbed the tears from his eyes. After a few seconds Lewis continued, "I have been suffering the last few months because I anticipated this would happen and so far I have not thought of any solution to my problem."

Francoise Diderot frowned as he replied, "You have very few alternatives to this difficult situation. The outlook looks grim and we should give careful consideration to what alternatives you may have right now so that you can prepare to answer the president."

Gov. Lewis' turned his head and asked the waitress to bring him a brandy, "To calm my nerves."

Diderot smiled and said, "Bring me one too."

In a few minutes the waitress returned with two brandy snifters. Diderot raised his snifter high and said, "Good luck Meriwether, I suggest you forget your predicament. Go out of office with your head held high. A little feminine companionship is my answer. We will go out and celebrate your new future."

The two men arose and exited their meal at one of the best restaurants in the world. It was gloomy and they hailed a carriage to go to Basin Street. Basin Street in the French Quarter was very crowded with revelers. The couples were happy and felt no pain as they had visited the cabarets and had too much to drink. The men were friendly and the women responded. It was a maudlin sight.

Francois said as he hugged his 'Lady of the Evening," "I have found my lady friend. Have some fun Meriwether. Bonjour." He waived and each went their own way.

Governor Lewis looked around to find another cabaret to visit where he hoped to make his connection for the evening. The place was packed. The ladies were dressed in scant dresses. Governor Lewis noted that their dresses were cut so low it was shameful. Obviously they were waiting to find their catch for the evening and it would be for a hefty price. Meriwether approached a redhead and said, "Hello my name is Meriwether Lewis."

She answered, "My name is Scarlett and I need a drink."

Realizing this would be his last fling, Merriweather said, "I am incognito today if you really want to know who I am let's go to your place and relax."

Scarlett said, "Come on honey we're on our way." They went next door to an intimate hotel and climbed the stairs to the front desk. Scarlett waived to the room clerk and took Lewis to a room down the hall. Governor Lewis followed her and the smell of perfume came out the door as they went into her fancy boudoir.

Scarlett walked over to her closet and selected a flimsy night wrap. She said, "Do you like this honey?"

Lewis replied, "Don't call me honey; call me Governor." He did it in that fashion because in London all gentlemen are called Governor.

Scarlett said, "Anything you say Governor, but again I ask, would you like to see me put it on?"

Lewis said in a sarcastic way, "Who could turn that request down?"

Scarlett went into the bathroom and came out with her filmy negligee wrapped around her shapely figure. Governor Lewis being a country boy had never envisioned seeing a woman dressed the way Scarlett was and so was definitely uncomfortable. He said, "That is something else, where do we go from here?"

Scarlett came over, grabbed his lapels, and pulled him down so that he could kiss her. Her lips were painted with scarlet lipstick and so was everything in her room. The color was to offset her white skin and scarlet hair.

Scarlett asked, "What is your first name honey? Lewis replied, "Meriwether, but just call me Governor."

She pulled him over to her bed and said let's take a little rest. The governor gulped and sat down on the bed as she said, "Let me help you get undressed."

It was hard for Governor Lewis to maintain his composure. She undid the Governor's tie and slipped off his coat, removed his shoes and stockings, and undid his belt. She helped him unbutton his breeches and removed them. Scarlett pulled him down into the bed and said, "You have a wonderful masculine body."

Lewis said "You also are a beautiful women, white body and lips as red as strawberries in season."

With that he pulled her to him and kissed her. She grabbed his hands and had him fondle her breasts. He became aroused as this was going on and they engaged in sex. Governor Lewis had never experienced this type of love making before and went to sleep.

Lewis expected to spend the night but after an hour or so she said "I have to get back to the cabaret as I'm supposed to entertain the other customers. Gov., that will be $10 dollars for my services, normally I collect right now. You can give me any tip you want."

Lewis said as he pulled his wallet out of his pocket giving her $10,"Thanks for a beautiful, a great time. I have to leave for Washington, D.C. and get another place to stay till morning."

Scarlett left the room and Lewis got dressed, straightened himself out, and went down the stairs passing the room clerk. Lewis said good night to the clerk, as he went out down to the street. Lewis looked to see if Francois Diderot was nearby, but he was nowhere to be seen. He wondered if Francois Diderot's advice would help him "face the music."

CHAPTER 69

Going to Washington

THE AUTUMN LEAVES WERE TURNING color. The Maple leaves were bright red and the yellow sycamore leaves twirled as they fell to the ground. These trees lined the banks of the Tennessee River on the Natchez Trail. Governor Meriwether Lewis went to the stable behind his hotel and hired a saddle horse to make the long trip to the nation's capital city. The horse he rode was frisky, buck skin in color and cantankerous forcing Lewis to rein him in. The Governor was traveling up the Natchez River trail. Lewis' mind was wandering. He could not help but think about what the next couple of weeks would bring to his life.

The 600 mile journey along the Natchez River Trail was winding its way through the rolling hills. It was a pleasant ride and Governor Lewis reflected on what had happened to him in the past year. It had been difficult for him because of his failure to establish the American Fur Trading Company as President Jefferson had desired. For some reason that Lewis could not explain, the people loved him as the Co-Captain of the Corps of Discovery; however, they did not have enough confidence in him as a businessman to do business with him.

Thus, when Lewis became President of the American Fur Trading Company he was pleased that his company was established to utilize the information and contacts he had made in the Northwest Territory. Captain Lewis was given the honor of becoming the president of the company to trade all furs trapped by Northwestern Indian tribes and American trappers. This company failed in 1807. Captain Meriwether Lewis was unemployed. As President Jefferson put it, "Captain Lewis is a great explorer, but could not sell Ice to Eskimo's."

And so, President Jefferson, still feeling that the three year trip by Captains Lewis and Clark was an earth shaking accomplishment, nominated Meriwether Lewis to be Governor of all territory that was purchased from France called the Louisiana Purchase Territory. This made the U.S. claim to the Northwest Territory valid. The Voyage of Discovery showed the world governments that the United States of America was a power to be reckoned with.

The Congressional approval of President's Jefferson's request to make Captain Lewis his Louisiana Territory Purchase Governor was passed by Congress in 1807. However, Meriwether Lewis performing this new governmental function had been spotty. In early 1810 Governor Lewis sensed that he was being recalled to Washington, D.C. to see the newly elected President James Madison. Lewis expected the worst. One factor had been His lack of progress in getting the benefits of the Northwest Territory's three year expedition.

Lewis knew his inability to have a coast to coast means of moving mail, merchandise, and people haunted him. The U.S. government's claim on the Northwest Territory was considered foolish and worthless in the eyes of the Federalists, of which the immediate past President John Adams was the foremost critic.

Lewis was having trouble sleeping at night because of his failures. Lewis had not created a positive image of President Jefferson's term. When the newly elected President James Madison took office he wanted no problems and everything in his administration to be run smoothly.

Governor Lewis had started to drink hot buttered rum at night. He had developed a taste for rum and would feel no pain by bedtime. He had not managed to meet the young lady of his dreams and was depressed by his future prospects.

His trip to see the President was "the last straw." Governor Lewis thought he would be out of a job momentarily. Lewis was approaching his 36th year and felt that he was at the high point of his life. It was reached with the completion of the Voyage of Discovery. His reputation was that he was a do nothing bureaucrat. Governor Lewis still had not completed his report to Congress about his findings while on the Voyage of Discovery.

The nebulous thought held by many Americans was that that Lewis' trip was worthless. Such beliefs were more presumptive the more time had passed. The benefits to this tiny nation were more difficult to recite. Lewis had taken copious notes, but had not organized anything either after the exploration or after taking the trip to encourage the presidential plan to form trading posts from St. Louis all the way to the Pacific Ocean.

Although he had not heard from William Clark Governor Lewis knew that Clark would get his own civilian life together. As soon both men had the Voyage of Discovery in the proper shape to be presented to Congress, the Lewis and Clark epic Voyage of Discovery matter would be closed.

These thoughts were rolling around in Governor Lewis' mind as he continued the ride to Washington, D.C. Every night Lewis would stop to stay overnight in an inn. These were called traveler's rests. Lewis would rest before continuing at daylight. As soon as the sun went down, Lewis wanted to have comforts with his nightly flagon of rum and pipe full of tobacco laced with opium, which he had used during his many visits while in New Orleans.

Governor Lewis dreamed of his Albemarle, Virginia home. He dreamed that the blue birds had started flying south. Thus he was expecting a cold and dreary winter. This was also his concern because he was not in good health. He was having dizzy spells. He thought it might be due to the alcohol he was consuming or the hashish he was smoking.

He had picked up his dog Seamen when he had left New Orleans and at least he had the dog for company. He had thought about taking a stage coach but none were available between New Orleans and Washington, D.C because of the road conditions. He only had the option of horseback. He had met some travelers going south on the Natchez Trail who had said that there were some bad spots on the road. The next location before continuing was Grinders Inn. He had heard that two more days on horseback would land him at Grinders Inn.

While on his horse Governor Lewis speculated what his future held. He realized that his life had been exciting when the Voyage of Discovery docked in September 1806. He had been a conquering hero for a week's celebration. Since that time nothing had gone right.

CHAPTER 70

The Teeter Totter

IT'S THE END OF SEPTEMBER 1806. President Thomas Jefferson has arranged to have a National Holiday to celebrate the U.S. flag flying over the Pacific Coast. Captain Lewis received a message from Thomas Jefferson. The President's message said, "Our country must establish a new post in the northwest territories. Friend and foe alike now know that we have completed and signed a treaty with France. Also, I have come to the conclusion that our nation is here to stay. The world must realize we have doubled the size and now reach from sea to sea (Pacific Ocean to Atlantic Ocean). The newspapers such as the Washington Post Intelligencer have reported to the world in a full front page explanation of this event which was just completed as have other newsworthy events of the past three years. The New York Times and the Boston Globe also reported this incident as front page news. Please notify the world of this, the Louisiana Purchase."

Meanwhile Captain Lewis had returned to his home in South Carolina. He was still unmarried and having to ignore the young women who had their eye on becoming Mrs. Meriwether Lewis. He had more invitations to dinner than he could ever eat. His only companion was Seaman his dog who had served him well in the Voyage of Discovery.

In the interim, after the end of the trip and the recognition of the accomplishment of this expedition, Jefferson planned to propose two measures to Congress as he signed the report given to him by Captain Lewis.

The President said, "This plan is about our country using the information we gathered on the Voyage of Discovery. I will ask Meriwether Lewis to reflect his findings in detail to Congress." The President added, "Realizing that I will need to get other help in the year of 1807 to read and execute its recommendations. This effort will be supervised by my new personal secretary and White House staff. The entire effort should be completed by the 1st of July, 1807. In the meantime Captain Lewis will be "my right arm" as he tours our expanding nation." Jefferson then said, "You gentlemen have other pressing duties; therefore, I hereby adjourn this body until next week.

Jefferson returned to office arm in arm with Captain Lewis. As President Jefferson took Lewis aside he said, "Well Meriwether, stand at ease and take a seat." He smiled and continued "I see that you should be ready for further events honoring your skills as an explorer. Men like you have discovered the world" added Jefferson offering a cigar made from Virginia Tobacco.

Jefferson asked "During your "winding down period" Captain Lewis you have spent three years of your life, and have weathered dangers from the Indian tribes and getting lost in the Rocky Mountain area. How did you find your way home?" Captain Lewis said, "It was not easy and we nearly froze to death."

The reason the President wanted to meet Lewis face to face was because he wanted Congress to pass legislation to fund the American Fur Trading Company activities, during the remainder of the 3rd President's term. It was at this time during early 1807 Captain Lewis toured the northeastern part of the US to secure Congress' approval of this new activity which would be headed by the President of the American Fur Trading Co. The two met at the White House where Lewis spent his days meeting with government officials. The evenings were spent by Lewis in entertaining young ladies and discussing his new appointment by Congress and the President to establish the American Fur Trading Company.

The first six months of 1807 was spent between Washington D.C. and Pennsylvania. This was where the American Philosophical Association was located. This was a very prestigious organization which invited the President of the American Fur Trading Co. to become a member. Lewis was more than happy to accept this honor without realizing how difficult it would be to make Jefferson's dream a reality. Lewis went down to the Missouri territory to proceed in establishing his own private office in the city of St. Louis.

Lewis worked extremely hard during the balance of 1807. After getting settled in the commercial district of the St. Louis city, Lewis setup his own organization. He visited Jefferson in Washington D.C. in January 1808 and made an official report to the President who was just finishing his 2nd term. Mr. Lewis as he was addressed in his meetings located an office in the commercial area. His permanent residence was in the nicer area in St. Louis. His mother, bother Tom, and families were back in South Carolina in 1808.

The year 1808 was a difficult one for Lewis. He realized he would have to take a trip up the Missouri to establish trading posts every 100 miles, following the route he had traveled in the "Voyage of Discovery." This trip was a combination of visiting old friends and old places along the river. He stopped at every town that had over 1,000 people along the Mississippi and Missouri. He met with mayors and other public officials to establish public relations. He was met by old friends and new friends alike. He was met with open arms and given keys to log cabins along the route. He was wined and dined and entertained by all. He also spent his time getting organized. The trip up the Missouri resulted in a celebration in each city as he went up the river by horseback. This was a trip for him to touch bases with compatriots in Kansas City territory.

On the way up the river Lewis came to the South Dakota Tribe located near the Black Hills of South Dakota territory. This was rugged country as the Black Hills were of granite and were not covered by fir trees or other trees and were covered with moss. The winter rain and snow keep the vegetation alive. Animals were limited to deer, bear, elk, and animals that could live on very little forage. It occurred to President Lewis of the American Fur trading Co. to start his expansion to the Pacific Coast. This meant going over the Rocky Mountains and down to the Clearwater River. As President as the American Fur Trading Co. it occurred to Lewis that he should establish trading post from the Clearwater junction to the Colombia River and proceed southward to Celilo Falls. At this point the Colombia went due west and headed toward the Pacific Ocean which was 120 miles away. This would bring the Northwest Territory into American commerce since the furs trapped by the Indian tribes would be sent by river over the great divide of the Rocky Mountains and down the Missouri to St. Louis.

The vision of this great addition to commerce for the young country would make trading with the European countries furs for any and all exports to the United States. For both parties the buyer and seller, Europe and US, would be beneficial to international trade. The President of the trading company would be stationed at his principal office in St. Louis, Missouri.

The venture of 1807 was disastrous. It was a typical Meriwether Lewis activity. Lewis would not meet expectations and became down beat and gloomy. Given this penchant for failure Lewis began all types of debauchery. He started using depressants and taking drugs, opium and the like. He would be gone for days at a time enjoying the evils available to men with nothing to do but to play with his health. He met no potential mate and very often would go down the Mississippi to New Orleans. By the end of 1808 the lifestyle of Lewis had deteriorated to his sleeping until midafternoon and going to gambling casinos, houses of prostitution, and other evil haunts of New Orleans. Places like Antoine's were not available to him anymore should he venture in for dinner and other activities. It looked like the end of the road for poor Lewis. Lewis was not nearly as far away as a man of 44 years of age. Lewis, the lush would want to stay up to dawn, lollygagging around with any man, women or child who would participate in such acts. Lewis thought of his mother located in South Carolina seldom and when he did he realized he was not worthy of her love. It was the same with brother Tom the tobacco plantation owner and leader of the family.

Meanwhile, President Jefferson had received news of the decline and falling health, wealth, and fortune of his former leader of the Voyage of Discovery. Jefferson had no time to waste and sent for Lewis to come to Washington D.C. immediately to meet him. It was not when but how fast and in what means he could do it. He sent a demand for Lewis to come to Washington D.C. as fast as he could. At this juncture Lewis started to return to being terminated without receiving anymore pay for his services as they were no longer needed.

Lewis gathered what he could of his belongings and took York, Clark's slave which Clark had abandoned, and of course the faithful Seaman his dog. They went down to the stable the first week in October and headed up the Tennessee River along the Natchez trail. It was fall, the trees had colored and represented a background of mountains red, yellow, and brown. They traveled up the river and some 50 miles until they approached Grinders Inn. This was a rest stop on the trip to D.C. As they arrived at Grinders they saw smoke coming out of the chimney, Seamen ran ahead to announce their arrival. York who was riding a horse and pulling the pack horse which had the memorabilia collected during the three year Voyage of Discovery. The weather was bad with intermittent rain; the travelers were exhausted and ready to "bed down" for the night. Lewis told York to feed the horses and stay in the stable until the morning in which time if all went well they would continue up the Natchez Trace. Natchez Trace was the path to D.C. After taking a hot bath Lewis went down to the area where all travelers met for their evening meal and a hot toddy of Havana rum. Lewis had taking up smoking a pipe full of Virginia Tobacco.

The troubles that Lewis had was a feeling of failure. Everything he had touched after his triumphant return in 1806 had been a failure. Nothing went right. It was downhill and had disappointed everyone who knew or had dealings with Lewis, but this evening was different. The tobacco smoke curled up to the ceiling of the resting place made of logs and dirt floor. Seamen was allowed in because of a hard day of keeping up with the horses. The hot toddy that Lewis was sipping and the pipe full of tobacco he was enjoying seemed to relax Lewis and everyone in the room was waiting for dinner to be served. It seemed peaceful and all the members of the Grinders Inn rest stop were enjoying the rest before bedding down before the next morning's departure. After dinner anyone who wanted could enjoy and card game called waist, a game made popular in London where the English settlers lived.

About ten o'clock in the evening Lewis had final toddy and went to his room. He was bedded down in a one bedroom room that had a small heating stove for heating the room. Mrs. Grinder gave Lewis a clean face towel and a pitcher of water in the wash basin. She told Lewis that she would be retiring at 11 and that everyone should be quiet by midnight. Lewis thanked her and proceeded to his room which was on the other side of a fireplace. Seamen stayed where he was until Lewis had gotten to his room and was told by Lewis to stay. Seamen was like human. Seamen watched Lewis enter his room putting a wooden board across the door keeping the door closed.

ARTHUR SWEET

The fire went down and all was quiet until midnight at which time there was a noise coming from Lewis's room. It sounded like two men arguing/talking to each other. After ten minutes of scuffling Mrs. Grinder came to the door and listened to two men arguing. She said, "You two quit this ruckus or I'll get my shot gun and it'll be bye-bye baby." The door would not open from the outside.

The 'missus' said in a loud tone, "Have it your way." She went out to the stable and called Sambo. Sambo was a slave. She told him to get out of bed and come out with her with the gun. "We will show the way Grinder's overnight guests get treated if they don't behave themselves."

The noise from the room stopped and Mrs. Grinders went back to her quarters. She thought that the ruckus was over. She wished Mr. Grinder was there. Everyone went back to bed, and quiet remained for three or four hours. Mrs. Grinder was awakened again by two shots. She yelled out for Sambo to come out.

Getting up to the door, Seaman was whining at the door. Mrs. Grinder knocked on the door. "Are you okay Mr. Lewis?" Mrs. Grinder heard no response. The door was locked from the inside. After a while everyone just proceeded to go to sleep.

The next morning Sambo got ready for any and all riders on the stage. Mr. Lewis had not come out from his room. Sambo went up to the room and yelled out, "I got your horse ready Lewis. The coach is coming. I have to take care of the stage and riders. So come get your horse out of my stable and head on your way." He waited a few minutes. Seaman was sniffing the door and whining. Mrs. Grinder came to the door to the guest room and listened. She said, "Come out, you'll miss your stage."

Mrs. Grinder then told Sambo to get an axe to cut their way through the door. He handed the axe to Grinder. As soon as the stage is finished we will break the door down. The stage came and Mrs. Grinder went to greet them. There were no guests and so she sent the coach on their way up Natchez.

Mrs. Grinder and Sambo came to door with the axe. Knocking on the door Mrs. Grinder yelled out "Your late Lewis and I'm getting itchy." Still silence in the room. Mrs. Grinder told Sambo to break the door down. After opening the door they saw a man sprawled on the floor with a bullet hole on his head and one on his knee. His eyes were one with blood on the floor. "My husband Grinder will not be back until Friday. What do we do?" Sambo told Mrs. Grinder to write a letter and he would head toward Washington D.C.

It was a mystery and was impossible to solve. A dead man Lewis sprawled on the floor with blood all over, one bullet hole in the forehead, one on this knee and two discharged pistols. How could a dead man shoot himself twice? Mrs. Grinder and Sambo were shaken in their boots. Seamen came into the room and sniffed the blood and master who was dead as a door nail. Mrs. Grinder said "I'll be glad on Friday when Mr. Grinder gets here. Meanwhile, we will lock the door and hopefully the flies don't get in. Stanger things have happened at Grinders Inn. But none as strange as this."

Mrs. Grinder said when her husband came back, "Grinder you missed a murder, a mystery. You must get the body buried. Sambo said he would get the two shovels and take the body up 500 feet up the Natchez Trace within the hour." The body of Lewis head pointed north toward Washington D.C. was laid to rest. His body was covered with a pile of rocks three feet high. The plaque said "Here lies "Meriwether Lewis October 10, 1810, May the Lord have mercy on his soul."